Land, Work and Resources

For Adrien De Backer, Industrialist, Economist and one of Europe's wise men

Land, Work and Resources

An Introduction to Economic Geography

Second Edition

J. H. Paterson
Professor of Geography in the University of Leicester

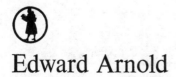

Edward Arnold

© J. H. Paterson, 1972; 1976

First published 1972 by
Edward Arnold (Publishers) Ltd
25 Hill Street, London W1X 8LL

Reprinted with corrections and revisions 1973
Reprinted 1974
Second edition 1976

ISBN 0 7131 5879 4

Text set in 10/12pt Monotype Plantin, printed by photolithography,
and bound in Great Britain at The Pitman Press, Bath

Contents

Introduction

There is something about the career of the subject known as economic geography that recalls Mark Twain's comment on the Mississippi steamboat traffic which he knew so well: 'At the end of thirty years it had grown to mighty proportions: and in less than thirty more it was dead. A strangely short life for so majestic a creature.' For, majestic or not, scarcely had economic geography emerged out of its predecessor, commercial geography, to take its place among the respectable academic disciplines than it began to break up again into a swarm of subdivisions—agricultural geography, marketing geography, transport geography and so on. Like its companion term, 'physical geography', it proved too broad to be useful as anything more than a general indication of purpose. It masked the specialist interests of a great diversity of workers, and today it survives mainly on the covers of textbooks and the outline timetables of classes.

Even during the days of its unity, economic geography does not seem to have developed any particular methodology: the classic debates on the nature of geography had little observable influence on its growth. Consequently, the textbooks on the subject reveal a rather bewildering variety of approaches and materials. The first task, therefore, of an author who presumes to add to their number must be to offer some clarification of his position within this very broad field. I should like to do this quite simply by making three points about economic geography, and indicating my view about each of them. Anyone interested in doing so can then carry out a form of triangulation—or, more properly, of resection—by reference to these points and obtain a fix on my position.

Firstly, then: there have been over the years a variety of accepted approaches to the field. This variety is immediately apparent if we turn to the ancestor of all our modern textbooks on economic geography—Chisholm's *Commercial Geography*, published in 1889 and happily still with us, in its nineteenth edition. This book is really three works in one there are 'General Facts, relating to the production, distribution and exchange of commodities'; there is a consideration of the individual commodities one by one and then we have 'Regional Geography', or the production and trade of individual countries. These three sections we might label as the factor approach, the commodity approach and the regional approach.

Most later writers of general economic geography textbooks have adopted an approach which in some way combines Chisholm's second and third sections: they have blended the 'commodity' and 'regional' approaches by the use of devices like the type-of-economy region, and they have produced such units of study as Commercial Grain-Farming Regions, or Delta Rice Economies. These are certainly useful forms of generalization, but there seems no particular need to add to their number. The first approach, by contrast, has until recently been curiously neglected, perhaps because of doubts about whether it was truly geographical or not. In the latest phase, however, it has come into its own; not, admittedly, in precisely the way Chisholm conceived of it, but as part of a general development of the theory of spatial analysis.

For today's 'accepted approach' to the subject is not to treat individual commodities or individual regions—nor, for that matter, necessarily to isolate one particular group of facts as belonging to 'economic' geography at all—but to build general theory: to treat the factors of production not as individuals but simply as factors—A, B or C. Generalizations about these factors can then be derived, either verbally or, more likely, statistically. By this means we are able to make, with the maximum degree of economy, statements in either 'language' about the distribution of activity—about static patterns or about flows of goods, people and ideas which go to make up circulation in the real world.

Where does this book fit into the structure which I have just outlined? As the list of contents will show, it adopts basically the 'factor' approach, but in the traditional manner treats the factors as individuals: beneath the anonymity of A, B and C it examines some specific characteristics of each, with particular reference to its limits and range of variation. If it is not too pretentious to suggest the parallel, I have thought of the work as doing for the factors of production and levels of activity much the same thing that Benjamin Britten did in his *Young Person's Guide to the Orchestra*—that is, to indicate the range and performance of each instrument (or factor) and its contribution to the whole score, or product.

This kind of study should not be thought of as running counter to the search of the theorists for new formulations. Rather, it complements the work done in the theoretical field. After all, it makes a difference whether our factor T (for Transport) is represented on the ground by a road vehicle, river steamer or railway truck; the physical properties and cost components of T are quite different in each case, and at some point or other in our work we are going to come up against the limits of T, which has now materialized as a railway line with single track, maximum gradients, minimum curvature, a loading gauge, a top speed of, say, 90 km an hour and a freight-rate structure based on the unit of a 40 ton load.

My claim that this kind of study complements the theoretical work being done in the field brings me, however, to my second point. In reality, as everybody inside the profession's magic circle knows, geographers are not such a happy and united band of workers as I am making us out to be. We have allowed new and old approaches, new and old 'languages', to breed disunity. The fact that there are virtually no formulae and few figures in this book—that it is couched in traditional literary terms—will already have been noted by some colleagues who lifted it idly from the shelf to leaf through its pages, and their judgement of it will already, therefore, have been formed on the basis of that observation.

But if this is the case, they will almost certainly have been over-hasty. For I share with them, and with most other professional geographers, an interest in valid generalizations. We all abhor the 'regurgitation of factual gruel' (a phrase for which it seems likely that we shall remember the late Professor Wooldridge for at least as long as we remember his work in geomorphology). There is, I trust, no regurgitation here. But it is possible to be interested in attaining an optimum level of generalization (and *optimum* rather than *maximum* is what we are all, surely, aiming at) without prejudging in what language those generalizations ought to be expressed. It is a simple fact that, by means of statistical methods, an areal generalization can be formulated which is more precise and, at the same time, contains a larger number of elements, than one arrived at by the traditional, word-based method. It *also* happens to be true that, for the present, it remains simpler to communicate with most people in words than in statistical symbols—symbols which normally have to be converted back into words if conclusions are being stated.

In any case, the whole point about a generalization is (and who better to quote on the point than William Bunge in his *Theoretical Geography*?[1]) that 'science . . . is willing to sacrifice the extreme accuracy obtainable under the uniqueness point of view in order to gain the efficiencies of generalization.' A generalization which is too precise ceases to be a generalization. When we are dealing with specific problems, we of course require specific answers. When, as in the case of the present book, we are looking for general statements, the verbal form of expression not merely may answer perfectly adequately, but may be preferable to the symbolic. For one thing, these verbal generalizations are themselves based upon

---

[1] *Lund Studies in Geography, Series C, Human and General Geography* 1, Gleerup, Lund, revised edition 1966.

and summarize a rapidly increasing volume of precise case work. For another, the use of mathematical symbols may well create an entirely spurious impression of precision in situations where our knowledge is precise only in a few specific cases, on which the generalization has been founded. If these verbal generalizations which we are using are invalid, by all means let them be replaced—not by a different language alone, but by better generalizations.

The third positional statement which can be made about this book concerns what I might call the historical element in economic geography. The factors of production with which we are dealing have applied to all economic activity over the whole period that a particular community has been evolving upwards from the start-line of mere subsistence or the margin of survival. These same factors produced the enclosure movement and the water-driven mills of eighteenth-century Britain just as they have now produced automation on the farm and nuclear power stations. Indeed, the application of these factors in their historical context is in itself a theme worthy of the closest study: at the lowest valuation, it permits us the academic pleasure of understanding past phases of development while it may, if we are fortunate, also enable us to save some of the less technically-advanced communities of the world from repeating European or American mistakes in the course of their own, contemporary development.

My own interest in this particular field is a strong one. Clearly, I am trespassing at this point on the historian's territory, but I have tried in every case to relate the discussion to the present landscape and its foreseeable transformation. The aim has been to take the various factors of production and comment on their application to changing patterns of economic activity over a period—generally a period of a century or rather more, leading up to the present day. The object has been to try to see why development has taken the form it has; why we have around us these cultural landscapes of ours rather than some other, different landscapes.

Obviously, this is an immense field of study and an over-ambitious venture for the writer of a single, relatively slim volume. I have been obliged to limit myself to considering only the most obvious or most important influences upon the production factors over the period. About the identity of most of these there is little ground for dispute. In the period since 1914 it is unlikely that anyone would question the impact of such events as two world wars, with their profound disturbance of rational economic patterns, or the rise of national consciousness in the third world, which has led nation after nation to reject the role assigned to it in an idealized division of labour between them. Perhaps most important of all has been the great increase in world population during the last half-century, which means that the efficient application of the factors of production is not merely desirable to maximize profits but essential to the survival of people who will otherwise starve.

But we cannot be content to place the economic activity of today against the background of twentieth-century events alone. In so many ways the nineteenth century is critical to our understanding too, because in so many ways it was an anomaly. It marked a complete departure from the slow and fairly consistent development of preceding years, and it contained at least two events that were of outstanding importance. One of these, as almost any student of the period would agree, was the main impact of the Industrial Revolution, with all that it involved—the re-ordering of production, the rush to town, the building of transport lines, the creation of markets for the products of remote and hitherto unrelated areas.

The other event has probably been accorded less space in the standard texts on the period before 1914 but it was, in a sense, more dramatic in that it was a single, non-recurring phenomenon. This was the opportunity which the century afforded for the occupation by ordinary settlers of huge areas of the earth's surface. Never before, and certainly never since, has there been in a few short decades such a glut of lands available: never before had the frontiers of settlement advanced with such speed. It was, in areal terms, roughly as if our own generation's landing on the moon had opened to us a surface available for immediate settlement and cultivation; by the same extent was the useful area of the planet's surface enlarged within a generation or two. In this era the common man came into his own: for the only time in his recent history was there land for him and to spare. For a brief period, this single factor of production— land—ran out of alignment with the other factors and, in the nature of things, it *could* only happen once. The situation was only temporary: in a free world economy with a brand-new transport network it was self-adjusting.

What all this amounts to is the proposition that, in writing a book on economic geography, one may either consider the factors of production acting against a hypothetical background of circumstances arbitrarily defined as normal, or else view them as operating in the historical context in which they did, in fact, operate at a specific point in time. I have no intention of criticizing either approach: I merely wish to record the fact that, of the two, I have adopted the second.

These, then, are my starting assumptions. The justification for writing this particular book lies in the fact that this particular set of assumptions is under-represented in our literature. What I have tried to do is to bring together a group of ideas which are logically consistent, which happen to interest me, and which have not been set out in just this way before. And that, surely, is all the justification that any of us would claim for writing as we do.

St Andrews

1971

Note on the Second Edition

Since this book first appeared in 1972, a number of users have been kind enough to tell me that they have found it serviceable, and that its particular content and approach coincide with their own requirements as teachers or students. This is, of course, highly gratifying to the author. What is a good deal less so, however, is the realization that, despite the short period of time that has elapsed since first publication, the writer has in a number of respects been proved a remarkably bad prophet. It is little comfort to reflect that a lot of other people, up to and including governments, have been caught out too; any academic worth his salt is sure that he can out-guess a mere government any day of the week. So revision is now necessary.

In carrying out the task, however, I have had to heed the publisher's warning not to add too much to the length of the book, and that is a hard discipline for any author. He is reluctant to throw out of his book any of the earlier, hard-won content; yet he has to find space for fresh ideas or insights, and for things which he now feels he should have explained more fully the first time, not to speak of new developments on the economic or political scene. But the revision has been kept to the minimum necessary and the structure of the book, with the sequence of ideas as originally conceived, has been left intact.

Also, we have gone metric.

Leicester

1975

1

Geography, Resources and People

If geography is concerned with the study of earth features, either natural or man-made, then economic geography is the study of those features regarded not simply as phenomena but as *resources*. The dictionary defines resource as 'a means of support'—support, that is, for the animal life of our sphere and, in particular, support for man. Economic geography is concerned with the usefulness of earth features to man, with the amount of support they can afford him, and with the measures which he may take to bring them into use. Economic geography is the geography of man making a living.

What constitutes a resource? And how might we assess the resources of a particular community? To be realistic, our calculation must include three main items. The first and most obvious of these is a set of natural conditions with which our planet in its various parts is endowed—rocks, minerals, soils, water, vegetation and wild life. It is normal to speak of these as 'natural' resources, in that they form a category whose existence is, in the main, independent of the actions of man: they were here on earth before he was and, although he may use or misuse them in such a way as to diminish their quantity, he cannot affect their basic distribution, which is an outcome of geological accident, position on the sphere, or age-long physical process. Rather, these natural resources are the data from which he has to proceed and plan. And he has to begin by accepting the fact that their distribution is uneven; that some regions are favoured above others—favoured beyond any possible bounds of compensation to or by the user.

No one has more successfully captured in a single anecdote the enormity of these inequalities of natural endowment than has Antoine de Saint-Exupéry.[1] He tells how the French arranged for a visit to France by certain tribesmen from their Saharan empire. On their return to Africa, he continues:

Memories that moved them too deeply rose to stop their speech. Some

[1] In *Wind, Sand and Stars*, Heinemann, London, 1939. The incident, here slightly abridged, is to be found on pp. 127-9.

weeks earlier they had been taken up into the French Alps. Here in Africa they were still dreaming of what they saw. Their guide had led them to a tremendous waterfall, a sort of braided column roaring over the rocks. He had said to them: 'Taste this.'

It was sweet water. Water! How many days were they wont to march in the desert to reach the nearest well; and when they arrived, how long they had to dig before there bubbled a muddy liquid mixed with camel's urine. Water! A thing worth its weight in gold! A thing the least drop of which drew from the sand the green sparkle of a blade of grass! And this water, this miserly water of which not a drop had fallen at Port Etienne in ten years, roared in the Savoie with the power of a cataclysm as if, from some burst cistern, the reserves of the world were pouring forth . . .

'That is all there is to see,' their guide had said. 'Come.'

'We must wait.'

'Wait for what?'

'The end.'

They were waiting for the moment when God would grow weary of His madness. They knew Him to be quick to repent, knew He was miserly.

'But that water has been running for a thousand years!'

And this was why, back at Port Etienne, they did not too strongly stress the matter of the waterfall. There were certain miracles about which it was better to be silent. Better, indeed, not to think too much about them, for in that case one would cease to understand anything at all . . .

This, then, is the first and most obvious category of resources. But the 'direct income' from natural resources, at least as measured by the proportion of national wealth contributed by the land and its products—agricultural or mineral—has tended to decline with the passage of time. In the U.S.A., for example, it has been calculated[2] that the proportion of national wealth represented by land fell from 36 per cent in 1910 to 17 per cent in 1955, while that of *agricultural* land fell from 20 to 5 per cent. The percentage remains highest in poor and backward countries and is lowest in rich and developed ones.

This last statement leads us on directly to our second category of resources: 'human' resources. If it is true that the volume of resources available to a community depends on the random scatter of features over the earth's surface or below it, it is also true that those features only become resources when the human population is in a position to benefit by them; that is, when man uses his hands to dig or cut or cultivate, his mind to conceive uses for natural objects, and his equipment to convert these objects from a form in which they are of no use to him into one which adds to the total of his support.

This means that the resource value of a natural object depends upon the discovery or extension of its usefulness. For most of man's history, for

[2] By T. W. Schultz in 'Natural Resources and Economic Growth', reprinted in *Readings in Resource Management and Conservation* edited by I. Burton and R. W. Kates, University of Chicago Press, 1965, p. 398.

example, the earth's great mineral resources were of little value to him; he did not warm himself with coal, and the use he made of petroleum products was limited to waterproofing (as with Noah's Ark in the Middle Eastern story), or medicine (as with the North American Indians). But as his technology has advanced, so man has discovered new resources because he has used his own powers to create new means of support.

Human resources may be applied either directly, by the labour of digging and building and fighting, or indirectly, by applying ingenuity to these and other tasks, especially by creating machines to do the work and, at the same time, to increase the labourer's capacity. Given a sufficient number of hands, human labour can fulfil virtually any constructional task, from building a pyramid to erecting a steelworks (the Chinese are reported to have employed 100,000 labourers to build their Wuhan steel mills). But the habit of thinking of human resources primarily as numbers of people belongs to the period when rival war lords or tribal chieftains built up their retinues for military purposes, and when one of the main 'resources' of the Scottish Highlands and the Swiss Alps was the fighting men they provided for lowland armies. Characteristically, societies progress by substituting human resources of ingenuity for direct labour, and machine power for hands. Not only do the machines multiply the labour of hands but they make possible some results—such as very high temperatures or the passage of electric currents—which are impossible to achieve without them.

By a process of substitution, in fact, a society can reduce the drain on both its natural resources and its labour force, for technological advance has a multiplying effect on both types of resource. The fuller the substitution, the wealthier the society is likely to become. One way of expressing this reality is to relate the average income of a nation to the amount of energy it generates or consumes (figure 1). The figure for energy consumption per capita gives a much closer correlation with income levels than would a map that simply showed how much coal or oil or rice each country produced.

The resources of a community, then, consist of a natural endowment plus a state of technological capacity. But there is still a third factor to consider, and the latter part of this chapter is concerned with it: what we may simply call a policy. Any community can decide, at a particular moment of time, *which* of its resources to draw upon, and at what rate. Its technology may be sufficiently advanced to provide it with a choice of means of support, and with the equipment to draw upon them very rapidly. It must then decide what it can afford to use in the present, and what must be kept for the future; which minerals it should extract or which forests should be preserved.

In practice, almost all communities, even the most technologically

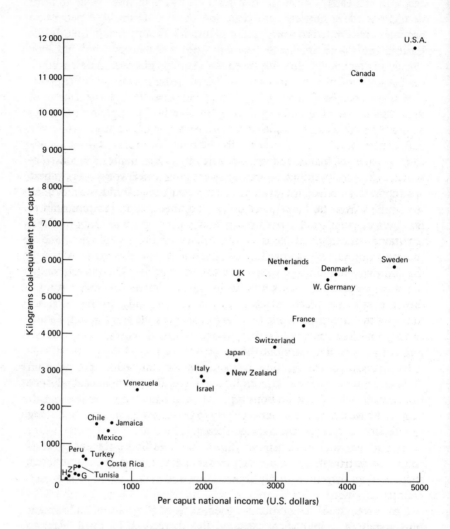

Figure 1: The relationship between energy consumption and wealth in a society: per caput consumption of energy (in kilograms of coal – equivalent) plotted against national income for selected countries, 1972 data. The countries identified by letter alone are: G Ghana, H Haiti, P Pakistan, Z Zaire. (Source: United Nations Statistical Yearbook, 1973.)

backward ones known to us, make decisions about these questions and enforce them by various means. And in practice, also, the number and importance of these decisions are growing all the time, as the number of people crowding onto our sphere increases and the valuation we place upon our resources becomes a more and more critical factor in survival.

RESOURCES, SPACE AND TIME

So far, we have been concerned with defining what is meant by the term 'resource'. We can think of the surface of the earth as possessing a resource 'cover', comprising the total support for man's existence that can be derived from any particular area, given his technical circumstances. It is obvious that this cover varies in density from place to place according to the distribution of natural phenomena; the Saharan tribesmen in Saint-Exupéry's story needed no convincing of that fact. At the poles, the cover is to all intents and purposes non-existent, because no matter what technical resources are brought to bear upon their ice and snow, they are at present incapable of yielding the least support to man. At the other end of the scale, there are areas so outstanding because of their rich endowment that they can only be described, as Russell Smith described the American Corn Belt, as 'a gift of the gods'—regions of temperate climate, smooth surface, deep soil, water in plenty above and coal seams or metals below, all exploited by technically-advanced peoples able to make the most of what nature has provided. The poles and the Corn Belt are the extremes, and it is with the thousand and one variations between these extremes that the geographer has to reckon.

But if it is true that this resource cover varies in *space*, it is just as importantly true that it varies in *time*. Since it is the application of human resources to natural endowment that gives it value, we always have to ask *what* human or technical resources are being applied. Are they those of the Stone Age? Then the metallic minerals have no value. Are they those of the Bedouin? Then the nomads may ride over *every* oilfield in the Middle East and still die of thirst, unless they have some way to extract the oil, sell it to those who can use it and, with the proceeds, buy themselves a water supply that will not fail them.

In other words, as time goes by the world's resource pattern changes, not because nature's basic provision alters (although on a small scale this may happen: we may recall how the unpredictable movements of the herring shoals have in the past affected the North Sea coastlands), but because of changes in what constitutes a resource. These changes have usually fallen into one of three main categories:

(a) There have been *changes in what man needs*, which have led to a revaluation of particular commodities. The best example of this type of change is, perhaps, the spice trade. The Great Age of Discovery which broke upon Europe in the fifteenth century saw the Portuguese round Africa and set up an empire in the Far East; it led the Spaniards westwards in search of the same eastern goals, and the English and Dutch to spend years searching for a northern passage to the Orient. At the heart of this immense, international effort was the desire to obtain control over the spice trade. Europe in the Middle Ages lived through its winters on salt meat, and spices were imported to make it palatable. Next to gold itself, and perhaps silk, there was no resource more prized than the roots and nuts of the East Indian islands. For the spice trade Europe fought war after war, just as it did, in the eighteenth century, for the sugar trade of the West Indies.

Today, no one is likely to fight a war over spices or sugar. The importance of spices has diminished because, with advancing technologies, it is now a simple matter to preserve food, in a perfectly palatable form, from one year's end to the next. A war today might be fought about oil, or conceivably about copper or uranium, but not about spices.

(b) There are *changes in sources of supply*, which affect the importance of particular natural resources. New ways of obtaining an endproduct are discovered and the old way, together with whatever raw materials went into it, is discarded. An excellent example of this type of change is provided by the extraction from kelp (that is, the ashes of seaweed) of the minerals potash, soda and—after its isolation in 1812—iodine. Seaweed, which had formerly been used for little else than as a crude fertilizer spread on seaside fields, gained a new resource value as a result of the chemists' work, and as a consequence there was in the early nineteenth century a meagre livelihood to be obtained, for example on the west coast of Scotland, by collecting seaweed.

But, as time went by, the chemists discovered simpler and larger-scale methods of extracting these substances from other materials. The market for potash and soda derived from kelp began to contract in mid-century. That for iodine kept seaweed gatherers in business for a while longer but, in 1868, Chile exported its first shipment of iodine extracted from the *caliche* of its nitrate beds, and the kelp-iodine market disappeared in its turn. We shall never know how many of the Scots who emigrated from the West Highlands in the later years of the century did so because this particular change in sources of supply finally tipped the economic scales against them. But this is the kind of impact which technical change is apt to make, even on relatively backward or isolated communities.

(c) Most commonly of all, there occur *changes in what man can find a use for.* From the economy of primitive peoples, who sought only for food, clothing and weapons, to the immensely sophisticated economy of modern societies which depend on thousands of different component materials, the story of technical advance has been that of a constant discovery of new uses for materials which previously had little or no value at all. A single invention, or a single discovery, has led to a revaluation of the materials on which production is based, and the resource pattern has changed almost overnight.

Once again, an individual example may serve to illustrate what happens. On the Pampas of Argentina in the mid-nineteenth century there roamed great herds of wild cattle. These cattle were hunted for their hides by cowboys, the *gauchos*. When the *gauchos* made a kill, they took the hide and left the carcass to the birds. There was a market for hides and, being relatively light, the hides could be transported to it, but for the carcass meat there was neither a market nor the means of reaching it had there been one.

And yet, within a few decades, the Pampas had become one of the world's great beef-producing regions. This could never have happened unless, at about the same time, three other developments had taken place. Firstly, the process of industrialization in Europe and the rapid growth of its urban populations after 1850 created a demand for meat. Secondly, the railway era dawned: the Pampas was covered by a broad fan of railway lines (figure 2), along which meat could be moved to market or to port just as easily as hides. Thirdly, refrigeration was applied to the transport of meat: the first frozen cargo left Buenos Aires in the 1870s. It was the coincidence of these three developments which produced the Pampas economy as we have come to know it, and without any one of the three the development could not have taken place.

The twentieth century has provided plenty of similar examples of the values created by new techniques. We may think of aluminium, a metal whose production depends on electrolysis and whose use scarcely antedates the first world war, or uranium, which emerged on the world scene in the second. Only a few decades ago, people found it amusing to realize that their picnic set was made from sour milk or their stockings from wood chips. Yet today all this is commonplace, for these were merely some of the first in a long line of so-called synthetic materials, made available to us by the scientist, and the appearance of each one has required us to reassess the resource patterns with which we had become familiar.

RESOURCES, POPULATION AND STANDARD OF LIVING

To the two world distributions which we have so far been considering—those of natural resources and technical resources—we must now add

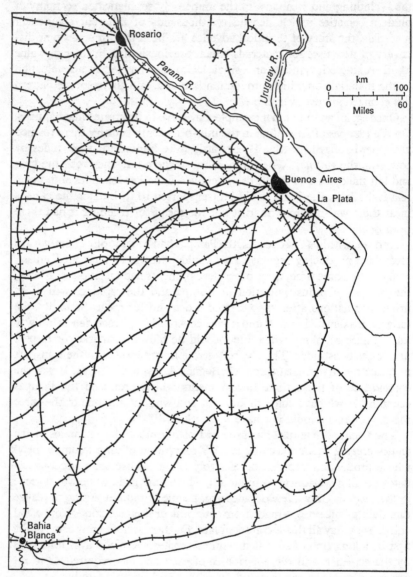

Figure 2: Railways of the Argentine Pampas. For further comment on this network, see p. 109.

two others. One of these is the distribution of population. Like the other distributions, it is manifestly uneven. What is more important, it manifestly does not vary directly with either of the other two. There are dense populations in naturally poor areas, and vice versa. There are dense populations enjoying a high standard of living even in naturally poor areas (as in Scandinavia or the Alps) because of the technical resources they can command, while in a region rich in natural wealth, such as central Brazil, a sparse population enjoys none of the comforts or luxuries of modern living.

How is it that these discrepancies can persist? The reason is, of course, that there is a fourth variable—the standard of living. The resource consumption or utilization of some groups is much greater than others. One has only to contrast the volume of possessions and the daily consumption of food, power, materials or newsprint of the average North American with those of, say, the Indonesian to recognize how vastly different in scale is the resource utilization of each.

So we have a quartet of distributions:

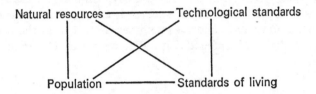

Our next task must be to examine the relationships, if any, between these four because, harmless as they may appear when set down on paper, their supposed relationship to each other has been the source of endless misunderstanding, political propaganda and wishful thinking in the quite recent past. In particular, we need to know whether, since the first distribution—that of natural resources—is largely foreordained, and the fourth distribution—standards of living—is one that everybody wants to alter, there is some way of manipulating the second and third of these variables to produce an optimum condition in the fourth; that is, a higher standard of living for all the world's peoples.

DISTRIBUTION: (1) NATURAL RESOURCES

As we have already seen, this distribution is largely given, and there is nothing we can do to affect it. It does not depend on any other variable within man's control. But what *is* within his control is the *discovery* of natural resources. The period of European exploration which began with the Portuguese voyages in the early fifteenth century is generally known as the Great Age of Discovery. The term 'discovery' applied not simply to new lands in Asia or America but to their resources: this search for commodities marketable in Europe formed one of the main enterprises of Europeans in the following four centuries, and rose to a climax when, in the nineteenth century, the Industrial Revolution enormously lengthened the list of commodities for which Europe had found a use. The discovery of overseas resources and their transport back to Europe underlay both the increase of the continent's population during these centuries and its rising standard of living. The vigour with which the search was carried out goes some distance to explain how, during the same period, Europe climbed to world pre-eminence while a more ancient empire, like the Chinese, decayed. Indeed, 'vigour' is perhaps too polite a word for Europe's search, which was both determined and ruthless: the spirit in which it was carried out was later captured by Ramsey Muir in the following words:

... the anarchy of primitive barbarism cannot be allowed to stand in the way of access to these vital necessities of the new world-economy.[3]

In the Congo Basin and on the Putumayo tributary of the Amazon, thousands of hapless 'barbarians' suffered from the onset of this ruthless search in the nineteenth and twentieth centuries, just as the natives of the West Indies had suffered with the coming of Columbus in the fifteenth.

DISTRIBUTION: (2) HUMAN RESOURCES
What determines the level of technological achievement which a particular human group attains? There is an ancient belief that the natural environment does. Certainly, this belief was explicit in the thinking of the Greeks, who attributed differences in intelligence, courage and initiative to the incidence of mountain, forest or climatic influences. Nor did the belief die with the classical age, for it has had two twentieth-century proponents of great influence and unquestioned scholarship. One of them is the historian Arnold Toynbee who, in his mammoth *Study of History*, devotes much of the second volume to the proposition that there is an *inverse relationship* between natural resources and human resources; that a harsh and unyielding environment has stimulated the peoples occupying it to greater endeavours than—and consequently to domination over—other groups who occupied more permissive environments nearby. The other proponent is Ellsworth Huntington, the American geographer, who developed the hypothesis that climate lay behind the apparently random patterns of human migration and mental energy and, in particular, behind

[3] In *The Expansion of Europe*, Constable, London, 1922 edition, p. 148.

the cultures, the religions and the imperialism of central Asia over the centuries.[4]

From such generalized statements, even when made with due scholarly caution, most of us instinctively recoil, and the recoil becomes a swift retreat when we consider how the twentieth century has witnessed the fuller outworking of doctrines that link human capacity with facts of geography—the doctrines of racism in all its disguises. Today, the deterministic controversy in geography, with which are associated such names as those of Friedrich Ratzel and Ellen Churchill Semple, seems remote and rather naïve; yet we should not underestimate either the volume of evidence that both sides marshalled to support them or the fundamental interest of the question, 'What *does* cause the difference in rates of technological advance?', complex or unanswerable though that question may be.

DISTRIBUTION: (3) POPULATION
In a community living close to nature, there is an initial and simple correlation between the distributions of population and of natural resources. There is a close control imposed on population numbers by the availability of game or fish or berries. But as soon as a community advances away from the level of mere survival, other factors come into play which distort the originally close relationship. Some of these factors are *permissive* and some are *restrictive*.

The principal permissive agent of change is, as we have already seen, technological advance, the first effect of which is to enable more people to subsist on a smaller area. As we shall see again in chapter two, the area needed to support one person may initially have been, in some unfavourable environments, several square miles. But with the development of new agricultural techniques this has been steadily reduced, while at the same time new forms of occupation, such as irrigation farming, mining or manufacture, have had the effect of bringing together dense clusters of population. Only so could 7–800 people support themselves by agriculture on a single square km of delta land in south-east Asia, and only by the introduction of the potato as the staple food of a large part of the population could Ireland support the $8\frac{1}{4}$ million people who lived there in the year of the great famine of 1846.

The other type of agency is restrictive; that is, it *prevents* the distribution of population from adjusting itself to current resource levels. The world's population confronts a multitude of barriers to such an adjustment, some of them political, and some social or cultural. Political

---

[4] A convenient single reference considering both these viewpoints is to be found in O. H. K. Spate, 'Toynbee and Huntington: A Study in Determinism', *Geographical Journal* 118 (1952), pp. 406–28.

barriers hold the Palestine refugees immobile in an area of Jordan which certainly cannot support them; at the same time they have barred the peoples of south-east Asia from entering a White Australia. At the end of the second world war, the density of population in what was left of Germany was increased by the arrival of millions more Germans, removed from the former eastern territories by the incoming Poles. On the social side, there are barriers imposed by land ownership and land policy, so that the great *latifundia* of South America occupy fertile valley lands and support a sparse population of estate workers while the barren hillsides are intensively occupied and cultivated by the 'free' Indians. Much the same landscape met the eye, even though the social background was quite different, in many of the plantation areas and the 'white highlands' of Africa and Asia in colonial days.

Sometimes, too, the barriers are technical; they are raised by the inability of a group to master a neighbouring environment to their own. Certain rice cultivators in Asia are notoriously unable, or unwilling, to transfer their rice growing from the crowded delta paddy land to the upland slopes which adjoin the delta, while in the Brahmaputra valley East Bengali peasants (who were accustomed to a way of life which was virtually amphibious) successfully colonized an area where the original Assamese cultivators had been obliged to give up owing to flooding and changes of river course.

DISTRIBUTION: (4) STANDARDS OF LIVING

Just as the distribution of population in a society subsisting on its natural resources will depend on the quantity and spread of those resources, so its standard of living will vary with the extent of its hunting-grounds and the hours its members devote to gathering supplies. It will compete with neighbouring groups for the richest hunting-grounds and the extra lands that will turn its poverty to wealth—for the *Lebensraum* which it covets, at the expense of its rivals.

But this simple correlation soon becomes overlain by other factors. Even although, for a brief period in Nazi Germany, the idea of *Lebensraum* by conquest became the doctrine of a technically-advanced nation rather than of a desert tribe, it is apparent now that, on a world scale, standard of living varies first and foremost with technological level and, in detail, with social structure. Technical advance in Europe and North America over the past two centuries has made possible *both* the support of a rapidly increasing population *and*, simultaneously, a huge improvement in the average standard of living of that population. Within the population the degree of dispersion about the mean commonly reflects the social climate, the strength of class barriers and the opportunity afforded to the majority to improve its living conditions, if necessary at the expense of the privileged few. In Latin America today, as in Europe at the beginning of the twentieth century, the degree of dispersion about the mean is very wide indeed, and calculation of an average national standard of living produces a figure which is virtually meaningless.

OVERPOPULATION

Between these four interrelated distributions there are, therefore, discrepancies. Sometimes these discrepancies become so pronounced that they create a condition of *overpopulation*.

This is a word which has become very familiar in a world where 65 to 70 million new inhabitants have to be accommodated each year. It is a term which we normally associate with 'teeming masses', probably in Asia, and with an abysmally low standard of living—all of which forms a human tragedy of immense size, and one which we shall be considering in a later chapter. But overpopulation is a concept which must be defined much more closely if it is to have an intelligible meaning.

Such a definition should combine all the four elements we have been discussing, for overpopulation represents a chronic state of unbalance between them at a particular point of time. In particular circumstances, then, an area may be overpopulated:

1   If the natural increase of the people occupying it leads to a fall in the standard of living, or
2   If an increase in the number of workers in the labour force leads to a decrease in production per worker, or
3   If technological progress at the current rate yields zero or negative change in the resource availability per capita.

It may seem strange that by this type of definition the sparsely-settled Scottish Highlands may be overpopulated while south-east England, with its growing towns and traffic jams, is not. But it is true, nevertheless, that the north-west of Scotland has more people than jobs, and that if the population should increase it could only be employed by sharing the limited amount of available work, so that each person did less, and earned less, than before. It is, of course, precisely because this has been the case for generations past that emigration has been necessary, not only from Scotland but from all the mountain fringes of Europe, so that the living standard of those who remained might be preserved: continuing emigration from a region is one of the chief indicators of overpopulation. It also explains the existence of government schemes and subsidies for regional development in these areas, the object of which is to *increase* employment opportunities.

In south-east England, on the other hand, despite the growth of population and the crush on the suburban trains, the standard of living continues to rise at more than the rate for the nation as a whole. This dense population, needless to say, does not support itself on the natural resources of the few square miles involved—most of nature is in any case buried beneath brick and concrete. But the application of *human* resources has been so great that this highly integrated society can support itself without difficulty by trading its resources of technique—its educational background and its manufacturing skills—for the material resources which it requires to maintain itself.

This subject of trade or exchange, however, more properly belongs to the discussion in later chapters. For the present, let us simply notice that the idea of overpopulation is always relative to the resources available to the community, and that these resources change as time goes by. There were complaints of overpopulation in Britain in Tudor times, when the country contained, probably, 3 million people; yet the same country supports 50 millions today. All this indicates is that Britain's sixteenth-century economy, supported by the technology of the period (and distorted by such changes as field enclosure and the transformation of ancient crafts) was incapable of absorbing and putting to use the whole volume of human resources available to it. With our own, much more advanced technology, we may still have the same kind of problem, but with fifteen to twenty times the number of people.

What are the possibilities of removing the discrepancies between people and resources which result in overpopulation? The traditional methods have been direct and violent—cattle-raiding, war and territorial conquest. These are, or were, methods which express the *competitive* nature of resource control; there was not enough for everybody, and the weakest suffered. As a means of eliminating discrepancies, however, they can hardly nowadays be looked on with approval.

An equally ancient and peaceful alternative is to solve resource problems by migratory movement. When hunger and shortages began to be felt, people would move to better-endowed areas elsewhere. Sometimes this migration has taken the form of a permanent transfer from one continent to another: this has been the basic European response to the problem of population pressure ever since the great nineteenth-century upsurge in the continent's natural increase rate. At other times, however, man overcomes the handicap of a very low resource value per unit area by movement of a different kind—by becoming a seasonal migrant or nomad and so obtaining from a large area the necessary total of support for life which he cannot accumulate in any one spot. In the desert, he moves from one patch of grazing to another, feeding his flocks for a month at a time and then moving on (figure 3). So, too, in the quite different environmental conditions of a mountain valley, he may spend each season of the year at a different elevation, herding, cultivating, cutting down timber. In either case, he has to move to survive.

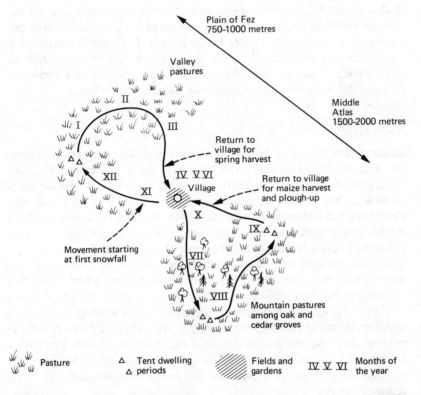

Figure 3: Annual migration of a tribe of the Middle Atlas, Morocco, with two harvest seasons and double transhumance. (Based by permission on H. Schiffers, *Afrika*, Munich: Paul List Verlag, 1962, p. 182.)

But to solve resource problems by human movement implies, of course, that there is somewhere to move *to*. It implies, also, that movement is possible on a scale appropriate to the degree of overpopulation. But for problems of today's magnitude, the old solution is simply out of scale. Migration on a scale sufficient to make a sizeable impact on the problem areas would involve tens of millions of people and an equal number of empty spaces on which they could settle. We do not have the reserves of empty space which the nineteenth century had, and we cannot expect to solve more than a small part of our resource problems in the future by this nineteenth-century means.

If war and migration are both unacceptable as solutions, what other possibility remains? The twentieth-century solution is to concentrate on the intermediate factor between people and standards of living: not to move people but to export technical aid; not to fight for higher standards of living but to achieve them by making better technical use of the resources available. It is no wonder that overseas aid to underdeveloped nations is so prominent a topic in these days. For, rightly understood, it is of immense importance. It is fulfilling the roles of both the old answers to population pressure. It is the modern counterpart of both the cattle raid and the emigrant ship—the rustler and the Mayflower.

RESOURCE POLICY

We must now return, in the concluding section of this chapter, to a theme that was mentioned earlier: resource policy. Since, as we have seen, the application of human resources of technology to the natural resources of an area can multiply its capacity to support population and, at the same time, raise the standard of living, it follows that the *manipulation* of the resource-yielding factors is a matter of the greatest importance. A wise policy will have a beneficial effect on the whole community.

All communities take decisions on resource matters. Generally, the more serious the pressure on resources the stricter the controls, but this control may be expressed in many different ways, small or large; by laws or simply by social convention. A community may express its resource decisions by means of rules about fishing or tree-felling; by laws governing the extraction of minerals and the treatment of industrial waste; by taboos on the eating of particular foods or acceptance of dates by which ploughing or harvesting are to be completed. All such decisions form part of its resource policy.

Most of these decisions originate where the resource situation is precarious, and they are designed to see to it that the individual does not jeopardize the welfare of the whole group. There is no question of any choice between alternative uses, because there is no margin of reserve. The extreme formality of community life in some primitive societies can probably be explained in this way; the group is too near the margin of subsistence to allow for nonconformists. All members of the group grow the same crops, plant and harvest together and take the same precautions to placate the tribal deity.

Where, however, there is a margin or surplus beyond mere survival level, the element of *choice* enters resource decisions. The community can then decide, for example, which of two or more forms of exploitation will be more economical, in the short run or in the long run. Because it has a surplus, it can afford to forego some of its choices. Some of these resource choices are discussed later, in chapters five and seven; the most obvious ones in contemporary society concern the use of alternative mineral and energy sources. They involve policy decision as to whether price alone shall determine the rates of use of alternative materials or whether other factors, such as strategic advantage or regional welfare, shall be allowed to play a part.

Where the resource margin is larger still, it is possible to introduce another factor into discussion—that of amenity. It becomes possible not to use resources in the most economical way possible, if to do so will spoil the view, disturb the sleep of citizens or interfere with their leisure activities. But the point to note is, of course, that only a resource-wealthy community can afford such decisions. Today in Western Europe and North America most resource decisions do involve the amenity factor; in many of them it is the overriding factor. But our present concern for amenity should not be taken as typical of mankind's resource use as a whole. Rather, it is the privilege of a community living, for the moment, in a resource-rich situation to concern itself in this way with the non-economic, non-profit aspect of its environment.

Some of the largest-scale, amenity-based resource decisions of modern times have been those establishing national parks, nature reserves and wilderness areas. By these decisions, the total resource potential of the area reserved has been forfeited to obtain the one value desired—that of environmental amenity. The community is saying, in effect, 'To obtain this value we are prepared to forego all the other values that the area may contain, now or in the future—minerals, timber, hydro-electric potential. We have enough without drawing upon the resources of this particular area. We can therefore afford to sterilize these resources.'

Only a society with a wide resource margin can afford to do this. The United States, as befits the world's wealthiest nation, has done it more than any other; not only does it possess a splendid series of national parks but, under the 1964 Wilderness Preservation Act, a start was made on a programme of 'wilderness' reservation which its advocates hope will eventually cover 20 million ha, or roughly the area of England, Wales and Scotland. If one were to try for a moment to imagine the government of, say, India making the same decision about 20 million ha of its territory, the contrast in resource situations is clear. Only in an affluent society is so wide a range of choices conceivable.

Underlying all the decisions and choices which have so far been mentioned are two assumptions. One is that the community has *the right to decide* matters affecting its resources, and the other is that it has *the responsibility to manage* them. The first of these assumptions has a long history, but recent developments have created a need to re-examine it. If the 'community' has the right to decide, how big a community should

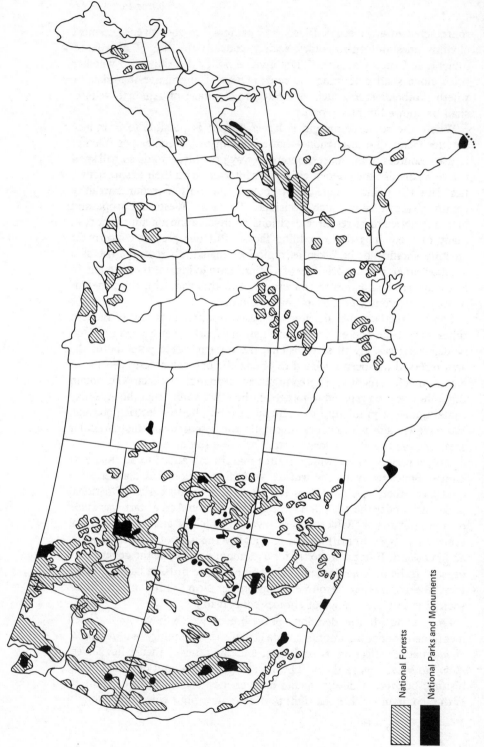

Figure 1.2 U.S. National Parks and Monuments, National Forests

National Forests

National Parks and Monuments

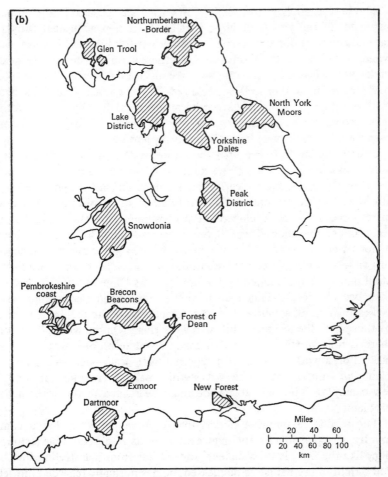

(b)

Northumberland -Border

Glen Trool

Lake District

North York Moors

Yorkshire Dales

Peak District

Snowdonia

Pembrokeshire coast

Brecon Beacons

Forest of Dean

Exmoor

New Forest

Dartmoor

Miles
0   20   40   60
0 20 40 60 80 100
km

Figure 4b: England, Wales and southern Scotland: national parks and forest parks.

do this? Since it emerged in Europe of the Renaissance, the nation-state has been the policy-making community in most matters affecting resources. But some of the most acute resource problems of the present day are purely local like questions of water supply or sewage disposal, over which individual communities claim the right to make their own decisions. Others, again, are regional. Within a federal system, for example, the interests of the nation and the province may conflict. The central government may wish to encourage nationwide use of a resource situated in a single province. The province, on the other hand, may want to preserve for its own use what lies within its territory.

The best example of this clash of interests is to be seen in the oil and gas states of the U.S.A. A large part of the nation at present runs its car and cooks its dinner with petroleum or gas from the Gulf States. But what shall Texas or Oklahoma do when these supplies run out? Is Texas under any *obligation* to sell its gas to Pennsylvania (which has plenty of coal for making gas) or to Wisconsin (which has no fuel at all of its own) just because, at this particular period of technical development, it is the most economical arrangement to do so? In twenty, or fifty, years' time the cost advantages will have altered completely.

Equally, today, it is true that the nation-state is not the ideal, or the only, unit of society by which resource decisions should be made because some of these decisions clearly call for *international* action. We have already seen that the nineteenth century knew a kind of internationalism in resource use—the developed nations assumed the right to exploit the resources of the undeveloped. Even as late as the 1950s, the developed nations were somewhat shaken when a Persian government challenged this view by saying, in effect, 'We would rather not have our oil exploited at all than have it exploited by foreign interests.' The assumption had by then become deeply embedded in the western mind that communities possessing natural resources would automatically desire their exploitation by those with the technical ability to work them. On the whole, however, there is today a strong sense that many resource problems can only be tackled on a world, or at least a supernational, scale—deep-sea fisheries, plant and animal pests, nuclear waste disposal and river flow are only a few examples. The right to decide must be related to the scale of the problem.

The second assumption underlying resource policy is that a community is responsible for the management of its resources. This assumption, like the first, is very ancient. Indeed, far from man feeling that he had a right to use nature as he pleased, he has normally regarded himself as a part of nature's own order, and not as standing over against it in the role of exploiter. It is a development of comparatively recent, western thinking to conceive of the 'exploitation of nature' as one of man's principal tasks.[5] That such an idea could emerge was probably the result of western technological progress and its spread to the vast empty spaces of the newer continents where immigrants from Europe, with no sentimental attachment to the soil, could 'exploit' to their hearts' content, untrammelled by conscience and, often enough, untroubled by neighbours. The great bonanza of this exploitive phase was certainly worse in North America: land was so plentiful and so cheap that it became the currency which

[5] On this point, see A. Spoehr's essay in Burton and Ka*.es, *op. cit.*, 'Cultural Differences in the Interpretation of Natural Resources'.

financed continental occupance. Being cheap, it was poorly esteemed, and being poorly esteemed, it was grossly misused. The worst abuses arose from what we should now call selective exploitation—logging out of a forest one or two species and burning over the rest, or using hydraulic power to cut away hillsides in a search for gold that brought with it devastating soil erosion.

Eventually, the abuses led to reaction and the reaction to the conservation movement which developed in North America in the last decades of the nineteenth century. The 'ecological' view of man, as forming a part of the total environment rather than its enemy or conqueror, was rediscovered through the writings of men like Aldo Leopold,[6] and heralded as if it had been a new idea, rather than an ancient one universally accepted until the ecological balance was temporarily upset by the events of the nineteenth century in a small number of national communities.

If these two underlying assumptions about policy-making are accepted, what should the goal of resource policy be? The simplest answer is probably: to maintain total resources in *a steady state*—to see that a society enjoys the highest standard of living possible without reducing the sum of its resource 'assets'. This clearly does not mean that no resources at all are used; by definition, it is necessary to consume *some* resources to survive. Rather, it means seeing that a society either uses its resources in such a way that they can be handed on intact to the next generation (as in the case of soils or wild life), or else that it ensures that they can be replaced in time by other resources made available by the technical progress of the group. In this way, coal can be substituted for exhausted supplies of wood; hydro-electricity can replace exhausted supplies of coal, and nuclear power can replace exhausted supplies of petroleum.

It is in connection with this idea of maintaining a 'steady state' that we can now introduce the word which has grown so familiar to us in recent years: *conservation*. It may be familiar, but it can also be confusing. Conservation is not the opposite of exploitation. The opposite of exploitation is *preservation* and, within the conservation movement, there have been constant clashes between preservationists, whose goal was to preserve *untouched* an area or its resources, and conservationists who merely wanted to *regulate* its use. Both exploitation and conservation refer to *rates* of use. If conservation is practised too rigidly, a society may depress its own standard of living by hoarding what it can perfectly well afford to use to increase its wealth. But the more common situation, historically, has been the reverse: to over-use resources, either through sheer carelessness or—and this is much more tragic in the long term—simply because the population of an area is so dense that it can only stay alive by supporting itself

[6] For further details, a useful source is R. Nash, *Wilderness and The American Mind*, Yale University Press, New Haven, 1967.

today on resources which properly belong to the generation of tomorrow.

Why has the idea of conservation come to occupy so prominent a place in twentieth-century thought? There are a number of reasons. One is that the figures of world population are now increasing so rapidly—and with an increasing volume of statistical evidence to make us aware of this growth—that their mere publication is a form of propaganda. To accommodate this increase, there are few empty areas remaining of the sort which were available in the nineteenth century: in that respect, as has already been suggested, the period between 1815 and 1914 provided a never-to-be-repeated opportunity to disperse the world's crowded populations into empty spaces.

Another reason for the prominence of the conservation idea is the increase in man's ability to control nature. The *rate* at which he can consume resources has been multiplied by the use of machines, and the *range* of use has been increased by modern means of transport. Technology, in a phrase of E. A. Ackerman's, 'extends the geographical reach of the population group.' Consequently, the rate and range of misuse have also been enhanced. If he chooses to do so, man can overwork his soil, overcut his forest and overfish his streams on a scale unknown in his previous history.

A third explanation is that 'conservation' is a reaction to the cult of conspicuous consumption and its partner-in-crime, planned obsolescence. Some wealthy societies have come to accept a deliberate under-use of resources, which has the effect of increasing consumption and throughput of new materials: they are 'waste-making' societies. Only a wealthy group, of course, can afford to do this. Until recently, it was the prerogative of kings and sultans.[7] But when a whole society acquires the habit, the rate of resource consumption rises astronomically.

Fortunately, this last tendency has been balanced by another: the growth of a social conscience in developed nations about resource levels in less favoured societies. Immediate film and television coverage of famines in Asia and Africa has brought home in a new way to the peoples of the developed nations the size of the gap that separates the haves from the have-nots. It is a phenomenon which has largely escaped comment that, in a few short decades (and in reality only since the end of the second world war), it has become a generally accepted proposition that it is the *duty* of developed nations to help the underdeveloped—a proposition that crops up, unchallenged, in such diverse places as papal bulls and

[7] Perhaps the democratization of waste-making might be dated from the party given in New York City in the 1920s, at which part of the entertainment was provided by offering the guests trays loaded with Dresden and Meissen china and held by bewigged footmen. The 'entertainment' consisted of throwing the fine china against a wall. For modern versions of waste-making, see Vance Packard, *The Waste Makers*, Longman, London, 1961.

communist literature, but for which there is little precedent in resource philosophy and almost none in resource practice prior to 1945. Certainly it is a viewpoint which provides a welcome change from that of the colonial era quoted earlier in the chapter.

It is perhaps also fortunate for the world's population that the excessive use of natural resources by societies which are technically advanced, and favoured by a high ratio of resources to population, tends to 'backfire' on the users. The conservation movement which grew up in North America at the end of the last century was the direct outcome of the devastation caused in earlier decades by careless exploitation: the evidence was so appalling that it brought about a reaction. In much the same way, the interest in conservation which is now building to unprecedented heights in both America and Europe of the seventies is a response to the evidence of pollution and destruction in the hearth areas of the most technically progressive cultures in the world.

It is probably significant, in fact, that, for the ordinary person in these areas, the need for conservation and care normally forces itself upon him first and foremost through loss of amenity rather than through any actual resource shortage. He finds his favourite beach closed, his drinking water tasting of chemicals and oysters off the menu, and becomes aware that all these inconveniences have a common cause. They are, however, inconveniences born not of poverty but of plenty. It is the newest, most complex synthetic substances which are the hardest to get rid of on the rubbish dump, and the culture which produces Megalopolis that has the greatest sewage problem.

The world of the 1970s is one to which the idea of conservation has returned—*returned* because only during a few decades of euphoric exploitation of the new lands of nineteenth-century settlement was the idea ever far distant from people's minds. It has returned with a vengeance. With the world's population increasing by something like two per cent per annum, there has been a flood of books and pamphlets written to raise the alarm: disaster looms ahead. Our earth, we are told, cannot contain us all, for its limits are set and we shall soon crowd each other into the sea. The alarmists have been opposed, however, by others who indignantly deny that we are anywhere near the limits: they see only the exciting possibilities which lie before us.

There is about all this more than a touch of the Mad Hatter's Tea Party:

'No room! No room!' they cried out when they saw Alice coming.
'There's *plenty* of room!' said Alice indignantly.

There is certainly no room for complacency in a world where so many are hungry, or ragged, or cold. Certainly, too, a two per cent annual increase in world population becomes more and more formidable as the absolute figure grows larger. But we must not allow ourselves to be blinded to the fact that to say 'Our resources will run out—next year . . . in ten years—and then we shall all starve' is quite improper, since no one knows what, in ten years' time, our resources will be. We know fairly accurately the limits of our present natural resources—how much meat or wheat we have available and how much coal or oil has been discovered. But we do *not* know what else there is to find, or what means of support our technology may in the future discover. We can only assess resources in the light of our ability to exploit them *now*.

Such an assessment is a complex operation, far removed from the crude simplicities of the pamphleteers. It involves technical standards, social attitudes and effectiveness of government control. Ackerman has attempted[8] to bring together all these factors and to express them in a single equation. It is obviously not an equation which, in the present state of our knowledge, can yield a quantitative answer. Each of the terms in the formula would require to be defined in ways agreed by the users, and the explanation of these terms would necessarily be lengthy. Nevertheless, it is reproduced here to form a summary of what has been said in this chapter so far. Ackerman's formula is:

$$PS = RQ\,(TAS_t) + E_s + T_r \pm F - W$$

where P = numbers of people, with a standard of living S; R represents the amount of resources available to them, and Q is a multiplier for the natural quality of these resources; T is a factor representing the physical level of technology and A is a factor for the standard of administrative techniques being practised; S_t is a factor for resource stability (i.e. the extent to which a 'steady state' is being achieved); E_s is the element of scale economies; T_r represents resources added by trade; F is the institutional advantage or friction loss consequent upon institutional characteristics of the community (e.g. loss through taboos, colour bar, etc.), and W is a 'frugality' element, representing amount of wastage in the use of resources.

Between the 1430s, when the Portuguese began in earnest their work on the coast of Africa, and the latter part of the nineteenth century, when the interior of Africa and High Asia were opened up to European view, each succeeding century brought with it the revelation of new natural resources, enlarging the rich endowment upon which the world's peoples could subsist. Today, we can no longer expect that the future will bring any such great discoveries of natural resources—apart, perhaps, from minerals— as those we have witnessed during the past five centuries; the boundaries

[8] E. A. Ackerman, 'Population and Natural Resources', reprinted in I. Burton and R. W. Kates, *op. cit.*, p. 128.

of the terrestrial unknown have been steadily forced back. For the future, it is upon technological advance that we must depend to increase the means of our support. But this is not some kind of sudden transformation of our situation: we have already been doing this for a long time. The scale of the task is undoubtedly greater than ever before. But this is not a prospect which we should allow to daunt us; rather, we should be challenged by it to greater effort, on behalf not only of ourselves but also of those who at present lag far behind us in the march of technical progress.

2

Inputs, Outputs and the Division of Labour

We have seen that the wealth and poverty of the nations of the world today bear little relationship to the distribution of natural resources. The well-to-do are not necessarily the most richly endowed by nature, nor are the poor lacking in minerals or fertile soils. The critical factor is rather the application of *human* resources to natural potential. It is in the spheres of technique, education and organization that the well-to-do excel. It is these factors which enable a small and crowded country, like Great Britain or Belgium, to make a very limited resource base support a dense population at an average standard of living far higher than that of empty, well-endowed lands like Brazil. In short, it is the technical capabilities which a community is able to put into its resource exploitation that determine the returns which it is able to take *out*.

Out of this proposition arises the concept of *inputs* and *outputs*, which is our concern in the present chapter. All production, of whatever kind, involves the input of some resource: land, raw material, labour, machine power, capital. But which of these factors is used will necessarily depend both on the range of resources at the disposal of the community and on the goal to be achieved. Not all societies, for example, have machine power available, and few of them have as much land as they would wish. They must therefore employ other factors of production in place of those in short supply. Then again, the society and its members have to decide whether they are going to combine their factors of production to yield the greatest possible output, or whether they will accept a lower output in exchange for working less hard; whether, in fact, they wish to maximize production or maximize leisure.

Input choices of this kind over the centuries of technological development reveal two trends. One is *substitution* and the other is *reduction*.

SUBSTITUTION

Primitive man could manipulate only two of the factors of production—the land over which he hunted or collected food, and his own labour. His output varied directly with the size of his hunting-ground and the hours he laboured. From this starting point, however, progress has taken the form of substituting for direct labour tools and, later, machines which have been produced by the input of other factors—technical expertise, education and capital. In this way the input of direct labour has been greatly reduced by the process now generally known as *automation*, a process of replacing men by machines which has become increasingly widespread in the last two decades, but has actually been going on throughout the period of industrial revolution.

The point of this kind of substitution is not, of course, merely that it eases the aching muscles of the labourer, but that the machine multiplies the effect of his labour. It can do the work of a hundred or a thousand men. Consequently, it is usually in the interest of the community as a whole to make the substitution, as soon as its resources allow for the capital investment necessary to put the process in motion. In fact, the main object of the input of human resources has almost always been to reduce the role of direct labour in the input mix, freeing the individual labourer and increasing the output at the same time.

REDUCTION
The object of substitution is to achieve the combination of inputs which, for any given output, reduces the necessary inputs to a minimum. Technical progress has given us more steel per ton of coal used in the furnace, more wheat per unit of seed planted and more food per unit of land, for the support of a population growing steadily more dense. Indeed, we can safely say that, if reduction had *not* been achieved, our earth would long since have proved inadequate to support its growing numbers of inhabitants. In practice, not only has this population been supported but, whereas much of mankind was once obliged to work a 72 or 90 hour week merely to subsist, in many parts of the world today people can enjoy a high standard of living while working a week of 40 hours or less.

What has happened is that man has exerted his ingenuity to economize in the use of his two scarcest or most prized resources—his land and his own labour—by employing resources of technique and capital in ever greater quantities.

INPUTS AND OUTPUTS IN AGRICULTURE

To understand the effect of these changes, let us at once move on from general statements to see how they apply to two main forms of production, agricultural and industrial. In agriculture, all production is a result of an input mix of three main factors—land, labour and capital. However, the proportions in which these are combined can and do vary very widely from place to place, according to conditions of technique, population density and available land. Rice, for example, is grown in both China and the U.S.A. In China, the yield is a little over 3,000 kg per ha, and in the U.S.A. about half as much again. But the input mix in the two cases is utterly different: in the Chinese situation, the labour of one man produces less than one ha of rice in each growing season, while in the U.S.A., where he is aided by aeroplanes and tractors with balloon tyres, one operator can farm 30 to 40 ha. The labour input in America is therefore, say, one fiftieth that of the Chinese. But this discrepancy is, of course, balanced by different inputs of the additional factor—capital. For many Asian rice cultivators, 'capital' means simply their seed, one or two hand tools and a right to use water. An American rice farmer, on the other hand, is encouraged by an advisory pamphlet[1] to consider, as a 'reasonable equipment inventory for a medium-sized farm', two tractors, a truck, two breaking ploughs, a disc harrow, a section harrow, a grader, a roller, a drill, a combine and a grain cart, as well as 70 to 150 kg of chemical fertilizers per ha. The astonishing thing is that, at the end of the day, such different inputs should yield so nearly comparable results.

Among the three factors of land, labour and capital, then, it is clear that in agriculture capital and labour are largely interchangeable. The way in which capital has been substituted for labour in the advanced agricultural economy of the U.S.A. is indicated by table 1 and figure 5. Over the 20 year period covered by the table, the area of land in farms was virtually constant, while the input of labour fell by a half and the output rose by about the same amount.

Table 1   Indices of inputs and outputs in United States agriculture, 1940 and 1960

(1947–1949 = 100)

Inputs:	1940	1960
Labour	122	62
Real Estate	98	106
Power and machinery	58	142
Feed, seed and livestock	63	149
Fertilizer and lime	48	192
Other	93	138
Output:	82	129
(number of commercial farms	120	71)

Source: Z. Griliches, 'The Sources of Measured Productivity Growth, United States Agriculture, 1940–60', *Journal of Political Economy* 71 (1963), p. 341.

[1] Louisiana Agricultural Experiment Station, *Bulletin* 491.

Capital, in fact, can either be used to *replace* labour, freeing workers for other tasks, or it can be used *in conjunction with* labour, to increase output. If we compare the agricultural systems practised around the world we find that it is this combination of labour-plus-capital inputs which forms the

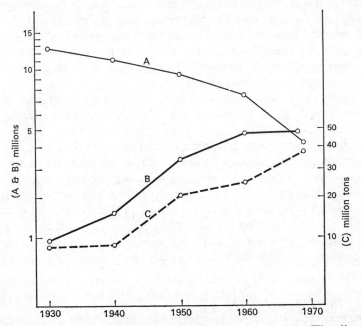

Figure 5: U.S.A.: Changes in agricultural inputs, 1930–1969. The diagram shows changes in the numbers of farm workers (A) and (B) tractors (left hand scale) and (C) in consumption of fertilizers in short tons (right-hand scale). (Source: *Statistical Abstract of the United States.*)

basic variable among them. At some points it is much higher than at others. On land where it is high, we speak of the farming as being *intensive*. Where it is low, the term *extensive* is used.

These familiar terms 'intensive' and 'extensive' refer, therefore, to *the volume of inputs per unit of area*. What decides how large the volume shall be? Although the question is both simple and logical, the answer to it is a complex one. To the prior question: 'How much land is needed to support one human being, or one head of stock?' there is, of course, absolutely no set answer.[2] In our human situation, in any case, the amount of land available is usually the starting point rather than the conclusion: the cultivator adapts his techniques to match the area at his disposal.

[2] In *The Economics of Subsistence Agriculture*, Macmillan, London, second edition, 1966, C. Clark and M. Haswell suggest that to maintain a minimum

Bearing this in mind, we can recognize three sets of factors which help to determine the level of intensity of agricultural inputs:

1 AVAILABILITY OF LAND AND CAPITAL

If land is in short supply, then every effort must be made to wrest from it a livelihood for the population dependent upon it. In other words, the first and most basic reason for farming more intensively is sheer hunger. The more marginal the livelihood, the larger the inputs of labour or fertilizers or waterworks must be to keep people alive, even although the land itself may be of inferior quality.

However, to intensify farming implies the existence of reserves, either of labour or of capital. The only way in which the farmer can intensify his own labour input (to keep up, usually, with an increasing population) is by working longer hours. But where natural processes of crop growth are concerned, there is a ceiling on this type of intensification; no matter how many hours a farmer works, his crop will not ripen any sooner. Nor is there any extra land for him to cultivate. In these circumstances only an increase in the capital input, in the form of either better seed or more fertilizer, is likely to affect the result of his labour. And to these things he has no access, nor any way of earning them. Only when capital reserves exist *somewhere* within the community can intensification of farming take place.

2 ENVIRONMENTAL QUALITY

Some areas lend themselves to intensive farming because of their natural condition—fertile soil, adequate water supply, smooth surface. Absence of these conditions results in low yields per ha, whether of crops or of stock, and in the kind of extensive pastoralism found in Patagonia or the western U.S.A. The individual rancher may be prosperous enough, but only on the basis that he can command the output of a large number of hectares, each of which individually has a very low output. In other words, the population which such an area can support is very sparse.

Natural conditions, then, condemn some areas permanently to extensive use unless, by his technical skills, the user can create what is in reality an artificial environment, by altering the natural conditions over a small

---

subsistence level requires about 300 kg of grain-equivalent per person per year (p. 53). It appears that, in primitive hunting communities, the area required to produce this amount of subsistence was of the order of 30 km^2 for the Australian Aborigines and 20–25 km^2 on the North American Prairies. With the introduction of agriculture, this figure fell to 1–5 km^2. Progress in technique and pressure on land have since conspired to bring this requirement down to 0·25–0·30 hectares (0·6–0·75 acres) per person among African and Asian shifting cultivators, and to as little as 0·06 hectares (0·15 acres) in present-day Japan, with its intensive rice cultivation.

area. The most obvious example is the use of irrigation in arid lands, by means of which intensive cultivation can replace extensive pastoralism. But there are other methods. One of the most intensively used agricultural regions in the world is an area of naturally infertile sandy soils in the Netherlands, which has been so enriched and cossetted over the years that it produces a world-famous bulb crop from what is, in effect, an artificial soil. Not far away from the bulb fields is the Westland region, where vegetables are intensively produced in the entirely artificial environment of acres of greenhouses. Over a limited area, then, the environmental obstacles to intensive land use can be overcome—if there is some reason for overcoming them.

3 ECONOMIC CONSIDERATIONS

In areas of subsistence agriculture—that is, where farming is being carried on for the support of the cultivator or the village community alone—intensity of output is likely to be governed almost wholly by the two considerations we have so far reviewed. But economic development beyond subsistence level brings with it changes in this simple relationship between type of land and input level. For one thing, the farmer now has a surplus to dispose of, in competition with other producers. For another, his occupance of the land is challenged by rival users who want to open quarries or build houses or erect factories. The value of his land no longer varies directly with its quality alone, but also with its *situation*— with its access to market and its suitability for purposes that compete with agricultural use.

Let us consider each of these complicating factors in turn. The existence of a market affects the farmer's decisions in two ways. (a) The producer who occupies the land nearest to the market has a clear advantage over producers further away—transport costs on his produce are lower. The desirability of this near-to-market land will mean that the price at which it changes hands will be bid up, and the purchaser will have to compensate for the higher price by a higher output; in other words, his use of the land must increase in intensity. The same is true not only of land close to the market but also of land near a port, a shipping-point or a railway line: the advantage of access to transport is in the same category as the advantage of access to market direct, and the land prices reflect this, falling off with distance from means of transport. The effect of this on input decisions can be traced on all the world's frontiers: as transport facilities become available, so farming becomes more intensive, partly because it is now *worthwhile* intensifying and partly because, with higher land prices, the farmer is obliged to intensify to meet his higher costs.

(b) The decision to increase his inputs and intensify his farming is linked with the farmer's market opportunity in another way. If we imagine—

which is generally the case—the market for agricultural produce as a point, then the best place at which to concentrate extra inputs is close to the market. Suppose that there are two farms, each producing 1,000 bushels of wheat, at distances of 10 and 50 km from the market point. An extra input of seed and fertilizer on either of them will double its output. If this extra input is applied to the distant farm, the resultant extra yield will have to travel 50 km; it will involve 50,000 bushel-km of extra transport. The same input applied to the farm nearer the market would involve only 10,000 bushel-km of movement. The net advantage gained by applying the extra input clearly increases as one approaches the market.

The effect of rival land uses is to give land a value independent of its quality. Some of the most valuable land in the world is on Manhattan Island, New York, which the original Dutch settlers found to be rough and broken by rocky outcrops, and of mediocre agricultural worth. But once a choice of possible uses exists, the agricultural user must be prepared to compete with the builder or the industrialist in paying a realistic rental for his land. To cover his expenses, he must then intensify the farm operation so that the output per unit area compensates for the higher rental. So where land is in greatest demand—and this normally means on the edge of built-up areas where there are a maximum number of rival users—farming takes one of a limited number of specially intensive forms: horticulture, poultry raising or 'dry-lot' livestock farming. Even so, there comes a point beyond which agricultural land use *cannot* be further intensified, and must give way entirely to other uses able to meet even higher rentals. Around a city, therefore, competition for land creates a series of concentric zones in which agricultural land use falls off in intensity from the inner fringes to the periphery. It was this pattern which was recognized and systematized as long ago as 1826 by Joachim von Thünen, and which is generally associated with his name (see p. 253).

These, then, are the factors which usually influence intensity of input and output in areas of agriculture.[3] We can now draw together some of the threads of the discussion by attempting to identify a number of major types of world agriculture and the input 'mix' characteristic of each. To this we can add an estimate of the local population supported by each system and the surplus produced for the support of other people elsewhere.

For the sake of simplicity these comparisons are expressed in the form of a table (table 2), and the range of values is reduced to a sequence of

---

[3] No attempt has been made, in this brief and simple account, to do justice to the general theory of rent, in either its classical form or modern variants. Only those aspects have been mentioned which bear on the theme of the chapter, and it would be necessary, for a fuller treatment, to consult one of the standard works on the subject.

letters, from *A* to *O*, in which *A* represents a high value, *E* a very low one and *O* an absence of the specific input or output factor. The actual range of values may be very large: as we have already seen, the ratio of labour input on Chinese ricelands to that on American ricelands is about

Table 2   Sample types of world agriculture: inputs, outputs, population and surplus

(*Note:* A rating of A or B in the table indicates a high value; E or O represent low or nil ratings)

		Inputs			Population	Surplus
		Labour	Capital	Output	locally	left for
Sample Type	*Land*	*per ha*	*per ha*	*per ha*	*supported*	*sale*
1 Shifting cultivation	A–B	A	O	E	E	O
2 Delta rice farming •	E	A	E*	A–B	A	O
3 European-organized plantation agriculture	C–D	C–D	A–B	A–B	O†	A
4 West European mixed farming	D–E	C–D	A–B	A–B	A–B	C–D
5 Southern European peasant farming	D–E	A–B	D–E	C–D	A–B	E
6 'New Lands' wheat farming	A	D–E	A–B	C–D	E	A–B

* Mainly in the form of irrigation canals or water works.
† Plantation crops not consumed by labour force or their families: food crops must be grown elsewhere.

50:1. But since all the values must be greatly generalized, the table merely serves to give orders of magnitude: the important point is that these variations in input–output combinations do exist, and that they have measurable effects on the world's food supply.

On this basis we could evaluate any of the other types of world agriculture or, for that matter, the land use of a particular region, and arrive at an estimation of its particular strengths and weaknesses. For what becomes apparent as we assess each type is that in most cases the input mix *could be improved*. How this can be done in any individual case is a subject which we shall consider later, in chapter seven.

INPUTS AND OUTPUTS IN INDUSTRY

When we turn from agriculture to industrial activity, the individual factors of production may alter in importance, but the pattern of analysis is exactly the same. We are concerned with inputs of labour, raw materials, capital in the form of machinery and plant, and power. Size of investment replaces intensity of land use as the basic variable between one operator and another, but the objective is still to achieve optimum output per unit of input, whether the output is to be measured in tons of steel or numbers of cattle.

There is, admittedly, one general difference between agricultural and industrial production, a difference pinpointed by Chisholm.[4] It lies in the relationship between production and location in the two cases. In agriculture, says Chisholm, 'the problem is to determine the optimum *production* for a farm the location of which is given.' With industry, 'the problem is reversed; given the type of production, what is the optimum location?' Although there are numerous exceptions to this general statement, it is certainly true that, whereas in agriculture land usually enters into calculations as a factor of *use*, in industry it enters as a factor of *cost*.

With this distinction made and qualified, we can consider the pattern of inputs that go to the making of an industry. All manufacturing is designed to do one or both of two things:

1   To replace hand labour by machines which are more powerful, more reliable or less costly to employ;
2   To apply heat, pressure or other processes to raw materials, in order to change their form.

We find, in consequence, in the period of industrialization which began in the late eighteenth century, and which has been continuing ever since, firstly that the share of labour inputs in the total operation has progressively declined, while the role of machinery has become larger and more complex, and secondly that industrial operations, because of either their scale or their nature, have increasingly required special premises to be built for them, i.e. factories. In the terms which we are employing in this chapter, the general trend has been towards a smaller direct input of labour and a much larger investment in both machinery and plant.

We saw earlier that, in agriculture, labour and capital were to a large extent interchangeable, if only because there is almost nothing in an agricultural operation, including pulling a plough, which human labour *cannot* perform if necessary. The substitution of machinery for men is largely a matter of convenience. This was equally the case in the earliest stages of industrialization: mechanical looms replaced handlooms and water mills worked bellows for the iron foundry, but the machine did nothing which the earlier manual operation could not achieve, if at a slower pace. Manifestly, however, it is *not* the case in most industries today; we do not have manually-operated cyclotrons. Most industrial effects are impossible to achieve without the input of considerable amounts of capital which becomes, therefore, not merely a convenient replacement for labour but the *essential* resource without which industrialization is impossible.

[4] M. Chisholm, *Rural Settlement and Land Use*, Hutchinson, London, 1962, p. 41.

The way in which the input structure of industry has changed over the period of industrial revolution (for there is no serious question but that the revolution is still in progress) is perhaps most clearly illustrated by the growth of the textile industry. Before the mid-eighteenth century, the manufacture of cloth was carried out by individual spinners and weavers in their own cottages, where they operated simple spinning wheels and handlooms. Material was supplied and collected by journeymen so that little warehousing was necessary; the investment represented by industrial premises and by machinery were both negligible. The only two significant items of cost were raw materials and labour. Production was small, and the productivity of the worker was limited by the speed of his or her hands.

The Industrial Revolution not only brought into use a whole series of machines which multiplied the effectiveness of each pair of hands, but also harnessed water power and, later, steam, to these machines. The machines were initially costly to install, but afterwards they greatly reduced the labour input and labour cost per length of cloth. Not only this but, to be effective, they had to be installed adjacent to the source of power —that is, in factories rather than cottages. It soon became clear that the cottage weaver could not hope to produce cloth so cheaply or so quickly as the factory weaver: the only barrier to the triumph of the factory was the need to build it and equip it with machines. Once this barrier was overcome, the new input combination of machine power with small amounts of labour produced more cloth, more cheaply, in relation to input than the old combination of large amounts of labour and negligible capital investment.

There has since occurred a further stage in the development of the textile industry—the swing to the use of synthetic materials. This marks the stage in which capital investment is undertaken not simply for the sake of convenience or productivity alone, but as an essential element in the industrial structure, for nylon and rayon and their relatives are not susceptible to production by hand like wool and cotton. Before it is possible to spin or weave nylon, there has to be a plant to manufacture the raw material; that is, there has to be a previous capital input in research and production.

Today, in most industries, the number of horse-power represented by installed machinery far exceeds the number of employees. In the U.S.A. the textile industry (which, as we shall see in a later chapter, is an industry which still employs a larger-than-average amount of labour) has about seven horse-power of machinery for every worker employed. In other types of industry the figure is much higher—36 horse-power in primary metals and no less than 90 in the petroleum industry. The Industrial Revolution of the last century can now be seen simply as the start of a process of automation whereby the labour input in industry is being replaced by machines; that is, by the input of technical resources to a point to which only a few of the nations of the world can aspire at the moment. Just as nineteenth-century Britain became, for a while, the 'workshop of the world' because she had access to technical resources possessed by no other nation, so today there is the same sort of gap between nations which have the technical capacity to go on generating and investing capital in new enterprises, and the many other nations which are at present only in the initial stages of their own industrial revolutions. The speed with which this second group of nations may advance depends very largely on the willingness of members of the first group to supply them with the capital and the educational build-up they need if they are to make technical progress.

THE INPUT OF LABOUR

So far in our consideration of input and output factors we have included 'labour' simply as one of these factors, a factor whose significance has changed very strikingly with the passage of time. But we must now recognize that labour is not a unitary 'it', but rather a collection of individuals with a living to make and a wage to receive, and it is of the utmost importance to a community that its manpower resources, like its natural resources, should be used in the most beneficial way. This usually means employing as small a number of workers for each task as is consistent with its fulfilment, and having the individual worker specialize in some particular occupation for the benefit of those employed at other tasks.

Such a division of labour becomes possible as a society advances technically from a primitive stage. We can observe this if we consider one of the tribes of Africa or western North America which, before the coming of the white man, lived exclusively by gathering berries and roots, or by trapping small animals, an existence so strenuous and unrewarding that it took the labour of every active member of the tribe through the whole daylight period merely to collect enough to subsist. Everyone was involved in the basic activity of food gathering: no one could afford to do anything else.

But if we now suppose that the tribe moved to slightly more favourable lands, or that a series of wet years increased the berry supply, a surplus of food might accumulate. Some members of the tribe could then, without starving, divert their energies to other occupations. Characteristically, the tribe would acquire a medicine man, who gave his services (for this was the first of the world's 'service industries') in return for food supplied by other members of the tribe. In time, other specialists would appear— smiths, shepherds, carpenters—who served the whole community, but only on the assumption and to the extent that the remainder of the tribe could produce enough food for themselves and the specialists too. In other words, only when there were surpluses of food or fuel available at the production level could specialization take place at the service level.

Today, we normally distinguish three categories of employment and sometimes four, according to their role in the economy:

Primary—the basic production of food, fish, timber or stone.
Secondary—the transformation of raw materials by manufacture.
Tertiary—the supply to the economy of services, mainly of a physical character, such as transport, and wholesale and retail distribution.
Quaternary—the supply of mainly intellectual services to the community, as in administration, research, education or finance.[5]

Once we have made this distinction between types of occupation, we can go on to the next step in our analysis—the richer the resource base of a society, and the more efficient the production, the smaller the proportion of a community which will be needed at the primary level. With the technical advances of the past few centuries, western Europe and North America have passed from a condition in which 100 primary producers could support only four or five 'specialists' (such as the landlord and the parish priest—it is worth recalling that, in Britain, the size of a parish was related to the area which could support a priest) to one in which the reverse is true, and four or five agriculturalists produce enough food for a hundred workers in non-primary occupations.[6] In the technically less advanced countries of Africa or Asia, on the other hand, the proportion of the population involved in primary production is much what it was in Britain three centuries ago.

The division of labour among the employed population of any country therefore reveals something of the level of economic development of that country. Table 3 gives this division of labour for a number of countries at different stages of development, and reveals the wide discrepancies between them.[7] And if to this table we add the figures for the food-gather-

---

[5] The proposal to recognize the fourth category—the first three terms are of much longer standing—came from Jean Gottmann, and arose out of his work on *Megalopolis*, the highly urbanized eastern seaboard of the U.S.A., where the quaternary occupations are, of course, very strongly represented. It makes good sense to distinguish between tertiary and quaternary services since, as we shall shortly see, the old 'services' sector has grown so large (60 per cent or more of total employment) that it badly needs subdividing.

[6] In the U.S.A., employment in agriculture is almost exactly five per cent of the total labour force. In Canada, the figure is about nine per cent, but these nine per cent produce enough not only for the nation but for a very large export market.

[7] Since there is often disagreement between statistics departments about the

ing tribe mentioned earlier, in which probably 97 per cent of the active
members were involved in the primary business of collecting food, two
per cent were specialist craftsmen and the remaining one per cent was

Table 3   Distribution by categories of occupation in selected countries,
as a percentage of total labour force

| | PRIMARY | | SECONDARY | TERTIARY– QUATER- NARY |
	Farming, fishing and forestry	Mining and quarrying	(including construction)	(including miscellaneous)
Belgium (1972)	4·0	1·2	39·5	55·3
Canada (1973)	6·6	1·4	27·1	64·9
Chile (1971)	19·3	2·0	31·6	47·1
Egypt (1966)	53·5	0·2	15·2	31·1
Italy (1972)	17·5	0·6	41·3	40·6
Japan (1970)	18·9	0·4	33·0	47·7
Spain (1970)	24·9	1·0	26·2	47·9
U.S.A. (1972)	4·1	0·7	30·1	65·1
West Germany (1972)	7·2	1·9	44·5	46·4

represented by the medicine man, then we can see the way in which employment structure alters with technical advance.

Those countries which have attained the highest levels of development
have in general the lowest percentage of their labour force in primary
activities; that is, the whole community is supported by a very small
number of people actually engaged in the production of raw materials.
Even in the U.S.A. and Canada, which are two of the world's major
surplus producers of primary products, this output is achieved by well
under a tenth of the labour force.

In a community at an early stage of economic development, employment forms a kind of pyramid, with a broad base of primary producers
and a rather precarious apex of specialized workers balanced on top. What
we have today, in the advanced economy, is precisely an *inverted* pyramid,
in which a small number of primary producers supports a larger number
engaged in secondary occupations and a larger proportion still in the service occupations. This inverted pyramid is seen most clearly in the statis-

---

placing of particular occupations (especially mining and the construction
industry) the figures in table 3 have all been calculated from a single source:
the *Statistisches Jahrbuch der Bundesrepublik Deutschlands*, Statistisches Bundes-
amt, Wiesbaden (annually).

tics for the U.S.A. in table 3, with those for Canada and Belgium revealing the same pattern.

In all the countries in the table, the figures for primary producers are steadily declining. In West Germany, for example, the 1972 figure of 7 per cent showed a decline from 23 per cent in 1950; in Italy the 1972 figure of 17½ per cent had been 26½ per cent only nine years before. Here we see the effect of an increasing replacement of labour by machinery in the primary sphere. In the U.S.A. in the 1970s, the capital investment per worker in agriculture was larger than it was in industry, an astonishing fact in a country which has given the world Ford, General Motors and the atom bomb.

A reduction in the number of workers required as primary producers sets an increasing section of the labour force free for other purposes: in the first instance, for converting raw materials into manufactured goods. In the long-industrialized countries of western Europe, this group of secondary activities employs about two fifths of the work force. In countries listed in table 3 like Chile, where industrialization on any large scale is a post-1945 phenomenon, the proportion employed in manufacturing is steadily increasing towards this figure of two fifths. At the top of the scale, however, the experience of the United States shows that there is an upper limit to this figure, and that increasing efficiency and automation will reduce the proportion employed in secondary activities, just as they will those in primary production. In the U.S.A. today, the nation which has the world's highest consumption levels and a great surplus remaining for export, only 35 per cent of the population is engaged on any type of production, either primary or secondary.

In consequence, an increasing weight of employment has to be provided by the tertiary/quaternary sector, or service trades. Some of the services are the direct lineal descendants of the medicine man's: in a society with an adequate margin of productive capacity we can, of course, afford to support many *more* medicine men than could our primitive tribe. Others of these services, such as the ones connected with transport and trade, are logical developments in an economy which is steadily growing in complexity, and which today demands a very wide range of materials for its operation. Others still, particularly the functions of government, have grown up because a complex economy calls for many more controls, and much more planning, than a simple one.

There remain, however, a large group of service occupations whose rise calls for special comment. In a very real sense their existence is an outcome of rising productivity on the part of the true producers: they exist because society has a large surplus of productivity and this surplus can be expended on embellishing life—on providing extras beyond mere existence. In another sense, however, these occupations exist to *increase*

society's consumption of 'extras'. Just because an advanced economy
has surplus-producing capacity, it is important that the level of consumption shall not fall, for the majority of people are consumers rather than
producers. In the U.S.A. where, as we have seen, only 35 per cent of the
population is involved in production, it is a very serious problem to find
something for the other 65 per cent to do. The solution is that they can
consume and, in order to ensure that they do so, a large number of them
are engaged in the process of selling—of creating demand. In the U.S.A.
in 1971, over $20,500 million were spent on advertising. This is a long
way indeed from the food-gathering tribe with which we began our
analysis.

What we have so far seen is that, as a country advances economically,
so its structure of employment changes. Most of the advanced nations
have only a small labour force in agricultural production, while most of the
backward ones have little else. This observation has, however, misled
some communities into thinking that the proposition can be reversed:
that if they are poor agricultural societies they can become wealthy
simply by creating industries. It is not, unfortunately, as simple as that.

There are, admittedly, good reasons for this misunderstanding. Perhaps
the main one is that, over the past century, the world's primary producers
have usually had the worst of the economic bargain. Apart from a few
short periods like the two world wars and the early 1970's, they have
found the terms of trade [8] consistently against them, their prices unstable
and their markets uncertain. Many of them were colonial possessions of
European industrial powers. Small wonder, then, that when they began
to seek independence for themselves the call for freedom was linked with
a call for industry. For industry, apparently, was what made the difference
between the 'haves' and the 'have nots'.

But this is a misunderstanding on at least two counts. One is that to be
an agricultural producer is not necessarily a sentence of economic doom:
the examples of Denmark and New Zealand point clearly away from that
conclusion and, indeed, the ex-colonies have now begun to realize this
themselves. The disability lies not in being an agricultural producer *per
se* but, as we shall see in later chapters, in two other conditions. One of
these weaknesses, referred to again in chapter six, is that of being an
unorganized agricultural producer, lacking the necessary marketing
machinery to enter the commercial arena. The other weakness is that of
lacking the power of independent *political decision* (which is implicit in
the very idea of a 'colony') and we shall have occasion to return in

[8] The 'terms of trade' describes a statistical device created several decades
ago to compare the prices of a sample group of imports with the prices of a group
of exports from a given country. As such it has, of course, no absolute value but
it does provide a guide to the *movement* of prices over a period of time.

chapter three to this point. But on a world scale industries have just as many price and market problems as agriculture, and there were more steelworkers and textile mill hands among the unemployed in the depressed 1930s than there were farm labourers.

The other count is that the call for industry involves the assumption that industrialization can be imposed on a community and have a magical effect on overall production. But as we have seen, it is only when there exists a surplus of productive capacity at a lower level, to act as a base, that a society can develop at a higher one. To express this in practical terms: if a poor country diverts labour from fields to factories, the workers who remain on the land must produce food both for themselves and for the factory workers. It is quite possible that this task will prove to be beyond them, unless the thinning out of the rural workers is followed by a thorough reorganization of agriculture (which in turn will lead to an increase in productivity per farm worker).

In the countries which have made the most rapid progress in industrialization since the second world war, this balance between industry and agriculture has been reasonably well maintained, and both sets of workers have benefited. In other countries, however, some of them in Eastern Europe, over-ambitious industrial plans drained workers off the land so fast that those who remained were unable to feed those who had gone. And outside Europe there are, unhappily, some cases where industrial growth, dictated more by political motives than by sound economic sense, has had no beneficial effect at all on the standard of living of either the factory worker or the farmer.

What is even worse is when a community becomes top-heavy at the tertiary level—when the primary and secondary base is required to support a large number of people who may be in services but are directly producing nothing. Characteristically, and especially in the East where considerations of status or 'face' weigh heavily, a person who has sufficient education to rise above the labouring classes is most unwilling to return to their level, even although there is no real use for him in the service occupations. A surplus of employees then exists at the tertiary or quaternary level, a swollen bureaucracy or a horde of unemployed lawyers, and each year college and school graduations release another batch of non-producers into a society which cannot afford them. This was notoriously the case under the British in India, when the openings for educated Indians were restricted both by the nature of the economy and also by imperial policy. Whatever other effects it may have had, the granting of independence to so many ex-colonial territories in the past two decades has eased this one problem at least.

Service occupations can only develop on a sound productive base; otherwise, a high proportion of the work force in this category is a sign not of strength but of weakness—a form of concealed unemployment. In West Berlin in the mid-1950s, for example, it was impressive to see, in every park and public place, road-sweepers in neat white coats pouncing upon the occasional sweet wrapper and brushing up the autumn leaves. Anyone familiar with the ratio of sweepers to leaves in, say, London or Glasgow could not help wondering how the city could afford this service.

In fact, of course, it could not. The productive base of West Berlin at that period was too narrow to offer employment to its whole labour force: in 1953, as a sample year, after bombing and dismantling had taken their toll, 21 per cent of West Berliners were unemployed. Massive relief funds were made available to the city by the West German and United States governments. Rather than hand these out in the form of dole, the city used some of the money to employ road-sweepers.

This single example is too specialized to have any general application but it may, perhaps, serve as a reminder that, on a world scale, no community can afford to pay road-sweepers—or indeed any other service workers—merely to keep them off the dole. It is, ultimately, the strength and soundness of the productive base alone that determines the quantity of services—the 'extras' of civilization—which a society can afford.

LABOUR SUPPLY AND LABOUR QUALITY

As a factor in production, then, labour cannot be regarded as a simple or unitary force; we need to consider its distribution between types of activity. Nor is this all. Equally important in a modern economy is its distribution (1) by sexes, (2) between skilled and unskilled occupations and (3) by ethnic groups.

I MALE AND FEMALE LABOUR SUPPLY

In most societies at an early stage of economic development, there is a very marked division of labour between the sexes. In this respect, the present-day interchangeability of male and female labour in many occupations must be regarded as a modern exception rather than a historic rule. But, even today, there remain types of labour for which either men or women are physically better suited—men for jobs involving physical strength, as in mining and metallurgy, and women for jobs—like electronics assembly—where dexterous fingers are an advantage. In an efficient economy, therefore, there should preferably be employment for both men and women, so that maximum use can be made of this human resource.

In view of the normal domestic responsibilities of married women it is not, of course, necessary to provide or expect jobs for as many women as men. In some highly industrialized societies, like that of West Germany, it is only the postwar shortage of male workers which has broken the hold of tradition upon German women—the tradition which relegated them to *Kinder, Kirche, Küche*—and has brought them out of the home into outside employment.[9] In Great Britain, the ratio of men to women in employment is about 10:6. But women represent a very important reserve of labour, and particularly of part-time labour. It is a reserve that has been drawn upon in two world wars at least, when wholesale conscription of male workers left wide gaps in the civilian ranks.

There is another consideration. Since for many years past the rates of pay for women have been below those for men, women have tended to form a source of cheap labour, especially for industries and occupations whose labour requirements are large; the textile industry is a well-known example. Although this situation is now changing, it still pays an industrialist who requires a considerable number of workers to seek out a location where he can draw upon untapped female labour supplies. In fact, for light industry today, such a source of labour is a prime attraction.

Where would industry be likely to find female labour available? One place would be in any previously non-industrial suburb; for example, on the edge of a large housing estate. Another would be in an area where there was a preponderance of male employment. For several generations past the coalfields have been in this situation—ever since, in fact, it was made illegal to employ women and children in the mines. The miners' wives and daughters have formed a largely unused source of labour. It was therefore to everybody's advantage to introduce textile or confectionery or electrical industries which would make use of the unemployed female labour, and this was one factor in the recovery of the coal regions from the depression of the thirties, as it has been a factor in cushioning them from the effects of dwindling markets for coal since 1950. Today, a name like Merthyr Tydfil or Pontypridd, which once stood for nothing but coal, is significant in the geography of half a dozen consumer goods industries.

2 LABOUR SUPPLY AND LEVEL OF SKILL

A further variable in the quality of labour is its range and level of skills. In a wholly agricultural or wholly hunting community, the range of skills is very narrow; all members, in fact, possess the *same* basic skills in varying degrees. But as the community advances and the economy is diversified, the range of skills needed is broadened and they are no longer all of the same kind. Training and education are involved, and the more sophisticated the economy becomes, the more highly skilled people are required to operate it. In consequence, a shortage of such skilled labour is today one of the main obstacles to further progress in the most technically-

[9] The ratio of males to females in the labour force of Germany was 10:2·5 in 1925 and 10:2·8 in 1933. In 1972, for West Germany only, it was 10:5·8.

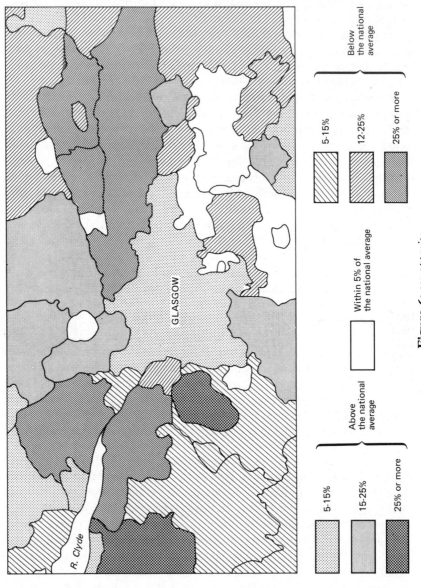

Figure 6: *see opposite*

advanced communities, and the education of labour has become a matter of the utmost importance to their governments. It is very generally recognized that the tremendous industrial progress made by Germany between 1870 and 1914 would have been impossible without the backing of the excellent German technical education of that period, while the converse is seen today in countries of Africa and Asia struggling to industrialize without the necessary cadre of trained personnel: hence the existence of the 'foreign expert'.

If we return for a moment to our theme of inputs and outputs, then we can say that technical progress has greatly reduced the demand for inputs of mere physical manpower, and increased that for human resources of technique, and this has altered the balance of labour input as between doing and thinking. These two subdivisions roughly correspond to the better-known classification, 'blue-collar' and 'white-collar' workers. In the earliest industrial establishments it was not uncommon to find the

Table 4　The U.S.A.: numbers and ratio of production workers to other employees in industry, 1927–1969

	Production workers	Other industrial employees	Ratio, Production workers: Other employees
1927	7,848,070	1,223,982	10:1·6
1937	8,569,231	1,217,171	10:1·4
1947	11,917,884	2,376,079	10:2·0
1957	12,838,889	3,782,251	10:2·9
1969	14,360,000	5,677,000	10:3·9

owner himself working on the production floor with, perhaps, one or two 'white-collar' clerks keeping the accounts in the office. Today's situation is much altered; the production workers' numbers are held down by automation and those of the office staff increase as the functions of research, advertising, marketing and welfare are enlarged. Table 4 shows something of this process as it applies in the U.S.A.

The point at which this changing demand for labour is most evident is at the level of the school-leaver looking for his first employment. There

Figure 6: The Glasgow region: variations in the proportion of female to male employment, by administrative areas, at the census of 1961. For Scotland as a whole the ratio of female to male employment at this census was 47·5:100, and the map indicates how, within a small area, wide variations occur about this mean figure. There is, however, a general distinction between the areas of heavy industry or former coal mining and a textile town such as Paisley, which lies to the south-west of Glasgow and has a high female employment level.

is a steady decline in the number of openings for the less well educated, and a growing demand for those with further training or higher skills. In a country as advanced technically as the U.S.A., a point has been reached where those who have been least privileged educationally—such as the Appalachian mountainmen or the southern blacks—may find it virtually impossible to obtain worthwhile employment, and so become a welfare problem immediately on leaving school.

As the structure of the economy changes, however, other problem groups are likely to emerge. One of these is sure to be made up of agricultural labourers, possessed of a single—if formerly important—skill and displaced by the mechanization of farming. It may be possible to turn the younger labourer into a tractor driver, but the older generation will become a social problem of more or less intractability depending on the speed of mechanization. Another such group which has become prominent since the second world war is that of unemployed coal miners. In the leading industrial countries of Europe and North America, a veritable army of miners (numbering more than two million men in the early twentieth century) were, perhaps more than any other section of the labour force, the burden-bearers of the Industrial Revolution. In the early post-war years, the late 1940s, the status of the miners within this labour force reached its zenith; recruiting was vigorous, and the miners in Britain were being cajoled by no less a person than the Foreign Secretary to produce more coal.[10] Then came mechanization and, even more important, oil and natural gas, to erode the market for coal and reduce the industry's labour requirements. In West Virginia and southern Belgium, the valleys of Wales and the Massif Central of France, the question began to be asked: what else can a coal miner do when the mine closes? The answer appeared to be: very little, except transfer to another mine which has not yet closed.[11] The size of the problem focused attention on it and obliged governments to take action: the Belgian government introduced special subsidies for Sambre-Meuse coal and the Americans set up the Appalachian Regional Commission. In the six countries which belonged to the European Coal

[10] The Foreign Secretary was Ernest Bevin. In 1947, he repeatedly called for more coal production as a bargaining counter in post-war diplomacy. Thus: 'If the miners could place behind him as Foreign Secretary 30,000,000 to 40,000,000 tons of coal a year, it would enable him more than anything else' to 'put this dollar business right' and 'make us more independent of the dollar grip' (*The Times*, 18.vii.47), or 'Give him the tools (money, credit, coal) and he would change the foreign policy of Europe' (*The Times*, 4.ix.47).

[11] In its early years, in the 1950's, the European Coal and Steel Community tried to get redundant miners from the fields of the Massif Central to move, on most advantageous terms, to Lorraine mines, but found that the French miners were unwilling to migrate away from their region. The alternative was therefore adopted of re-training them (as bricklayers, etc.) in their home area.

and Steel Community, the High Authority concentrated on this problem and, in securing a reduction of the mining work force from 927,000 in 1950 to 414,000 in 1971 (of whom only 220,000 were underground workers), dealt with it perhaps more successfully than any single government has done.

But the miners form only one group, if a very large group, affected by changes in the economy and so by *structural unemployment*. Such changes are taking place all the time. Their effects can be eased by retraining programmes, given time and resources, but no society can ever take for granted that it has available the right skills, in the right proportions, for its labour needs in a year's or ten years' time, or that labour can be transferred automatically from one occupation to another.

3 LABOUR SUPPLY AND COLOUR BAR
In some societies there is a third variable in the character of labour— the colour of its skin. If we recognize that the origins of this distinction are physical—the inability of people from the temperate zone to do hard manual work in tropical climates—we must also concede that the colour bar has long since taken on a social character and has, indeed, spread in some cases to temperate lands where climate forms no sort of obstacle to equal labour at all.

The effect of a colour bar in employment is to reserve particular occupations for members of a single ethnic group. Normally, those who are employed in the less skilled jobs are barred from the higher grades and from the professions. Instead, therefore, of there being one set of skills available for the whole range of jobs to be done, the skills of the work force are arbitrarily divided into two—or sometimes more—categories, according to the race of the individual who possesses them. Inevitably, some skills are wasted because a man with the potential to be an engineer, or a doctor, or a physicist, is confined by the colour bar to some menial or undemanding occupation. At the same time, the task which he might have fulfilled is being carried out by a member of the race for whom the job is reserved, but less well than it would have been if the job had been given to the best man, regardless of the colour of his skin.

Such arbitrary misuse of the labour resources of a society may be the product of other forces; the most notorious case probably is, or was, the caste system of India. An example nearer home for the European is the refusal of Roman Catholics and Protestants in some communities to employ each other. But whatever the grounds for discrimination the effect is the same: to reduce the efficiency of labour and to misapply this all-important human resource.

3

Bases of Economic Activity: (1) Exchange and Trade

A division of labour such as we have been considering in the last chapter is only possible if it is accompanied by an *exchange* of goods or services between the community's various specialists. By an extension of the same principle, as the community's standard of living rises, or the economy becomes more sophisticated, the range of its needs will broaden until it has to draw some of its requirements from other communities, differently situated in relation to environment or resources. Out of these exchanges, regular trade is born. The more advanced an economy then becomes, the more dependent it is likely to be on trade. Conversely, without the exchange of goods few if any parts of the earth's surface are so endowed by nature as to be able to sustain a twentieth-century society in all the multiplicity of its requirements. The whole economy is threatened when trade is interrupted by bankruptcy, war or blockade. We witnessed the effects of this kind of interruption during the last world war. In Great Britain most foods were rationed, many raw materials were unobtainable, and the nation's agriculture had to be abruptly converted to fresh types of production. Meanwhile, Nazi Germany was obliged to invent or develop a whole range of *ersatz* materials—substitutes for commodities no longer obtainable, like petroleum derived from coal and coffee made from acorns.[1]

Long before commodity exchanges could be dignified by the name of trade, they were a common occurrence between communities in differing environments—between mountain and valley dwellers, or between the desert and the sown. The earliest formal recognition of these exchanges was usually the establishment of a market where they all took place: the individual producers attended with their goods in a central location chosen for reasons of convenience, or security, or control. While this type of exchange arrangement has become largely a curiosity in Europe, it continues to be the basis on which the economy of, say, rural Africa operates above the subsistence level.

In due course these local exchanges grew to form the basis of the much

---

[1] A person served with this coffee might well believe that he had been given the petroleum instead.

48

more extensive commerce of the Ancient World, with trade routes running through the Fertile Crescent of the Middle East and across the Chinese empire. Subsequently, a new dimension was added to what was now a genuine 'world' trade, by the discovery of sea routes and the rise of the seafaring middleman—Minoans and Phœnicians, Arabs and East Indians. In Europe, the Roman Empire saw the first organization on a grand scale of commodity exchanges. Later, it was the Norsemen who were the standard-bearers in European trading ventures; not the raiders along the continent's western coasts but the traders, mainly Swedish in origin, who worked eastwards from Wisby to Novgorod, and who from Novgorod opened up the so-called Varangian route south and east through Russia to Constantinople.

But meanwhile in the East there was occurring a development which was probably even more remarkable since it did not depend, as the Roman trade had done, on unified military control. It was admittedly made possible by the remarkable organization of the Chinese empire but it involved trade routes that ran far beyond the bounds of the empire—the overland routes through High Asia (of which, later on, in 1340, Pegolotti was to write, 'The road you travel from Tana to Cathay is perfectly safe, whether by day or by night'[2]) and the maze of sea routes that focused on the East Indies, with Arabs trading between there and the Middle East, and an astonishing range of products moving north to the Chinese markets.[3]

Very far, then, from the European nations having themselves pioneered in world trade, it was precisely their desire to break into an already-established trade pattern which, aroused by the reports of returning Crusaders, monks and merchants, prompted them to set sail for the East and so ushered in the Great Age of Discovery. The coming of the Europeans may, in fact, be said to have largely *disrupted* an orderly process of exchange, for all too often force of arms rather than commodity value was the true arbiter of exchange.

[2] Quoted in *Travel and Travellers of the Middle Ages* edited by A. P. Newton, London, 1926, p. 144.
[3] See P. Wheatley's 'Geographical Notes on Some Commodities Involved in Sung Maritime Trade' (A.D. 950–1200), *Journal of the Malayan Branch of the Royal Asiatic Society*, Singapore, 1961, and especially the review of it by J. E. Spencer in *Economic Geography* 38 (1962), pp. 374–5, which is worth quoting: 'What does this study add up to? On the one hand it is a wonderful antidote or counter-irritant to the theory of some modern economic geographers that a far-flung pattern of trade is modern European only. To read, even briefly, of the trade in kingfisher feathers out of Cambodia, sulphur out of Java, asbestos out of Asia Minor, myrrh out of Arabia, and dragon spittle (known in the trade as ambergris) being palmed off on the Chinese by secretive Arabs is a welcome diversion. . . .'

During the three centuries which elapsed after the Portuguese rounded the Cape of Good Hope and entered the Indian Ocean, virtually all the commodities entering long-distance trade were luxury articles, with a high value to bulk ratio and a limited market. Bulkier cargoes were generally found only on the shorter routes, such as those of the Baltic and North Sea trades, where timber, wool or wines moved in quantity. It was only with the rise of the tea traffic in the mid-eighteenth century that the East Indies trade can be said to have developed a 'bulk' phase; both the volume and the value of tea carried increased rapidly to eclipse all other commodities. Meanwhile, probably the earliest long-distance bulk traffic had developed on the famous 'triangular' routes of the North Atlantic. These ran between Europe, west Africa and the European colonies in North America, Central America and the West Indies. From Europe (and especially the port of Liverpool, whose rise was based on this traffic) manufactured goods were shipped to West Africa, where they were traded for a cargo whose 'bulk' formed one of history's most tragic horrors —slaves. In all, probably 9 to 10 million slaves were imported into the Americas between the sixteenth and nineteenth centuries.[4] From the Americas came sugar, rum, coffee, tobacco, timber, fish and (once Whitney had invented his spinning machine in 1793) cotton, while their demand for European manufactured goods rose by ten or twelve times in the period 1700 to 1775 and soared paradoxically even higher after the American Revolution.[5]

With the coming of industrialization in Europe and the prosperity which it generated, the nature of world trade began to change. For one thing, industry generated a demand for raw materials in bulk. Commodities which formerly were of insufficient value in relation to weight to stand the cost of long-distance shipment now were needed in great quantities by the manufacturing nations to keep their factories supplied. Some of these raw materials could, in any case, only be produced in tropical zones. It was necessary, therefore, not only to find a source of these raw materials, but also a cheap means of bringing them to market. At the same time, rising standards of living for the new middle classes enlarged the old luxury-goods markets and transformed many of the luxuries, like sugar or tea, into commodities in everyday use. And industrialization in its turn created a demand for food supplies for the new cities and towns, whose

[4] The figure is taken from the most recent and thorough count, P. D. Curtin, *The Atlantic Slave Trade*, University of Wisconsin Press, Madison, Wisconsin, 1969. The figure refers, however, only to slaves actually landed in the Americas, and not to those embarked but dying on the voyage.

[5] G. D. Ramsay, *English Overseas Trade During the Centuries of Emergence*, Macmillan, London, 1957, p. 225.

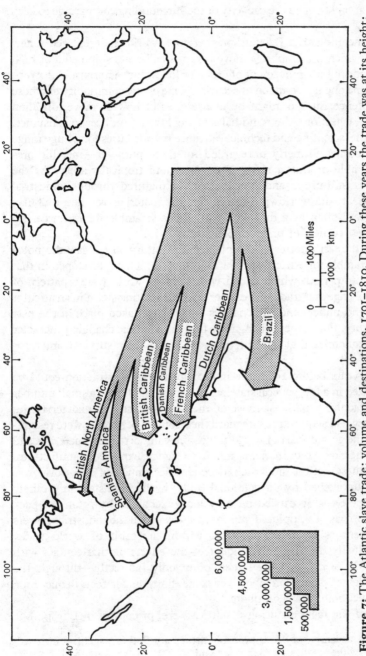

Figure 7: The Atlantic slave trade: volume and destinations, 1701–1810. During these years the trade was at its height; some 60 per cent of the slave shipments of the whole period from 1500 to 1870 took place during these 110 years. (Reproduced by permission from P. D. Curtin, *The Atlantic Slave Trade: A Census*, Madison: University of Wisconsin Press, 1969, figure 14.)

growth far outstripped the capacity of the surrounding countryside to keep them fed.

With the Industrial Revolution, therefore, world trade entered a new phase in which the emphasis moved from small-scale shipments of high value goods to bulk movement of crude or low value materials. The problem became one not so much of securing some exotic commodity of whose very existence Europe might be unaware, as of how to move a million bushels of wheat or a thousand bales of wool from producer to consumer. Meanwhile, scientific and technical advance revealed uses for a huge range of commodities formerly unregarded for trade purposes—metallic ores and vegetable products, refrigerated meat and tropical rubber. As the economies of Europe and North America matured through industrial development, the worldwide search for raw materials reached a climax as it spread, often as a thoroughly infamous scramble for resources, to the furthest corners of undeveloped lands.

It was the last quarter of the nineteenth century which saw the notorious 'scramble for Africa' and for its resources. There developed in that now-remote period, which ended with the first world war, a pattern of world exchange and trade that can serve as our starting-point in an attempt to trace and understand the changes which have taken place in the past half-century. For in these changes we find reflected the changing character of the economies that depend upon trade for their survival and progress.

In the years before 1914, the international trading situation could be summarized in a few general statements, rather as follows: a small number of manufacturing nations, most of them possessing colonial territories which they had acquired to safeguard their sources of supply, were responsible for the greater part of world trade. They imported raw materials and some of their food requirements and, in exchange, exported manufactures. Outside these nations and their dependencies, much of the world was virtually untouched by international trade; it either existed on a purely subsistence basis or carried on only local exchanges by means of pack animals or coastal shipping. Even in the areas which the industrial powers had, sometimes by force,[6] brought within the orbit of world trade, only gradually did the population feel the effects of this contact with the outside world, and even then often only indirectly—through the conscription of plantation labour, or some dimly-understood demand for the production of crops on quota.

Most of the manufacturing countries were, of course, in Europe but

[6] The best example of this is probably the Treaty-Port arrangement imposed on China by the treaties of 1842–1843 and 1858–1860, whereby the European powers, the U.S.A. and Japan assured themselves of the freedom to extend their trade areas into the moribund Chinese empire.

by 1914 they had been joined by the U.S.A., which had virtually completed its economic transition from colonial status to mature nationhood
(and even possessed a few colonies of its own) and Japan, the newly-
emergent industrial power of the Far East. But even allowing for these
exceptions, in 1913 the European countries were responsible for almost
exactly three quarters of the world trade which reached the level of
statistical registration.[7] And among all the trading nations of the world it
was Great Britain which played the leading role. In the mid-nineteenth
century she dominated both world manufacturing and world trade. By
the end of the century there were a number of rivals in manufacturing—
the U.S.A., Germany, Japan—but in the sphere of trade she still reigned
supreme, her tariff levels low or non-existent, her currency the medium
that insured the smooth working of a whole system of world exchange.

FACTORS OF CHANGE

In the half-century or so since 1914, much has altered—the number and
importance of the trading nations, and the commodities exchanged. If
we first consider the actual participants in world trade, we can identify
some of the reasons for these changes.

I THE ALTERATION IN THE ROLE OF GREAT BRITAIN

The leadership of Britain in trade, as in manufacturing, was far too
striking to last. With the rise of other industrial nations her share in world
exchanges has diminished. Trade with Great Britain no longer occupies
a dominant position in the economic affairs of more than a handful of
countries, most of them in either the Commonwealth or the European
Free Trade Association.

This relative decline may have been inevitable, but it was certainly
hastened by the events of the post-1914 period. For one thing, two world
wars drained away the overseas assets of Great Britain, which had formed
the best guarantees of future trade between her debtors and herself. For
another, the dominance of Britain had depended to a significant extent
on the doctrine of *free* trade, a doctrine which, as we can now see, was
peculiarly British in conception and to which a number of other trading
nations paid at best only lip service. The hard years of postwar recovery
in the 1920s and of depression in the 1930s led, by contrast, to the erection
of a multitude of barriers to trade and to the replacement of the old,
free-moving, sterling-based world trade by what was in many cases simply

---

[7] They imported 74 per cent of the primary products and accounted for 73 per
cent of the exports of manufactured goods. These figures, and a number of those
that follow, are to be found in P. Lamartine Yates, *Forty Years of Foreign Trade*
(1913–1953), Allen and Unwin, London, 1959.

barter between governments. Such a situation was bound to be unfavourable to Britain.

2 DEVELOPMENTS AMONG THE NON-EUROPEAN NATIONS

Here, three things have happened. One is that the number of participants in world trade has been increased by the appearance of new trading commodities. Of these, the most important is certainly oil. In 1914, Venezuela, Saudi Arabia, Iran and Kuwait were hardly serious participants in international exchanges; today, no trade survey could possibly overlook them, nor could any political calculation omit them. In the same way bauxite (for aluminium) brought the Guianas into international trade eclipsing their former sugar exports, while phosphates brought in Morocco and nickel the remote French island of New Caledonia. Gradually, then, the involvement of states and communities in world trade has been broadening.

The second development among the non-European nations which we need to note is their growing unwillingness to act merely as suppliers of raw materials to other, industrialized countries from which in the past they have received back their own materials in manufactured form. We saw in chapter one how, for better or worse, independence in Africa and Asia has been accompanied by a surge of industrialization. Some of these newly-industrialized nations have entered the export market on their own account, using their low wage-rates and small overheads as weapons to help them to undersell the older industrial powers: as we shall see in chapter eight, from an economic standpoint the older powers may be thankful that more have not done so. There are thus many more manufacturer-members of the world trade circle now than there were, for example, before the second world war. And the trade of industrial nations is quite different from that simple exchange of consumer goods for raw materials that characterizes a colonial dependency.

The third development may, in the long run, exceed the other two in importance but, at the moment, it is the most recent of the three; too recent, in fact, for us to be able yet fully to assess its impact. This is the discovery by the primary producers, and especially the former colonial territories, that they possess a measure of power over market conditions far greater than they or their customers previously recognized. Almost by definition, the market conditions for colonial producers are set by the metropolitan consumer, and this has been true not only in areas which were colonies by legal status (like most of Africa before the second world war) but in countries which were nominally independent in their political status (as several Middle Eastern countries have been throughout the twentieth century) but which were economically dependent on the same colonial powers. In practice, the price levels for colonial produce of all kinds were set by the consuming countries: even individually, each was more powerful than its colonies and, if they acted together, they could in effect set any price level they wished. Comparable action by the producers to *raise* the price of their produce was not a serious possibility, and *concerted* action by groups of colonies was out of the question.

Political independence has completely changed this situation, although the first major exercise of 'producer power' actually came from a group of states which politically were already non-colonial and in which, coincidentally, a great world resource is heavily concentrated—the Middle East. Here, the oil states have shown the way; they have decided upon a price level for their product just as unrelated—though in the opposite sense—to real costs as the prices offered by the former colonial powers, which obtained cheaply the products of native labour paid only a few pence a day. By concerting their action, and by holding between them a large enough share of world production, the oil exporting countries have forced up the price of oil. And given the political freedom to do so, the sugar-producing, or cocoa-producing, or coffee-producing states can attempt the same kind of agreement, and no doubt will. Even a single primary producer may successfully force up prices, if only it controls a sufficiently large share of the world's exportable supply of a commodity.

3 THE CHANGING POSITION OF THE U.S.A.
For one nation at least, the U.S.A., the year 1914 marked a turning-point in its trade relations which was of the utmost importance. The early American colonies, like colonies elsewhere, were heavily dependent on the mother country for markets and the supply of manufactured goods: indeed, the affair of the Boston Tea Party and the War of Independence which followed were nothing if not protests against this economic dependence. But although the colonies gained their political freedom (to be followed half a century later by those of Spain and Portugal in southern America) their economic status was less simple to change. For at least a century after 1776 the U.S.A. continued to depend on Europe, not so much now for manufactured goods—for those it began to produce for itself—as for capital, the capital needed to settle a continent. This dependence reached a peak in the 1860s, when the U.S.A. was simultaneously fighting a major war and expanding its settled areas westwards (the first transcontinental railway, it may be recalled, was completed in 1869). Huge amounts of capital were required and, in return for these, the U.S.A. supplied Europe with food and raw materials like cotton. Whatever the political situation, the economic relationship of the United States to Europe was not greatly different from that of colonies elsewhere.

Between the 1860s and 1914, the American economy matured. Without ceasing to export primary produce, the U.S.A. became a great manufacturing nation. In the 1914–1918 war it played the part of 'arsenal of democracy' and emerged from that war with a huge productive machine and a volume of credits which completely reversed its former position as a capital-hungry, underdeveloped nation. From now on it was the U.S.A., and not Britain, which dominated world trade relations; it was American productivity which set the world standard; it was the problem of trading with the United States which was uppermost in the thoughts of European ministers of commerce.

The second world war produced a repetition of the situation arising out of the first, but on a still larger scale. Europe, which owed the United States such vast sums, could not afford to pay old debts; nor could it, in its war-torn condition, avoid incurring new ones. The Americans forgave and forgot to the extent of many billions of dollars, but the basic imbalance remained: they could outproduce all other nations, either in agriculture or in industry, and this made them permanently difficult trade partners.

While these changes were taking place the *direction* of American trade was also changing. The old links with Europe declined in relative importance, while those with Canada, Latin America and Japan were strengthened. In 1850, Europe supplied 71 per cent of the United States' imports and took 75 per cent of its exports. A century later, the figures were 19 and 22 per cent.[8] The raw materials which formed the U.S.A.'s main imports were largely drawn from the western hemisphere: its exports, whether of food, cotton, coal or machinery, were distributed throughout the world.

4 THE REORIENTATION OF THE COMMUNIST NATIONS
The other great change in world trade patterns, which dates from 1945 (although the process began with the Russian Revolution) is the withdrawal from free and full trade participation of the Communist countries of Eastern Europe. At the end of the second world war, the U.S.S.R. organized its European satellites into a separate trade bloc, as far as possible self-contained and bound together by reciprocal trade agreements, and planned to give each state a specific role.

Although, in the past 30 years, the satellites have succeeded in reasserting some measure of economic freedom, and the bloc as a whole has come to play a much larger part in trade than it did in its early years, nevertheless the present situation bears little resemblance to that of the

[8] In 1971, thay had recovered, from the European point of view, but only to 28 per cent for U.S. Imports and 33 per cent for U.S. exports.

pre-war period. Traditionally, eastern Europe had supplied primary produce to western Europe in return for manufactured goods. Austria and Czechoslovakia lay on the borderline, economically, between the two halves of the continent, and Germany was the leading trade partner of each of the Balkan states. After 1945, however, all this changed: not only had Germany as such disappeared, and eastern Europe been taken out of the general circle of trading nations, but the Communist-dominated states were now committed to a policy of industrialization which meant that, as and when they re-entered the trading circle, they would do so with radically altered characters, and not as the old-style primary producers of the pre-war years.

Since 1945, both eastern Europe and the Soviet Union have confined themselves to limited and government-planned interventions in world markets, usually by way of barter agreements with other states. Even so, their share in world trade has increased, and there is certainly no reason on other than doctrinaire grounds for their continuing absence from the markets. On some of these commodity markets their full-scale intervention could have profound effects.

Table 5 indicates the impact of some of these changes on the direction and volume of world trade. It has to be recognized, of course, that the figures in the table for 1938 reflect the lingering effects of the great depression of the thirties, while those for 1953 relate to a Europe where post-war recovery was far from complete, and to a U.S.A. which was engaged in stockpiling in connection with the Korean war. 1913 and 1963 were as 'normal' as any years could have been, but the data for 1913 are very far from complete. What we can, however, assume is that, whereas before 1913 world trade was highly polarized, it has become more broad-based both geographically in terms of participant areas and economically in terms of commodity flows with, for example, manufac-

Table 5   Participation in world trade 1913, 1938, 1953, 1963

	Per cent of imports				Per cent of exports			
	1913	1938	1953	1963	1913	1938	1953	1963
U.S.A. and Canada	11·5	11·3	18·0	14·4	14·8	16·7	24·1	19·2
Latin America	7·0	6·1	7·7	5·4	8·3	7·3	9·2	6·3
Western Europe	51·7	50·5	39·1	45·3	46·5	39·3	34·8	41·2
United Kingdom	15·2	16·8	10·7	8·1	13·1	10·3	8·6	7·4
Eastern Europe, including U.S.S.R.	13·4	4·6	7·4	10·7	12·4	8·7	8·2	11·0
Other	16·4	27·5	27·8	24·2	18·0	28·0	23·7	22·3

Source: 1913 figures—P. Lamartine Yates, *op. cit.*, pp. 32–3; 1938–1963 from R. S. Thoman and E. C. Conkling, *Geography of international trade*, Prentice-Hall, Englewood Cliffs and London, 1967, p. 12. The definitions used by the two sources for western and eastern Europe do not precisely correspond, especially in relation to the Mediterranean countries. Comparability is therefore somewhat restricted between column 1 and columns 2–4.

tured goods travelling *both* ways along traffic routes on which the movement was formerly in one direction only.

COMMODITIES IN WORLD TRADE

When we come to consider the commodities which enter world trade we
must recall the discussion in chapter one about the changing resource
value of particular items. Since 1914, many new items have appeared in
international markets, while the importance of others has dwindled, just
as that of spices or silk dwindled in centuries gone by. In other words,
there is a constant process of replacement occurring among the 'top
twenty' items in world trade. The most stable items are foodstuffs, but
even among these there have been some marked fluctuations over the past
50 years, while the widest swings have occurred among the figures for
minerals.

Before 1914, the two items which provided the largest *volume* of goods
in international trade were coal and wheat (or wheat flour). Today, wheat
still maintains an important position, and accounts for 50–70 million
tons of cargoes each year, more than double the volume of the second
agricultural item, sugar. But coal has fallen from its leading position, to
be replaced by the commodity whose movement dwarfs that of all other
goods in volume—*petroleum products*. International shipments of these
have now reached the colossal total of over 1,600 million tons a year—
two-thirds of the world's production, in fact, moves in international
trade, and more than one out of every two tons of cargo on the high seas
is petroleum. Some two thirds of this traffic originates in the Middle
East, a region which, in the early thirties, exported less than 15 million
tons a year.

Although it is by far the largest single element in world trade, this great
traffic in petroleum products takes place almost independently of the
remainder of that trade. The cargoes are loaded at special terminals, transported in tankers designed for this one purpose and unloaded at refineries
situated, for the most part, away from the older dock areas of major ports.
World trade in petroleum has, in fact, a geography all its own. Its focal
points are terminals in remote places or on reclaimed coastal marshes—
on the Persian Gulf or the shores of a Scottish loch; amidst the mournful
flats of the Thames estuary, or the lagoons of the Rhône delta. Its vessels
and loads are both far larger than those to be found in other types of trade.
It moves along a few main routes, between key supply-points and the
market areas of oil-hungry Europe and Japan. It is a trade unlike other
commodity trades and it dwarfs them all by its magnitude.

Commodities entering world trade are commonly grouped into a small
number of main categories:

1 food products
2 agricultural raw materials
3 minerals, and
4 manufactures.

Each of these groups of products has undergone changes in make-up and significance in the recent past, and some of these changes we must now consider.

1 FOOD PRODUCTS

This group of commodities attained its greatest importance in world trade in the second half of the nineteenth century, the period when grain and meat (kept fresh by the new refrigeration process) were pouring out of the 'new' lands of the world and into a Europe which was running short of food for its rapidly-expanding population. Thanks to the opening of huge areas of cheap land in the Americas and Australasia, and with tariff levels low in Europe, the industrial countries could feed their peoples with an ease which had never been known before. (Rather more crudely expressed, cheap food meant that they could pay low wages and so keep the price of their manufactures down.) To pay for this food, Europe exported textiles and machinery—cotton cloth for native populations, and railway engines for the pioneers who were constantly pressing forward to bring new land under the plough.

In the twentieth century, however, world trade in food products has declined somewhat in relative importance, particularly considering the enormously increased number of mouths to be fed. In value terms, it currently accounts for about one fifth of all trade, while in 1913 the figure was probably about 27 per cent.[9] Partly, this change is due to increased demand in the producing countries: independence and land reform have given the producer greater control over his own crop, leaving less to be exported. Partly, also, it has been due to changes of policy in Europe, the principal food-importing area. The 'cheap-food' policy of the mid-nineteenth century was one which overrode both the interests of the home farmer (who could not hope to compete in the open market with American or Australian farmers whose production costs were much lower than his own) and the demands of national security. Before the nineteenth century was out, a number of states, led by Germany, had adopted the alternative policy of protecting their own agriculture by tariffs and of working towards self-sufficiency. It required the first world war, blockade and food shortage to convert Great Britain; although it is only fair to add that with her overseas possessions and her system of imperial preference tariffs she had most to gain from the old arrangement. But the

[9] Yates, *op. cit.*, p. 44.

risks inherent in such an arrangement have become clear, and Europe as a whole in this century has reverted to what was, after all, its historic attitude of encouraging its own farmers so as to reduce dependence on outside food supplies.

Upon this background of rather fluctuating demand for some food products we must now superimpose the other uncertainties of agricultural production: natural variations in yield, and the difficulty of co-ordinating the efforts of thousands of independent wheat, sugar or coffee farmers with the state of the market. Taken together, these factors help to explain why some food commodity markets have undergone such violent upheavals in recent decades. A half-century which has covered two world wars, when the farmer was wooed and rewarded for all the food he could produce, has also included the depressing spectacle of piles of unsold crops being ceremoniously burned and the establishment of quotas for individual crops to curb over-production.

So far as temperate food crops are concerned (and the principal one is wheat), the basic problem is that there are too many countries involved in production, each committed to helping its own farmers and protecting them from foreign competition. Four traditional exporters of wheat—the U.S.A., Canada, Argentina and Australia—between them place an annual average of 40–50 million tons on the export market, but most of this has to be sold in Western Europe, whose farmers also grow wheat. Much the same is true of meat or apples: the main foreign market is in Europe and the size of that market depends on the policy decisions of the importing countries, and on the amount of protection which their governments decide to afford their own farmers. The exporting countries have therefore to be constantly on the alert to discover and penetrate new market areas in which to dispose of their export surplus.

With tropical foodstuffs, the problem is rather different: farmers in the non-tropical, importing countries are not usually in competition with the producers (except, perhaps, in the case of cane and beet sugar). Here, the problem is much more on the supply side than on the market side. The market for sugar or coffee or cocoa is dominated by a few big consuming countries, headed by the U.S.A., and is relatively stable in its demands. What causes fluctuations is the problem of keeping peasant producers informed about marketing and about production techniques—information which, in any case, they may well lack the education to assimilate. As a result, they are subjected to the full effects of crop failure or overproduction, with only the thinnest screen of assistance from their revenue-short governments to protect them.

There are one or two major food products which play only a minor role in international exchanges. Of these, the best example is rice. Although

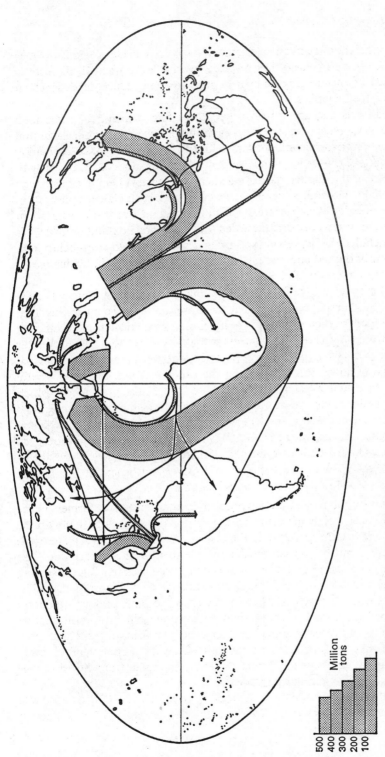

Figure 8: World export trade in petroleum, 1969.

Million
tons

500
400
300
200
100

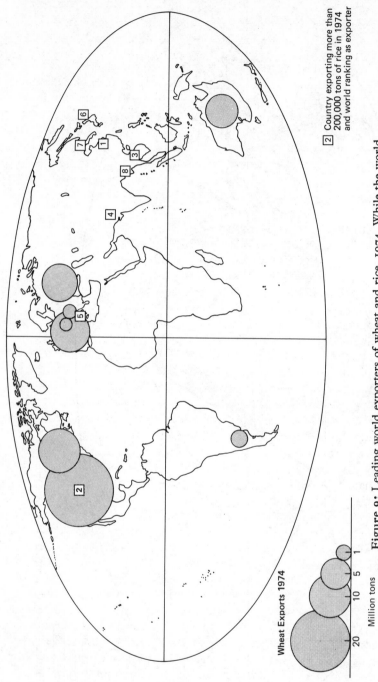

Figure 9: Leading world exporters of wheat and rice, 1974. While the world total of wheat exports exceeded 60 million tons in this year, the volume of rice entering world trade was small: the eight countries shown in order of importance were the only ones exporting as much as 200,000 tons each. (Source: *Trade Yearbook*, 1974, F.A.O., Rome, 1975, Tables 36 & 38.)

Wheat Exports 1974

Million tons

2 Country exporting more than 200,000 tons of rice in 1974 and world ranking as exporter

it is the staple food of so large a part of the world's population, with an annual production of over 300 million tons, only 7–10 million tons normally enter world trade each year (or, say, 2½ per cent of world production, compared with 17–20 per cent of the world production of wheat), and of this export an increasing share is provided by the U.S.A. rather than the Asian countries whose staple is rice. The remainder is, of course, consumed within the country of origin and much of it by the cultivator of the crop. What is true of rice is even more markedly the case with other vegetable staples, like millet or cassava, some of which never travel more than a few miles from the plot where they are grown. Thus the appearance of a commodity in world trade gives only a very crude indication of its importance within the world economy as a whole.

2 AGRICULTURAL RAW MATERIALS

Not all agricultural products are grown for food: some of the major farm commodities entering world trade are destined for the factory as raw materials. Of these, the three most important are cotton, wool and rubber, and they are followed by lesser, but still valuable, products such as jute, sisal and flax. Within the producing region trade in these products is often vital to the well-being of the economy—jute to Bangladesh, sisal to Tanzania, cotton to the Sudan and Egypt.

This being the case, it is necessary at once to add that, over much of the half-century which we are reviewing, the world market for this group of commodities has generally been disappointing to their producers. There have been brief periods of prosperity, such as that in 1950-51, at the start of the Korean war, and in the early 1970's, when a number of sudden shortages developed in world markets. But on the whole the opposite tendency has been apparent: for each of these products substitutes have been introduced, and the substitutes have reduced the market for the natural commodity. Cotton and wool confront a whole range of fibres beginning, in pre-war days, with 'artificial silk' or rayon, and continuing with nylon and the family of synthetic polyesters based on chemical products and marketed under trade names. Silk itself has almost disappeared from world export lists. Jute and sisal face competition from plastic sheeting and nylon rope.

But the clearest illustration of the process of substitution is to be seen in the rubber market. At the beginning of the century world production of natural rubber was a mere 50,000 tons. By 1960, it was over two million. But even steeper has been the rising curve of synthetic rubber production. Introduced generally during the second world war, when the Japanese invasion of south-east Asia cut off supplies of natural rubber to the West, the synthetic product today accounts for some 75 per cent of consumption in the U.S.A., the main market (table 6); this in spite of the fact that, as is clear from the table, the U.S.A. deliberately cut back its synthetic production in the first few post-war years to give the producers of

Table 6   U.S.A.: supply of natural and synthetic rubber, 1945–1971 (in thousands of tons)

	1945	1950	1955	1960	1965	1967	1971
Production							
Synthetic	820	476	970	1436	1813	1912	2241
Reclaimed	243	313	326	293	280	243	199
Total	1063	789	1296	1729	2094	2155	2440
Imports							
Natural	135	802	638	411	445	459	617
Synthetic	10	26	11	9	40	41	127
Total	145	828	649	420	485	500	744
New supply, total	1208	1617	1945	2149	2579	2655	3184

natural rubber a chance to recover their position. The large, and expanding, market for rubber products has consequently not led to anything like a proportional increase in production and world trade in the natural article.

The difficulty for the producer caused by this process of substitution has been compounded by an increase in the number of producing countries operating in the market. Cotton, in particular, has spread to new commercial growers in South America and Africa where it is cultivated, often under irrigation, in competition with older areas such as the U.S.A., India and Egypt. Within the U.S.A. itself, where a quota system has been in operation on and off since the 1930s, the same process can be seen: the old cotton states of the south-east have to share the quota with newer areas in the south-west—California, Arizona and New Mexico—where the crop is irrigated and yields per ha are two or three times as high.

In the meantime, another process has been at work. It is seen in the fact that, while world *consumption* of cotton rose by 56 per cent between 1938 and 1960, world *exports* of this commodity rose by only 10 per cent. What this reveals is that today a growing share of the output is being used and processed in the producing country itself. In the 1850s much of the world cotton crop found its way to Lancashire. There it was turned into cotton cloth, and exported back to the areas where it had been grown. Today, this double journey has in many instances been eliminated: the producers have their own textile industries. Cotton cloth is produced in

Egypt and Brazil and some of Bangladesh's jute travels only as far as local mills, instead of making the long double trip to Dundee in Scotland and back in the form of sacking. For this reason also the overall movement of agricultural raw materials in world trade has diminished in relative importance.[10]

3 MINERALS

Because of their bulk in relation to value, and even without the huge volume of petroleum products already mentioned, minerals occupy more shipping space than any other commodity group in world trade, although they do not constitute the most valuable cargoes. Today, about 300 million tons of minerals—iron ore, bauxite, copper—move across international boundaries each year.

Since all these amounts represent considerable increases over pre-war figures, they serve to offset a big decline in movements of coal. The coal trade reached its peak in 1913, with 150 million tons of exports. This was in the days when most ships and almost all railway engines burned coal, and when it was necessary to maintain coaling stations all over the world, often many hundreds of miles from a coal mine, in places like Aden or the Falkland Islands. Great Britain was the chief exporter (73 million tons in 1913), as the now-empty collier's berths in Fife or South Wales eloquently testify; the U.S.A. and Germany were other major participants and so, after 1920, was Poland, which had gained possession of much of the Silesian coalfield and had little enough use for the coal at home. The trade continued into the years after the second world war (see p.46), but in the past decade it has fallen off into insignificance at the international level.

The volume of trade in other minerals and mineral ores depends largely on how and where processing is carried out. There are two factors to consider:

(a) *The relationship between weight of ore before processing and weight of metal obtained.* With an iron ore of 60 per cent iron content, the advantages of smelting the ore at or near the market outweigh the disadvantages of hauling 40 per cent of waste with the metal. A huge and growing quantity of iron ore therefore moves in international trade, some of it over long distances, to the blast furnaces of the industrial nations which are the consumers. By contrast, the ores of most base metals have a metal content of one or two per cent, and treatment of some sort at the source is essential

[10] The elimination of the double journey can also be seen *within* a country: the best example is the decline of the New England cotton textile industry in the U.S.A. Almost the whole of the industry is now concentrated in the south-eastern states, adjacent to at least one section of the cotton-growing region.

if the metal is to reach the market at a reasonable price. The commodity which enters trade is therefore small in volume and is likely to be either the refined product or one smelted to within two or three per cent of the required purity.

The importance of weight reduction in governing this trade in mineral ores is seen in the recent development of the process known as 'benefication', applied to the famous iron ores of the Lake Superior region. After a century of use, high-grade ores in this region are running out, although there are plenty of lower-grade ores left. The benefication process is designed to concentrate these leaner ores. From 35 or 40 per cent their iron content is raised to 55–60 per cent so that they can travel down the Great Lakes and through the blast furnaces of Pittsburgh, Cleveland or Chicago in company with the high-grade ores being supplied by Labrador and Venezuela. Only by this means is it economical to use lean ores at such a distance from their source (it is well over 1,600 km from Duluth to Pittsburgh). The low-grade ores of the English Midlands or Lorraine are almost all smelted within a few miles of their source.

(b) *The type of industrial use to which the mineral is to be put.* In this respect, there is a contrast between iron and most other minerals. With iron, the smelting process is usually only the first step in a long and complex industrial operation, in which the ore is converted to pig iron, the pig iron to steel and the steel to a multitude of different shapes or sheets in one integrated process (see p. 224). The economics of integration are such that there is no point in having one part of the process at the source of the ore and all the others at the market or the fuel supply. Certainly this was once the case, in the days before integration in the steel industry, but today iron ore is normally shipped to the consumer even when the latter is thousands of km away: from Venezuela to Pittsburgh, and from Swaziland and Western Australia to Japan.

Most other metals, by contrast, are used in smaller volume and by a wide variety of customers. It is normal to produce them in ingot form, a unit suited to the scale on which they are used. There is no single point of consumption demanding—as a steelworks does—a million or two million tons of the product a year. Trade in these other minerals is therefore both smaller in scale and much more diffuse in character than that in iron.

The economical movement of great volumes of minerals has only been made possible by the development of cheap means of transport. We shall be considering this subject in the next chapter, but we should note here, at least, that it is the emergence of the bulk carrier which has made such movements possible—the single-purpose ship (or, in some cases, railway train) which handles only one cargo and often runs only between two specially-built terminals. The Great Lakes ore carriers—the 'Whalebacks'—are probably the best known, as they were some of the earliest, of these specialized bulk carriers, which have now grown to include the world's oil tanker fleets.

With time and technical progress, these minerals tend to replace each other as items of trade: in particular, the light metals—aluminium and magnesium—have displaced copper, lead and zinc in a number of uses. But the total volume of traffic generated by this commodity group is likely to rise rather than fall since, whatever its actual components, it is essential to the support of the advancing tide of world industrialization.

4 MANUFACTURES

The items of trade which fall within this category are so varied that it would be futile to try to consider even the main groups individually. About three fifths by value of world trade are composed of manufactured goods. But it is possible to trace over the past half-century two or three general developments in this sphere, and so to indicate the overall character of these trade movements.

Manufactures are normally divided into two types: *consumer* goods, or articles which are directly used by the individual who buys them, and *capital* goods, which are themselves used (as in the case of machinery) to produce other articles. In the early days of the Industrial Revolution, Great Britain achieved a long lead in the supply of both types of manufacture. The consumer goods category was represented, first and foremost, by textiles—Lancashire cottons, Yorkshire woollens, Irish linens or Dundee jute sacking, which between them accounted for some 37 per cent by value of British exports in 1913. Capital equipment consisted of railway stock, machine tools and mining gear, the essentials for the development of a world four fifths of whose area were only now being brought within reach of nineteenth-century technical possibilities. Although other nations—and in the first place Germany—followed Britain in the export of manufactures, the same pattern generally held good up to 1913.

Since that time, world trade in consumer goods has changed in a very marked way. The prominent place held by textiles has been lost, and the type of manufactures entering trade has become much more sophisticated. The reason for this change is not hard to see. Textiles, with food, are the basic essentials of human existence in most societies. Textiles also happen to represent a fairly simple and early phase in industrial development. As soon, therefore, as a developing country moves into its own industrial revolution, it is likely to begin with textile manufacture. Today, we have a situation in which there are very few nations which do *not* possess their own textile factories, and this small number is steadily decreasing. As a result, international trade in textiles has fallen sharply. Over the 40 year period from 1913 to 1953, for example, the share of textiles in the total imports of a number of developing countries fell in the proportions set out in table 7a.[11] The remaining trade is concentrated

Table 7a   Percentage of total imports by value represented by textiles: selected developing countries 1913 and 1953

Country	Per cent in 1913	Per cent in 1953
Egypt	26·0	7·1
Belgian Congo	23·9	9·5
Venezuela	30·9	7·7
Mexico	12·5	2·3
Colombia	41·2	5·0
Brazil	10·9	1·4
Indonesia	36·7	14·3

at the two extremes of the value scale. It consists either of textile luxury goods, which sell because of prestige and individuality, or of very cheap cloths (and apparel) exported by manufacturers whose wages and over-heads are low, as is the case in much of Asia and Latin America, as well as the Mediterranean countries including, in this context, Italy.

What have been the replacements for textiles? The consumer goods in world trade today are generally more complex than has ever been the case in the past, and have a higher value to weight ratio. This is in keeping with the fact that the simpler manufactures can be produced by the newer manufacturers, and with the fact that the more experienced industrial countries, like Britain, must increasingly concentrate on products of advanced design, in order to stay in the export business at all. Their advantages lie in their resources of skill and education, and it is these which they must exploit if they are to overcome the handicap of higher costs of production. Of all consumer goods the most complex is probably the motor car. Perhaps for this reason exports of motor vehicles have attained a special prominence in the thinking and the statistics of the older trading nations. They form an index of industrial maturity. To become an exporter of motor cars is for any nation to join an exclusive club: it marks attainment of a status level, like the earlier industrial stages of possessing a steelworks or building a railway locomotive.

In the field of capital equipment, the export trade has not shown the same radical changes as in that of consumer goods. It is true that, today, the equipment is different: the steam locomotives for which Britain and Germany were famous have been replaced by diesel or electric engines,

[11] The figures are taken from P. Lamartine Yates, *op. cit.*, p. 251.

and all three have been overshadowed by the growth of the market for aeroplanes, but the basic needs to be met are much the same as they were fifty years ago. These needs are for transport equipment and for machinery to construct, manufacture and develop. Capital equipment exports, in fact, can be thought of as the service which an advanced nation can render to a more backward one. Since the second world war, and quite outside normal commercial exchange, the European and North American powers have made available to the less developed countries a great volume of capital equipment, together with the necessary technicians, as a gesture of goodwill. It will be a considerable time before the need for this action disappears, for there is much still to be done, and little of it can be paid for at present by those whose need for capital is greatest.

What has been said about trade in manufactures can be stated in another form. A country's trade in manufactured goods normally goes through three phases:

1   A period when it imports simple consumer goods, manufactured elsewhere, and pays for these by the export of primary produce.
2   A period when the import of consumer goods continues, but is supplemented by the import of capital equipment necessary for economic development. Much of the latter cannot be paid for out of exports. Rather, it represents investment by the established industrial country in the developing one, and the investing country has often retained effective control over the investment—the British or Germans ran the railways or operated the streetcar lines.
3   A period following development when the country joins the 'club' of industrial nations and itself begins to export manufactured goods.

One of the striking features of world trade during the period when the 'club' has been rapidly increasing its membership is the way in which trade in manufactures has grown *between* manufacturing nations. Growth in the number of club members may affect the *nature* of the manufactured goods entering trade (as we saw in the case of textiles), but far from stifling trade, as might at first sight be expected, it has led to an increase in total value. To illustrate this, it is interesting to notice the figures in table 7b. These show that all three of the regions listed increased their share of world imports of manufactures over the 40 year period. While we should have expected this in the two developing regions, it comes as a surprise, probably, that the third, the most highly-developed industrial region in the world, should fall into the same category. But trade in manufactures between manufacturing nations is today one of the main growth areas in the whole field of international trade.

Table 7b   Imports of manufactured goods: percentage shares of world totals, 1913 and 1953

	1913	1953
U.S.A. and Canada	13·8	19·1
Latin America	13·7	14·7
Africa	7·0	14·0

Source: P. Lamartine Yates, op. cit., p. 49. The figures exclude, however, the Iron Curtain countries.

TRADE PROSPECTS FOR THE FUTURE

The total volume of world trade is steadily increasing. In 1964, and making allowance for value changes, it was three times what it had been in 1938, and had increased at about six per cent per year since 1950.[12] There seems to be no reason why this increase should not continue, in the absence of major world disturbances, but the *rate* of increase will depend on several factors which we must consider before concluding this chapter.

I RATES OF DEVELOPMENT AND STANDARDS OF LIVING

The volume of international trade has increased because standards of living in many countries have been rising and, as they do so, the range of the individual's wants broadens. Once it was only the wealthy—and even then only the wealthy in a limited number of countries—who could command the resources of other lands at their tables or in their homes. Today, the consumption of products from other continents and climates is a commonplace in the more backward also. In this respect, the appearance of the Coca-Cola sign or the Shell petrol emblem in virtually every city from Singapore to Santiago is a symbol of change: it reminds us that a rising standard of living calls for an increasing volume of trade, and that there are, today, truly universal consumer goods.

With rising standards of living, then, we may expect a corresponding expansion in the circulation of goods. What is true of individual standards of living is also true of national development and especially of industrialization. A country's participation in world trade increases as it advances technically, and, what is more, developed countries are showing a higher rate of percentage increase than underdeveloped countries. This is made clear by the statistics in table 8, which divides the nations arbitrarily into developed and underdeveloped. From the point of view of the underdeveloped areas, this failure to expand their foreign trade at a rate at least equal to the world average is a serious problem; so, too, is the fact that

[12] R. S. Thoman and E. C. Conkling, *Geography of International Trade*, Prentice-Hall, London and Englewood Cliffs, N.J., p. 11. For later figures, see also Table 8 adjoining.

many of them depend for their exports on a single staple, demand for which may be relatively inelastic. But since, on any showing, the destiny of most of the underdeveloped areas of today is to graduate into the

Table 8   Quantum index of exports of all commodities entering world trade

	1958	1966	1969	1972
(1963 = 100)				
All participants	71	127	167	213
Developed countries	70	130	173	220
Developing countries	75	118	147	186

(Source: *United Nations Statistical Yearbook,* 1973, p. 410.)

'developed' category in the years to come, we may safely assume that we have here a multiplier of the rate of increase in volume of future world trade.

2 THE RAISING OR LOWERING OF BARRIERS TO TRADE

The flow of trade depends also on the number of artificial barriers it has to surmount. These barriers are normally set up by governments, and their erection has been a normal activity of governments, even very local ones, for centuries. Sometimes the barriers are erected to obtain revenue, by charging customs duties on passing goods. A trade route like the medieval Rhine became notorious for the number of 'toll' points erected along its course by robber barons in picturesque castles, and its usefulness for trade was greatly reduced. At a more respectable level, the Romans charged tolls or *portoria* at intervals along their imperial road system, and the British financed the defence of India from the Indian customs.

More usually, however, the object of these barriers to free international movement is to protect home producers from foreign competition, either by preventing the entry of foreign goods or by artificially raising their price. The range of devices by which this can be done is very wide. In the reign of Edward III in England, the English clothiers were protected by a law which forbade all but the upper classes to wear foreign cloth. In Western Europe before 1950 the same kind of effect was created by requiring all freight crossing a frontier by rail to pay an extra charge, as if it had been unloaded from one truck and loaded into another, even though it had actually crossed the frontier without halting (see p. 105). Other common devices have been the quota system by which a country permits only a limited quantity of goods from abroad to enter its markets and then cuts off the flow, and exchange controls by which governments prevent importers from obtaining the foreign currency necessary to buy from abroad.

The effect in each case is the same: the home producer benefits by these varied forms of protection, even although the price to the consumer may well be raised in the process. So normal has protection been in the annals of trade that periods when trade has been *free* of restrictions stand out as striking exceptions. The best-known of these periods occurred in the mid-nineteenth century, when international trading was dominated by Great Britain and when free trade suited Britain's case. With a huge force of factory labour to feed as cheaply as possible, and a world market to supply with manufactured goods, free trade was to her advantage on both counts. But as rivals arose, they did not hesitate to protect their own infant industries behind tariff walls, nor did they care to see their own farmers driven out of business (for this is what was happening in Britain) by the cheap farm produce of Australasia and the Americas. In time Britain, too, retreated from free trade; indeed, it is quite possible to view the whole episode as a form of mid-Victorian madness, a by-product of the euphoria of those expansionist times, after which things gradually reverted to normal.

The years since 1913 have seen two periods, apart from the world wars, when trade has been particularly restricted by institutional barriers. One of these was the period of the great depression between 1929 and 1933. For most governments, protection was a reflex action when the economy began to falter: especially was this the case in the so-called 'succession' states of Europe (the small countries brought into being by the break-up of the pre-1914 empires and the peace treaties of 1919–20) which had not had the time to establish their economic viability before the depression struck them. World trade, already faltering as production fell off, was further reduced by this host of new restrictions. Over the period 1926–29 world exports had been averaging about $31,700 million a year. For 1930, the figure was $29,000 million and it then fell to below $14,000 million a year for the whole of the period up to 1935. Such a contraction naturally had enormous side-effects: the estuaries and sea lochs of Britain were filled with out-of-work shipping, just as the labour exchanges were filled with unemployed transport workers and stevedores.

The second period of intense restriction occurred after the second world war, when the nations involved were all trying to make good the effects of the war and a number of them in addition were engaged in reforming their economies to new patterns of central planning. In this period the movement of every commodity and every banknote of foreign currency was rigorously controlled. The old multilateral trading system, whereby one nation could pay its debts in the currency of another, or through credits held in a third country, was at a virtual standstill.

It was in the midst of these myriad obstacles to the free movement of goods that the policy was courageously launched of regaining that freedom. The instrument of release was the General Agreement on Trade and Tariffs (G.A.T.T.) and much of the encouragement came from the U.S.A., a nation whose tariffs had for years been among the highest in the world. A series of 'rounds' of tariff negotiations have taken place, as a result of which the barriers to trade have been gradually dismantled. But experience shows that while it is a slow and difficult process to remove barriers, it is all too easy to replace them: political pressure from groups affected by tariff reduction, or cries of 'dumping' when import quotas are abandoned, can very swiftly undo the patient work of the negotiators.

The situation today, then, is that all the subscribers to G.A.T.T. are committed in principle to the concept of freer-flowing trade, but reserve the right to apply 'temporary' restrictions, in the event of a sudden threat to their economy or trade balance. It is unlikely that, in today's conditions, world trade will ever again move with the freedom that it did in the era when it was dominated by Britain and the pound sterling. Not only was that an era when the colonial producers exercised little or no control over their own economic interests, so that the smooth flow of trade was to some extent purchased at their expense, but it was in the period before the planned national economy became fashionable; it was an era of *laissez-faire* and pre-Keynsian economics.

3 THE PROGRESS TOWARDS CUSTOMS UNIONS

While progress has been slow, if steady, in negotiating for the removal of the economic barbed-wire entanglements hindering world trade, the post-war period has seen the development of a far more spectacular, if restricted, solution to the problem. This is the customs union between a group of states. It was not, of course, a post-war invention. The first article of the Constitution of the U.S.A. laid down that 'No State shall, without the Consent of the Congress, lay any Imposts or Duties on Imports or Exports.' The Hapsburg Empire in Europe was transformed between 1700 and 1850 from a series of kingdoms and crownlands with their own customs duties into a single economic unit. Probably the most famous customs union of all was the *Zollverein*, which united Germany economically during the mid-nineteenth century and paved the way, in doing so, for the political unity of the German Empire.

By contrast with these earlier unions, the distinctive feature of the post-war initiatives has been that they bring together independent nation-states, and not merely sections of a larger empire or federation. Since a customs union involves a common tariff on the outside and the elimination of all tariffs on the inside, it also demands the surrender of some measure of sovereignty by its members; it requires agreement on external relations, and acceptance of the free movement of goods between members, even when this may mean disaster for a particular national industry or group of producers. So far reaching, in fact, are the effects of even a simple customs union, let alone those of a full economic union (in which people and capital move as freely as goods) that post-war proposals for union in western Europe were treated with widespread scepticism. It seemed altogether unlikely that nation-states which had fought so bitterly—in some cases against each other—to assert their individuality in the recent past could ever agree to surrender their individualism, even in part.

But from 1952 onwards, this is what has been happening. In that year there was launched the 'pilot project' of European integration—the Coal and Steel Community (E.C.S.C.). It was confined, as its name indicated, to a particular sector of the economy of six countries in western Europe, but its success was sufficiently striking for the six member-states to move on, in 1958, to a commitment to full economic union. Since 1958, this union of the Six, the European Economic Union (E.E.C.), has pioneered the way towards integration, followed cautiously, and at some distance, by the European Free Trade Association (E.F.T.A.) and by skeleton customs unions in Latin America and the Middle East.

The problems encountered along the way to union are not our immediate concern. What is important is the way in which the volume of trade has expanded between the E.E.C. and the rest of the world, but especially between the member countries themselves. During the first decade of the life of the E.E.C. (1958–68), a period during which internal tariffs were being progressively reduced to zero, the community's imports and exports from and to *external* partners increased by 109 and 122 per cent respectively. *Internal* trade in the same period, between the six members, increased by no less than 320 per cent. Trade between members, which in 1958 had accounted for just 30 per cent of their combined foreign trade, had grown by 1968 to comprise 45 per cent of the much larger total in that year.

The evidence of the E.E.C. experience and, to a lesser extent, that of E.F.T.A. certainly suggests that one of the quickest ways to increase the flow of trade is to form a customs union. In practice, of course, there are any number of other considerations to be borne in mind. But governments and peoples can now find some kind of encouragement for the belief that the relinquishment of the right to control or limit foreign trade, which is one of the oldest and most cherished instruments of national policy, is worth making.

The volume of world trade, then, may be expected to increase. The number of participant countries in that trade will continue to rise, until all are involved. Once they are all represented, we may expect to see this involvement spreading *within* the nation, so that those sections of each which at present operate within a subsistence economy will gradually be brought —for better or worse—within the scope of the world economy. In the past, this involvement—this transition from a subsistence to a commercial economy—has often proved extremely painful and disturbing to the community concerned. It will be up to the developed countries, as senior partners in world trade, to see to it that the entry of the more backward into twentieth-century economic life is made as painlessly as possible.

The directions of flow of world trade will become more numerous and varied in the future. For several centuries, there were only two significant 'poles' of world trade—south-east Asia and western Europe. They were joined in due course by eastern North America and virtually all the world's important trade routes ran to one or other of these poles, while the most important routes of all ran between them. But although these routes will always be of major significance, the growing participation of other nations in international commerce is steadily increasing the traffic on other routes and its concentration at new poles. Japan is a clear example. With its advanced technology but very limited natural resources, Japan draws food and raw materials from a score of trade partners—wheat from the Americas; iron ore from India, Australia and even distant Swaziland. This is the peaceful, post-war equivalent of the Greater East Asia Co-Prosperity Sphere, the imperialistic Japanese design of the 1930s whose object was to integrate the resource use of the entire Far East in the service of the Japanese 'pole'. In the present context it is interesting to realize that the whole grandiose scheme was foundering through lack of shipping to maintain the necessary trade links, even before military defeat brought it down.[13]

Not far from Japan, Hong Kong, Manila and Singapore gain steadily in importance as trade centres in a region where, as we have already seen, water-borne trade has been well developed for centuries past.[14] Half a world away, trade is increasing across the Caribbean, between the developing countries of the South American littoral and the ports of the southern U.S.A. This is in keeping with another observable trend in

[13] See C. A. Fisher's fine paper, 'The Expansion of Japan: A Study in Oriental Geopolitics', *Geographical Journal* 115 (1950), especially p. 188.

[14] Singapore, with its strategic location on the Straits of Malacca, now seems, like Chicago in another setting, predestined by nature to be a focus of traffic routes and trade. In fact, both Malacca and Penang took precedence over it, and its modern rise dates from 1819, when Sir Stamford Raffles established it as a free port. Since then, its primacy has been assured.

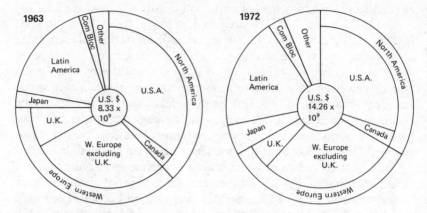

Figure 10a: Latin America: direction of exports by the countries of the Latin American Free Trade Association, 1963 and 1972. Note the diminishing share of export traffic to the U.S.A. during these years and the small (though slightly increasing) proportionate share of regional exchanges *between* the Latin American countries themselves.

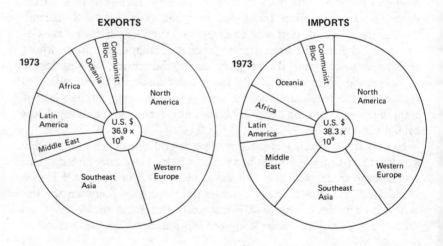

Figure 10b: Japan: direction of foreign trade by imports and exports, 1973.

international commerce: the tendency to what may be called the 'regionalization' of trade, or the expansion of trade with neighbours, in place of the nineteenth century's pattern in which routes from all over the world led to and from European ports, and local commerce hardly existed. And across the whole map of world commerce there is meantime superimposed the most remarkable of all modern trade flows, from another new 'pole'—the great oil route from the Persian Gulf, westwards to Europe and eastwards as far as Japan.

4

Bases of Economic Activity: (2) Transport

In the exchange of goods which we have been considering in chapter three, the critical factor is clearly transport: the openings for commerce are limited by the available means of moving the goods. This is obviously true with regard to the physical provision of roads and railways and canals; trade between Europe and the Far East multiplied after the opening of the Suez Canal, just as wheat production on the grasslands of the New World waited on the coming of the railways. But from the point of view of the economic geographer, the *cost* of such transport is a factor just as important as its initial provision. For the price at which a commodity can be delivered at the market will determine the size of that market and the competitive strength of a particular supplier. In the market price, the cost of transport is one of the most significant variables.

How, then, do transport costs vary? Firstly, and most obviously, they vary with distance. If two suppliers are linked by road, rail or pipeline to a market, we should expect that the supplier nearer to the market would have the cost advantage. But in reality life is hardly ever as simple as that because of the number of other ways in which transport costs may vary. The main variables are (1) the *type of terrain* which has to be traversed, (2) the *type of carrier* and (3) the *competitive policy* adopted by the carrier— to be more precise, the ratio between the carrier's costs and the price he asks for the transport provided. In practice, these other factors give rise to any number of special cases and local advantages, so that mere distance from market tells us little about the ability of a particular supplier to operate competitively in it. That ability is likely to be governed by his choice of carrier as much as by his own productive capacity.

It is clear, then, that transport is a factor of the greatest importance in all economic activity. But for the geographer there is more to the matter than that. Just because of the importance of transport in making possible particular traffic movements, it is often true to say that the structure of the transport network tells, as clearly as any history book would, the story of economic development within an area. On the map of routes, each line has its own significance: it reveals the projects and ambitions of the builders, and their efforts to shape the future of the region. Often these projects have been absurdly grandiose, and little is left behind but a grassy embankment or a half-finished viaduct, as a mute testimony to unfulfilled hopes. But network analysis should find as much interest in the links that fail—and their reasons for doing so—as in those that survive.

There is still a further aspect of the geography of transport which is important. Each of the main types of transport so far developed—road, water, rail, air or pipeline—operates in a different manner and places particular areas or sites at an advantage over their neighbours. Water and rail transport, for example, offer maximum access to points along their lineside—the river bank, the canal wharf or the railway track. Away from the lineside, some other form of transport is necessary. Air transport, on the other hand, creates a pattern which gives the maximum advantages of access and cost to a circular area centred on a major airfield. As these relative locational advantages operate over a period of time, they create different patterns of activity which correspond to the various stages of transport development. Activity, in turn, shows up on the map in patterns of settlement, and so it is possible to allocate these patterns to the transport period to which they belong. In the nineteenth century, for example, the canal and the railway had the effect of aligning industry and settlement along their routes in ribbons of development. In the twentieth century, road transport has produced a pattern of much freer dispersion while air transport has led to the development of some quite new industrial nodes, of which the best example is, perhaps, that at Shannon in Ireland.

All these aspects of the geography of transport require fuller examination. In the body of this chapter we shall therefore consider in turn (1) the various means of transport so far developed and the particular advantages of each, (2) freight rates and competition in transport services, (3) transport policy and (4) transport networks, as a geographical expression of regional development.

MEANS OF TRANSPORT

I RAILWAYS

On land the railway, despite growing competition from road hauliers, is still the major carrier of goods over medium and long distances. It was the vehicle *par excellence* of the Industrial Revolution, and there are few regions which have developed to economic maturity without its help. To appreciate its importance in nineteenth-century expansion we have only to recall the faded photographs in books and museums which document the jubilation in a thousand cities and towns of Europe, America or Australia on the day when the first train arrived. In the flourish of oratory which marked the occasion, someone was sure to declare that a new era of progress had begun. And so, indeed, it had.

But today we can afford to be less swayed by the oratory and a little more precise about the character of the railway as a means of transport, if only because some, at least, of those towns which welcomed the coming of the railway have since seen it depart. The railway, with its specially prepared roadbed, provided the first, and for several decades the only, low-friction means of moving freight in bulk overland, and the only means of moving larger numbers of passengers swiftly. Its usefulness, however, has always varied according to its *capacity*—the amount of traffic which can pass over its tracks in a given period.

This capacity is, in the first place, a function of the number of tracks laid. Since trains can only overtake or pass each other when they are on separate tracks, the provision of a double line gives a railway at least twice the capacity of a single line—and in practice a good deal more, since on a single line a certain amount of time is inevitably wasted in waiting. Yet the construction of a second track adds to the cost of building the railway, and there are very few countries, as table 9 shows, in which as much as

Table 9   Percentage of railway route-kilometres (excluding private railways) which had two or more tracks, 1973

Belgium	62·8	Netherlands	55·2
France	46·1	West Germany	42·3
Poland	33·3	Italy	30·8
Czechoslovakia	21·3	U.S.A.	12·4
Bulgaria	6·0	Spain	6·0
Norway	2·1	Turkey	1·5

(Source: *Annual Bulletin of Transport Statistics for Europe, 1973,* United Nations, New York, 1974, Table 6.)

half the total route mileage is more than single-track. (Great Britain, with well over three-quarters, is quite exceptional in this respect.) If traffic increases, it is necessary to double these stretches of single track. In Europe, this action has most recently been taken on the trans-Alpine route that uses the Lötschberg Tunnel, a route on which the traffic, especially in summer, has become far too heavy to be handled smoothly over a single line.[1]

Capacity also depends on other aspects of construction, such as track

[1] This line has always been privately-owned, but was obliged by the Swiss government to bore all its tunnels, including the nine-mile Lötschberg itself, for double track. In 1913, when the line was built, the company could only afford, however, to lay one track. The recent engineering works have not, therefore, been as serious a problem as would otherwise have been the case.

alignment and gauge. The few really high-speed stretches of railway track in the world are easily outnumbered by the many winding, poorly-laid lines where curvature and gradient keep down speed. In the days before the bulldozer, only a very well capitalized line could afford to cut through a hill rather than go round it, and it is interesting to study track alignment on the ground or on the map and to estimate, as one often can, how well-to-do a particular railway company was at the time of track-laying. Because of their alignment, some railways have been built on narrow gauges, which limit the loads that can be carried; indeed, in hindsight it can only be regretted that so many of the world's railways were laid out on a 'standard' gauge as narrow as 4 feet 8½ inches (1·44 metres), for no better reason than that it was supposedly the distance between the wheels of a Roman chariot. Sometimes, because of terrain or, much worse, because of the whim of government or contractor, countries operate a railway system of mixed gauges, where trans-shipment between gauges adds to the cost of movement. For this inefficient state of affairs Australia has until recently been notorious: standardization is not yet complete.

The last important factor which determines the railway's capacity is the type of train movement over it. Highest capacity is achieved by running all trains at the same speed and with the same stopping points. When this happens, no train has to overtake or to wait for another. Conversely, however, if the traffic is mixed—as it usually is—line capacity is reduced. Figure 11, which is a simplified version of a train diagram, illustrates this feature. At the left-hand side of the figure a number of trains are shown operating on a regular-interval basis with a few identical stops. With such a schedule, it is a simple matter to increase the number of trains running in a given period, up to the limits imposed by the type of signalling employed and the length of the intermediate stops. On the right of the diagram, however, the regular-interval service is augmented by (1) a local train, travelling slowly and stopping more often, and (2) an express train which has priority. Since overtaking is only possible where loops occur in the track, the movement of all the trains is impeded, with delays at the points marked, even assuming that the route is double-tracked and that return traffic is not involved.

Traffic capacity, then, is the critical factor in railway operation, and the type of traffic best suited to this form of transport is the movement of goods in bulk quantities but of moderate individual size (for very large objects will not fit within the loading gauge), preferably on a regular basis between the same two points. In passenger service, the railway's advantages are greatest when the number of people to be transported is large, as it is likely to be between two cities, and where the distance between them is not more than 300–400 km, beyond which point the competition of air transport

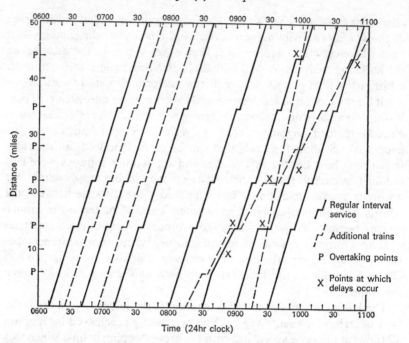

Figure 11: A train diagram: a simplified and uni-directional version of the train-movement planning diagram, as used for timetable construction. For explanation, see the adjoining text.

becomes much stronger. The advantages of rail transport diminish, conversely, as the passenger traffic becomes smaller in scale and the individual destinations more numerous.

What is the pattern of activity which the railway creates? Since the train is confined to its tracks, the railway offers overwhelming advantages to lineside locations. Admittedly, the main line may be extended by branches or sidings, but the presence of the tracks is everything. In evidence of this situation, we need only think of the fate of some of the communities which, in the early days of the railway era, mistakenly refused to allow the lines into their town.[2] Even a distance of a few miles from the railway

[2] One of the clearest British examples was the refusal of the citizens of Stamford, in Lincolnshire, a town of great antiquity and a population in 1841 of 6,385, to grant access to the London to Yorkshire line which became the main stem of the Great Northern Railway, i.e. the east coast main line. The adjacent town of Peterborough (1841 population—6,107) welcomed it, however, and it was built leaving Stamford 5 kms off to the west. For comparative purposes, the 1971 populations of the two towns were: Stamford – 14,662; Peterborough – 70,100. For another example, see V. A. Hatley, 'Northampton Hoodwinked? How a Main Line of Railway Missed the Town a Second Time', *Journal of Transport History* 7 (1965–6), pp. 160–72.

proved a severe handicap to future growth. To take advantage of the railway's presence, industry and commerce need to be as close to it as possible. It exerts a positive attraction and, in practice, may well end by exerting so strong an attraction that congestion results.

In spite of its limitations and drawbacks, then, the railway remains the best method of moving by land either large numbers of passengers or large quantities of goods, with the reservation that, to fit within the loading gauge on most world railways, individual items cannot have a cross-section of much more than 9 feet or 3 metres. In particular, it is valuable where there is a steady flow of bulk traffic (such as coal or iron ore) between two areas, for the laying of railway tracks, like marriage, tends to commit the partners for life. It creates a fixed investment, not merely in transport generally but in transport between two individual points, so that the railway and the canal are the least flexible forms of transport in face of any change in traffic conditions.

2 WATER TRANSPORT

When we come to consider transport by water, we must make an immediate distinction between ocean transport and inland waterways. That such a distinction is important is at once obvious from the fact that although Great Britain has dominated ocean-going trade for several centuries, her inland waterways are largely disused. In Britain, goods which arrive by sea are not often distributed beyond the port area by water. Yet across the North Sea, only a few score miles away, there flourishes a whole system of navigable river routes and canals which extend the influence of Rotterdam, Antwerp and Dunkerque far inland.

What is the reason for this difference between the two sides of the Channel? The answer to this question is one that calls our attention to the character and advantages of water transport in general. On the British side, the distances involved are short. It is usually possible to direct an ocean-going vessel to a port on the east coast rather than bring the vessel into a west-coast port and trans-ship its cargo onto a barge for delivery by river or canal. In any case, the distances from a major port to a British industrial centre are seldom great—Bristol to Birmingham, for example, is 150 km; Hull to Bradford is 105 km. In addition, few of the British rivers are deep enough, long enough or sufficiently free of obstructions to make navigation worthwhile, and British canals were for the most part constructed in a period when the unit of traffic was a horse-drawn barge carrying, perhaps, 30 tons of cargo.

Across the Channel, by contrast, distances from the sea are much greater. From the seaport of Rotterdam to the river port of Basle is 850 km; from the steel mills of Lorraine it is 480 km to Le Havre and 650 to Rotterdam. Over distances like these, the advantages of using water transport can make themselves felt. And this is, of course, still more true of the semi-continental distances within the U.S.S.R. or the U.S.A.

There is also the factor of size of waterway. The West Europe network is based on broad rivers, between which the canals form links. Since the rivers were—or could be made—capable of carrying heavy traffic, there was an obvious purpose in constructing the canal-links to scale. Today, as a result, there is a system of major waterways on which the standard 'loading-gauge' is the vessel of 1,350 tons burden.

This contrast between the British and the West European developments reveals the economic advantages of water transport. Compared with other forms of transport, movement by water becomes increasingly competitive with increases in

1   distance involved
2   size of vessel load.

Short distances and small loads—as on the British inland waterways—represent one extreme: a 250,000 ton oil tanker plying between the Persian Gulf and Milford Haven *via* the Cape represents the other—at least until the 500,000 ton tanker is in service.[3] These conditions make water transport a suitable choice in situations where a commodity is moving over long distances and in sufficient bulk to justify the use of a large vessel.

The drawbacks of water transport are twofold. One is that it is usually slow, and cannot be employed in the movement of perishable goods unless refrigeration is used. On transoceanic routes this factor of speed is accepted, and the refrigeration of perishables is normal. On inland waterways, however, it is a factor which tends to divert cargoes to road or rail, leaving the canal traffic to handle the non-perishable bulk goods. The other drawback of water transport is the need for trans-shipment between ocean-going and inland waterways craft. If this need can be eliminated, the advantage of water transport and of communities served by it is greatly increased. This was clear to the builders of, say, the Manchester Ship Canal, just as it was to the advocates of the St Lawrence Seaway half a century later. In both cases the object was to give inland points direct access to ocean-going vessels without the need to trans-ship.

There are therefore two important but opposing trends visible in the shipbuilding industry: on the one hand, to build ever larger ships to gain the economies that go with size, and on the other to develop a *smaller* class of vessel, which will be able to operate equally well at sea or on the major inland waterways. With both the object is the same—to reduce costly handling at points of trans-shipment.

Like the railway, the canal and river tend to create linear patterns of

[3] On the economies of using large tankers, see p.26.

settlement and industry. They did so in the early phases of industrialization, when they brought china clay and coal to the Staffordshire potteries that lined their banks, or wool to the warehouses of the West Riding, and filled the valleys of the Pennines with mills and weavers' cottages. They continue to do so today. Along the Intracoastal Waterway that follows the Gulf shoreline of the U.S.A. are some of the choicest plant sites for America's new industries, in what was once a wilderness of sandbars and lagoons. In the barren Campine of eastern Belgium one of Europe's newest industrial concentrations is growing up—along the banks of the Albert Canal. Even in Britain, on the hard-worked rivers of the Trent–Humber system, the siting of electric power stations was based, at least in part, on the use of water transport to bring in coal supplies.

But the main form of settlement attributable to water transport is, of course, the port. It is a form which has evolved since the time when the term covered any staith or anchorage, up through the scores of small medieval ports that lined the shores and rivers of Britain or France, to the present situation in which, while the volume of goods in world transit steadily increases, the number of ports between which the goods move as steadily declines.

The major determinants of the fortune of ports are the size of vessel and the bulk of cargo. Since both have increased strikingly over the years of the Industrial Revolution, the number of ports in a position to participate in trade has been greatly reduced. Even if their harbours have not silted up—and this has often been the case—their depth of water has become insufficient to float the larger vessels of today. At the end of Fenland canals in East Anglia lie the grass-covered wharves of tiny villages, with names like Commercial End as a testimony to their former role. The waterway linking Commercial End with the outside world is a canal or 'lode' 3 metres wide and very shallow, adequate for a punt or small wherry laden with grain or reeds but totally out of scale with any modern freight movement. Although the heyday of Commercial End lies far back in the past, the process whereby it became derelict is still continuing, and today affects much larger port-towns. Today, in fact, we are close to a nightmare situation in which the biggest tankers are too large to enter any existing port, and are condemned either to anchor and discharge far offshore or else roam the seven seas for ever like a modern *Flying Dutchman*.

The advantages of the big, deep-water port are compounded because the bigger the port, the more frequent the services using it are likely to be. Size alone, therefore, tends to attract business away from the smaller, less well-served, ports and to increase the lead of the larger, by a process that applies equally to ports, towns, industries or supermarkets.

These same increases in size of vessel-load have made it necessary for some old ports to develop *outports*, to avoid losing traffic too bulky to penetrate into the original dock area. Normally, the outport grows because the old port has become too involved in its local economy to be abandoned: it has attracted business and industry which it wants to retain. Commercial End, on the Fens, could be abandoned as a port because it was merely a transit point, and nothing else depended on its survival except the livelihood of a handful of local workers. But Bristol, or Rotterdam, or Bremen are far too integral a part of the regional economy to be dislodged by a mere increase in the draught of the ships using them. Consequently, they develop deep water facilities nearer the sea—Avonmouth, Europoort, Bremerhaven. Shipping companies avoid the slow and costly business of working ships upstream to inlying docks while the region, for its part, avoids the loss of business which would result if the cargoes were landed at ports elsewhere.

In chapter three, reference was made to the growing volume of bulk cargoes entering world trade. One result of this has been the growth of specialist ports; that is, ports dealing in a single commodity, with facilities built for that one purpose. The clearest examples are the oil terminals at either end of the tanker routes—on the Persian Gulf, the estuaries of western Europe, or the Gulf Coast of the U.S.A. They are followed by the iron ore ports—Duluth on Lake Superior, Sept Iles on the St Lawrence, Puerto Ordaz on the Orinoco. Within the larger general cargo ports, of course, the same kind of specialization is found between the individual docks, so as to obtain the greatest possible efficiency in cargo handling.

This development of specialist ports is actually only one side of the coin: the other is the emergence of specialist ships. Before the first world war, although there were admittedly specialist vessels plying their trade— the tea clippers, or the grain ships from Australia—much of the world's seaborne traffic was carried by tramp steamers, general-purpose vessels which sailed wherever a cargo was to be found. Today, tramps account for less than 20 per cent of the world's tonnage of cargo ships, and we have witnessed the appearance of the bulk carrier and the freight liner; that is, the single-purpose vessel and the regular freight service. As a result, the chances of finding that a particular ship, even (to recall John Masefield's lines) a dirty British coaster, was carrying such an assorted cargo as road rails, pig lead and cheap tin trays *as well as* Tyne coal and iron ware have, statistically, greatly diminished.

If the cargo is assorted in this way, the chances are that it will be containerized, for this is the most recent development in handling small freight. The smaller items are loaded, often by the shipper himself, into a container which is of standard size and which can travel interchangeably by road, rail or water with maximum ease of handling by standardized equipment. The container is designed expressly for this purpose. The growth of container traffic has been one of the transport phenomena of the past decade.[4]

A particular case of specialization in port and 'cargo' is offered by passenger traffic. The passenger forms an exceptional cargo because he normally wishes to spend as small a part of his journey at sea as possible. While the object of freight movement is usually to carry goods as far inland as navigation allows, in order to obtain the maximum advantage from low freight rates on movement by water, the case of the passenger is the reverse: he is carried as far as possible by rapid land transport before beginning his voyage. This gives the passenger port a distinctive setting— often remote and isolated (as at Holyhead, or at Port Vendres on the France–Algeria crossing), and normally where the water crossing is shortest (as at Folkestone and Dover). It also helps to explain why so many passenger ports—including the largest of them, Southampton—owe their development to the railway companies in whose territories they lie.

3 ROAD TRANSPORT

Transport by road is of great antiquity, but transport by road *vehicle* is another matter. Prior to the eighteenth century in Europe it was the pack animal which, from time immemorial, had plodded over the trade routes of the Ancient World, that was responsible for moving goods along the continent's roads. Any freight-laden vehicle was liable to endless delays on appalling roads, and the freight itself was usually transferred to the waterways at the first suitable point.

The two earliest incentives to road improvement were not commercial need but (1) military requirements and (2) profit for the builder. The first of these motives has given the world a whole series of networks, from the Roman roads to the French *routes nationales* and the German *autobahnen*. The second motive underlay the construction of the eighteenth-century turnpikes, in lowland Britain the first passable highways, on which tolls paid for upkeep and made the enterprise profitable.[5] It was not until it became generally accepted that road maintenance was a government responsibility that commerce could economically take to using them.

---

[4] Among other advantages of containerization are the fact that unloading time for a ship may be reduced to less than one tenth of that for a conventional type of non-container cargo, with a proportional increase in the throughput per berth in the docks. One of the balancing drawbacks, at least in old and crowded ports, is the amount of 'back-up' space needed behind the quayside, where the containers are assembled.

[5] The case of Highland Britain, by contrast, belongs largely to the military category of road construction. The 1715 and 1745 risings led to the building of a network of military roads, with which the name of General Wade will always be associated. In England, the number of turnpike trusts multiplied between

Even so, in the Industrial Revolution they played only a minor role: the railways could handle heavier loads and move them faster for, although road surfaces might have improved, nothing had as yet superseded the horse.

It was the invention of the motor vehicle which enabled road transport not merely to supplement the railway, but to compete with it. In fact, it is probably simplest to think of road transport after the motor car as an entirely new form of transport—new in range and new in speed. This will enable us to see in its proper light the next problem that confronted transport men—that of providing a suitable network of roads on which this new form of vehicle could operate. For it is precisely because the motor vehicle has *not* been regarded as essentially new, but merely as a swifter version of the old horse and cart, that the motorist has been condemned to use horse-and-cart roads for so long.

Today, one nation after another is facing the real situation: that while the old network of country lanes and city streets was adequate for road transport which was merely acting as feeder to railways and canals, the newer, competitive role of the road carrier requires a system of long-distance trunk routes to which the side roads can again act as feeders. Under the special circumstances offered by National Socialism in the 1930s, it was the Germans who first embarked on such a system of trunk routes. Today the Americans have the 70,000 km of their Interstate Highway system, while what is, probably, the densest trunk network created anywhere up to the present is to be found in the Netherlands—very appropriately in the nation whose population density is the highest in the world. Despite decades of campaigning for better roads, however, Great Britain's showing in this respect is distinctly poor.

As an increasing volume of goods and passenger traffic has taken to the roads, the characteristics of this type of transport and its effect upon settlement patterns have become clear. The advantage that road transport possesses over the railway and canal is that it can operate door to door, without any necessity for trans-shipment; that it can economically handle small part-loads while, paradoxically, it is better than the railway at handling outsize objects which would not fit inside the loading gauge. Every motorist knows the frustration of following slowly behind a giant road vehicle, with which he is obliged to share the highway, while alongside him a railway track—that is, a highway built expressly for the movement of heavy goods—lies empty and unused. There seems a distinct possibility that, within a decade or two, it will be sensible to build separate

---

1750 and 1800, to reach a maximum of about 1,100, controlling 35,000 km of roads. But despite high tolls these roads were often allowed to fall into a shocking condition. It was almost the end of the nineteenth century, however, before the last of the trusts was wound up.

traffic routes for freight vehicles; they might even run along the old railway roadbeds.

The effect of road transport on settlement and industrial locations has been one of liberation from the confinement of the canal and railway eras. Not that proximity to a motorway is an advantage to be overlooked by an industrialist: very far from it. But the dense road network which is to be found today in most industrial areas offers a much wider range of choice for a plant site than in the days when heavy materials could only be moved by water or rail. In the same way, with the spread of private car ownership, it is possible to develop residential areas which are widely dispersed around the employment focus. If there was one feature more than another which epitomized the early industrial era it was the terraced rows of labourers' cottages clustering drably round the mill gates. Today, with a population whose individual mobility is steadily increasing, such a settlement pattern is unnecessary and, indeed, intolerable. For the mobility of the individual, and the dispersal that results from it, road transport is largely responsible.

4 AIR TRANSPORT

Modern air transport possesses two obvious and outstanding advantages: speed, and freedom from hindrances caused to other transport media by physical features. It also possesses some less obvious advantages which, on occasion, play an important part: the vehicle load is generally small, so that air freight may be used with cargoes which are not large enough to interest shipping lines, while this same small size of unit load makes air transport extremely flexible.

These advantages are offset by high cost. If, therefore, other means of transport are available, airlines will have to rely on speed for any competitive advantages they obtain. Since weight is the critical factor, the air route is suited to movement where a light, valuable cargo is to be moved quickly. As it happens, few 'cargoes' meet these conditions better than passengers, and in Great Britain some 90 per cent by weight of the loads moved by air are people. The other 10 per cent consists of mail, perishable goods, precious metals and single items (such as spare parts for machines) needed in remote places at short notice.

The air freight business made a rather slow beginning. In fact, air transport is still in what may be called the 'exploratory' phase of cargo-seeking, largely by a process of trial and error. But two types of freight seem likely to increase the airlines' business in the future. One of these is the movement of flowers, fruit and vegetables—commodities whose sales potential depends very largely on the speed with which they can be marketed. Already a number of regular delivery services operate, in the case of Great Britain especially from the islands—Jersey, Guernsey, Scilly

—to the mainland. The other type of business that has come to rely on air freight is what is called in America 'central warehousing'. Manufacturers find that, instead of having to maintain stocks and spares in depots in the various regions of North America they can hold a single, central supply and air-freight parts in a few hours to any point in the continent.

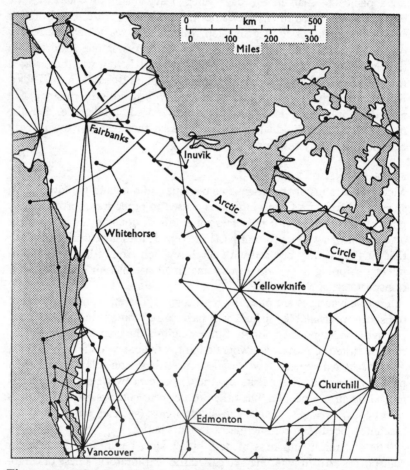

Figure 12: North-west Canada and Alaska: the air service network. A short distance north of the Vancouver–Edmonton–Churchill line, the road network becomes fragmentary and communications depend on these air services, which link many small settlements having no road or rail connections with the outside world, and only seasonal water transport. For the sake of clarity, all other detail except the coastlines is omitted. (Source: *Arctic Development Digest* Route Map 1971.)

Passenger traffic by air has increased very rapidly since the second world war,

1   as a means of long-distance travel
2   as a means of crossing water barriers, even on quite short routes
3   to maintain contact between business installations in dispersed centres, by the use of private or company planes, and

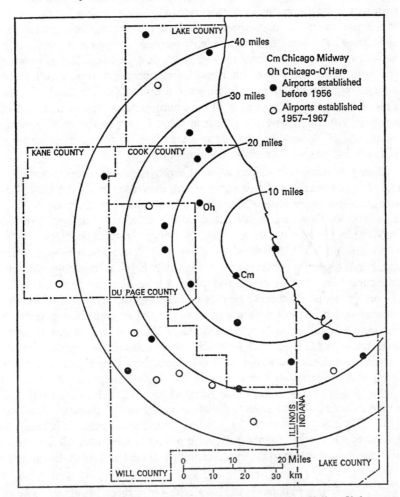

Figure 13: Chicago: location of airports, 1967. Scheduled airline flights were originally routed to and from Midway, until congestion on the runways and the constriction of the surrounding built-up area made necessary a move to O'Hare, now the world's busiest airport. (Based by permission on E. C. Kirchherr, 'Variations in the Number and Distribution of Commercial Airports in the Chicago Region, 1951–1967', *Michigan Academician* 3, p. 88.)

4   for catering for irregular and often cross-country passenger movements.

The best examples of this last kind of service are the pilgrim flights to Lourdes and Mecca, but the same applies to charter flights for football supporters and holiday makers.

So far, we have assumed the existence of other means of transport, with which the aircraft is in competition. But in some areas of the world this is not the case. In northern Canada, for example, there is often no alternative to movement by air except 'packing' into an area on foot. In such cases, air transport becomes 'normal', despite its costliness, because any true assessment of comparative costs must take into account the savings represented by *not* building a rail or road link instead. So the aircraft bears the main burden of communications. This is true also of northern Australia, where even cattle move by air to the meat-packing plant, and of Venezuela, which has a very limited road system and has virtually by-passed the railway era altogether.

Heavy air transport depends on the provision of adequate airfields and, as the number of fields increases all over the world, there has developed a hierarchy ordered according to size and service. In the U.S.A., for example, there are about 4,400 public airports,[6] but they vary in importance just as much as once did the railway stations which they have often now replaced. Speed is essential in air communications, and the number of stopping points is therefore usually held to a minimum for any particular service. Choice as a stop on a long-distance route gives an airport immediate status, since it is certain to bring with it the 'feeder' services which connect with the main flights. Most [countries in western Europe are small enough to have developed a single international route focus but in the U.S.A., with its much greater size and its large number of competing airlines, the situation is more complex. There have emerged a number of primary air traffic centres 800–1,500 km apart, which cast a traffic 'shadow' over other cities lying within their orbit (see table 10). These in turn fall into several ranks according to the quality of service which they enjoy: it may be frequent but in the lower ranks it is likely to consist of short-stage flights only, terminating at the major airport; that is, of flights equivalent to the local, stopping train in the days of the branch-line railway.

[6] It is interesting to notice that Alaska, with 537 of these, has almost twice as many as the next state, California, although it has only a hundredth part of the latter's population. Alaskans, in fact, fly many more air-miles per capita than other Americans, for the same reasons as do Canadians in the Northlands. The state of Texas, on the other hand, has over 1,100 airfields but three-quarters of them are private: they are owned by, or cater for, the ranchers and oil men with their private planes.

Quality of service, then, is likely to determine the relative locational advantages of a particular airport or its surroundings. But these

Table 10 World airline passengers: airports handling the largest numbers in 1973

(Figures in millions)

1	Chicago, O'Hare	35·5	2	Los Angeles, International	23·5
3	Atlanta, Ga.	23·3	4	New York, J. F. Kennedy	21·4
5	London, Heathrow	20·3	6	San Francisco, International	16·6
7	New York, La Guardia	14·0	8	Paris, Orly	13·9
9	Miami, International	12·8	10	Osaka	12·0
11	Boston, Logan	10·7	12	Frankfurt am Main	10·6
13	Denver, Stapleton	10·4	14	Washington, D.C., National	10·3

advantages may change, and change quite rapidly, as aircraft themselves develop. Airports around the world are at present transforming themselves in preparation for the next generation of larger jet planes, which will require more parking space, larger passenger facilities and, perhaps, longer runways. Any airport which cannot or does not provide for this growth in size will quickly find itself by-passed, and industrialists or companies located around it will lose the advantages of its main-line services. The same thing may happen if airline stages continue to lengthen. Thus Shannon in Ireland and Gander in Newfoundland, in the 1950s the two buttresses of the Atlantic air bridge, are no longer actually necessary as stopping-points: more and more planes fly over them instead of calling. Much the same is true of the South Atlantic bridge between West Africa and Brazil, and of the 'stepping-stone' route from Europe to the Far East. In other words, the advantage conferred on a locality by air transport may, through technical change, prove just as transitory as that once afforded by the canal bank or riverside.

5 PIPELINES

The last form of transport is the pipeline. Apart from its use in carrying water it has so far been employed almost entirely for moving petroleum and gas, from producer to refinery and from refinery to customer. This is not to say, however, that it cannot be used for other products—a coal and water mixture, for example, that replaces the orthodox coal train or coal barge—but these developments lie mainly in the future.

The U.S.A. has by far the greatest pipeline mileage in the world, with nearly 200,000 km of oil trunk lines and more than 450,000 km of transmission lines for natural gas, apart from gathering and distribution pipes.

This network extends across the border into Canada, so that there are at least the beginnings of a genuinely international 'grid'. The U.S.S.R. has some 47,000 km of pipelines. In the Middle East, although the mileage of pipes is small, each line is of strategic importance to the operation of the fields and the economy of the countries involved, as witness the frequency with which the pipes have been cut during the troubled years of the past three decades. In Europe, both West and East, the pipeline is a phenomenon of the past ten to fifteen years. Only since the late 1950s has anything resembling a network begun to develop. Since there are few oil or gas fields within the continent itself, and Europe depends largely on petroleum imports, the pipes run from the coastal refineries and ports into the industrial areas and cities of the interior, and from the oilfields of the Soviet Union and Rumania into the oil-less states east of the Iron Curtain. At present, only the trunk lines exist: local distribution is carried out by rail, water or road. At present, too, we see only the skeleton of a gas-pipe network around the North Sea, where extension of the net is certainly going to occur as more strikes are made.

FREIGHT RATES, COMPETITION AND MODAL CHOICE

Carrier companies of every kind in the business of transport are in competition with each other to secure a larger and more profitable share of the traffic. Their profit is gained by charging freight rates and passenger rates for moving goods and people, and these rates are often extremely complex and varied. Even where—as is the case in some parts of the world —there is only one railway company or one road, the cost to the carrier of providing the transport service varies according to the type of terrain, the type of goods carried (including passengers as a type of 'goods' which requires highly specialized treatment), the quantity of a particular commodity involved and the frequency of shipment of that commodity. Freight costs are at their minimum when the carrier is handling a bulk consignment of a non-perishable, non-breakable commodity (like iron ore) in a regular daily service between two fixed points. At the opposite extreme, costs are highest for passengers, who demand to ride in comfort, to travel as and when they please, and to board or leave the vehicle at the stopping place of their choice. If the carrier can arrange that the loaded iron ore wagons travel downhill and the empties travel uphill, he can reduce still further the cost of moving bulk freight. If, on the other hand, his passengers expect to be carried high into snow-covered mountains for winter sports, and set down in heated stations, these factors will further increase them. In between iron ore and passengers in the range of costs and the table of freight rates come a host of other items with their own particular requirements—fish which must be frozen, bananas which must be heated, or precision instruments which must be protected from shock and vibration while in transit.[7]

The basic freight rates are therefore fixed by carriers according to the class of goods to be moved and the care needed in handling it. This *class rate* is then modified according to the quantity involved. If the quantity is small, and occupies less than a whole vehicle, the rate will be higher because of the extra handling involved and the risk of the vehicle travelling half-empty; to such rates the term *less-carload* is applied in North America and some other countries. On the other hand, if the quantity is large and the movement frequent or regular, the carrier will very probably estab-

Table 11a   Steel manufacture in the U.S.A.: Assembly of materials required to place on the market one ton of finished steel products

1 *Per ton of finished products—Materials moved*

	Tons	Percent of total weight
Coal	1·42	34
Iron ore	1·74	42
Finished products	1·00	24
	4·16	100

2 *Per ton of finished products—Transport costs*

	Amount as above (tons)	Unit cost per ton-mile of movement	Percent of total costs
Coal	1·42	1·04	25·7
Iron ore	1·74	0·70	21·1
Finished products	1·00	3·06	53·2
	4·16	4·80	100·0

Source: A. Rodgers, 'Industrial Inertia—A Major Factor in the Location of the Steel Industry in the United States', *Geographical Review* 42 (1952), p. 58. It should be noted that, as the British figures in table 11b show, in the years since these data were assembled, the amount of coal required per ton of steel produced has been steadily reduced by technical improvements to the process, and there has been some replacement of ore by scrap in the furnace. The result has been to strengthen the influence of the market over plant location. See also pp. 225–6. All data in miles: 1 mile = 1·6 km.

[7] A famous *Punch* joke of a past period, often reprinted, offers a comment on the problems of freight classification:

Railway Porter (to old lady travelling with a menagerie of pets): 'Station-master say, mum, as cats is "dogs" and rabbits is "dogs", and so's parrots; but this 'ere Tortoise is a insect, so there ain't no charge for it.'

lish a lower rate (sometimes called a *commodity rate*) which is, in effect, a special quotation for a particular cargo and a specified journey—a kind of excursion fare for freight.

Where this is the structure of freight rates, two things normally follow:

(a) The basic variable in transport is not distance but *cost-distance*; that is, the distance multiplied by the freight rate per ton per km. If we substituted cost-distance for geographical distance in world commodity movements, then we should require a separate globe for each commodity, and that globe would be distorted out of all recognition. Places hundreds of miles apart would be brought together because of the carriers' habit of grouping a number of separate destinations under so-called 'blanket-rates'. The quays of Liverpool or Bristol would suddenly become as broad as the Atlantic Ocean, because the per-ton cost of unloading a cargo across them was as great as that of carrying it from New York to the dockside. Places equidistant from a market point would be displaced out of line with each other, because one possessed some transport route denied to the other, on which a preferential tariff was available for delivering goods to the market.

An example of an industry in which freight *cost* overrides the simple consideration of *volume* of movement is that of steel making in North America. As the figures in table 11a show, in the manufacture of steel

Table 11b   Steel manufacture in Great Britain: Assembly of materials required to place on the market one ton of finished steel products

1   *Per ton of finished products—materials moved*

	Tons	Percent of total weight
Coal	0·90	25·5
Iron ore	1·60	46·0
Finished products	1·00	28·5
	3·50	100·0

2   *Per ton of finished products—transport costs*

	Amount as above (tons)	Unit cost per ton-mile of movement	Percent of total costs
Coal	0·90	1·08	26·5
Iron ore	1·60	0·94	41·0
Finished products	1·00	1·19	32·5
	3·50	3·21	100·0

Source: Author's calculations from generalized data for 1970 supplied by British Steel Corporation.

the bulkiest item moved is the iron ore. On these grounds, we should anticipate that the steel-making process would be drawn towards the ore source. But in cost terms the most expensive item to move is the finished product. It is therefore to the manufacturer's advantage to minimize this particular movement, and so it is the location of the market rather than the location of the ore which exerts the more powerful attraction on the producer (see also figure 35b, p. 212).

In Great Britain, where the steel industry uses a considerable volume of low-grade ores, and where the differentials between the freight rates are less pronounced than in the American example (table 11b), the ore supply dominates on grounds both of volume and of movement costs, but the importance to the manufacturer of the cost-of-movement calculation is just as critical.

We shall return to the subject of industrial location in a later chapter. For the moment, our concern is to notice how the freight-rate structure may benefit producers in a particular locality, and influence their decision to operate there. Of course, there is no guarantee that their advantage will not be transitory; if a new means of transport is provided, or if a new rate level is offered, they may regret their choice. And this brings us immediately to the second consequence of a freight-rate structure of the kind we have been considering.

(b) Since distance is not the sole criterion in fixing freight rates, there are limitless opportunities for competition between transport media and between individual carriers. The carrier charges for his services on the basis of his own costs plus a profit margin. But there is no reason why, over a particular route, his charges should reflect the true cost of *that individual service* which in any case may be impossible to determine accurately. He may decide that, in order to capture the traffic and increase his business, he will trim his charges on the route in question, and perhaps recoup by charging more on another route where competition is less intense.

It is under these circumstances that 'rate wars' develop: competitive price-cutting brings down the charges for transport services until one or more of the competitors is forced to give up. For his part the shipper, if the volume of his business is large enough, can play the carriers off against each other, and secure very favourable freight rates on his goods. In the 1870s in the U.S.A., for example, it became common practice to quote special low rates for individual shippers: in an extreme case the privileged shipper is said actually to have received rebates amounting to the difference between what he paid the railway and what his competitors paid.[8]

---

[8] The shipper's name was John D. Rockefeller.

Such jungle warfare inevitably brought intervention by governments. Today, the *amount* of competition possible usually depends on political rather than economic factors—upon the degree to which a government permits competition on internal routes (and, if it owns all forms of transport, it will probably permit very little), while on international routes it has in most cases been decided by agreement between the nations involved.

Generally speaking, the transport industry has passed from an early era of *laissez-faire* and free competition into one of increasing control, in which transport is regarded less as a business making profits and more as a service provided for the public. That nineteenth-century era of competition has certainly left its mark. It was epitomized by the steamboat races on the Mississippi and the Race To The North between the east coast and west coast railways in Britain in 1888 and 1895; by the rate wars on North American railways and the sale of stock in bogus transport companies on both sides of the Atlantic. Policy in Britain and North America in this early period permitted the construction of a series of competing routes between every pair of towns of reasonable size: first a canal, then a turnpike and then not one but two or three railways. Usually, the traffic was quite inadequate to support all these companies. The canal and the turnpike were superseded, and the railways fought each other to the point of bankruptcy. It was an expensive method of achieving the survival of the fittest, and seldom in the long-term interest of the public.

Elsewhere, for example in France and Germany, this situation was modified at an early stage by the creation of national transport plans— that for the *routes nationales*, or the railway plan which both countries adopted to ensure that necessary lines were built and that wasteful duplication was avoided. Transport increasingly came under government supervision, if not outright ownership, even in those countries where competition had been fiercest, and public bodies like the Interstate Commerce Commission in the U.S.A. (1887) were set up to secure the orderly provision of transport services. So today we have a country like Switzerland, where there is normally only one public means of reaching each particular place: it may be a train, postbus or cable car, but it is a unique link in a fully integrated system. On land, more and more freight rates are being set strictly on a basis of distance and freight class, although it also sometimes happens that governments use their regulatory powers to see that road, rail and water routes *can* compete with each other on the assumption that, while unrestrained competition is not in the public interest, a decorous amount of it is good for all concerned.

With governments increasingly 'holding the ring', where do the advantages in transport lie? Half a century ago passenger traffic was almost exclusively in the hands of the railways on land and the shipping companies on overseas routes. Since then, both have lost ground. On land today, the great majority of passenger-miles are covered by private car—90 per cent in the U.S.A., and 70–75 per cent in western Europe. Even of the remainder, the railways obtain only a limited share. They have lost their lower-income passengers to the bus, and their wealthier patrons to the plane.[9] At sea, the passenger ship still carriés a few who either have too much luggage for the plane, or who deliberately choose the slow route, but in numerical terms the airlines have forged right ahead: on the North Atlantic route they carry well over 95 per cent of all passengers.

In freight movements there is the same swing away from rail transport, although as yet the ship has little to fear from the plane in trans-oceanic traffic. In Great Britain, the railways accounted for 51 per cent of ton-km of freight moved in 1955, but only 24 per cent in 1973. For the U.S.A., the figures were 50 and less than 40; for the U.S.S.R., they were 89 and 76. Most of the lost traffic was taken over by road carriers, although in countries of the size of the U.S.A. and U.S.S.R. the competition of waterways—which in each case fully maintained their percentage share of freight ton-km—must not be overlooked.

To all this competition the railways have responded by measures intended to improve their competitive position. These include

1   closing down uneconomical services, mainly on little-used branch lines
2   seeking new forms of traffic, of which 'car-sleeper' services in Europe and 'piggy-back' road–rail services in America are good examples
3   conversion from steam to diesel or electric traction
4   cutting labour requirements. Since labour accounts for 50–60 per cent of all railway costs, there is a broad area of potential economies available.
5   increasing the speed of their services.

The railways' efforts at improving their situation are reflected in the figures given in table 12. There have been some encouraging efforts on individual systems: the growth of Inter-City traffic in Great Britain, and the increase of 18 per cent in the single year 1973–4 in passengers carried on AMTRAK services (AMTRAK is the name given to the government-backed inter-city services which now make up almost the entire passen-

---

[9] In the U.S.A., where these tendencies are most fully developed, the statistics show the number of road passengers rising—at the railway's expense—to a plateau, and then gently falling off in favour of the airlines. Evidently, this is largely because of a decline in the number of people in the lower-income groups in a wealthy society, and not because of the air hostesses and 'free' meals.

ger-carrying operation of the United States railways.) But it seems clear
that, in their present form, the railways in developed areas will continue
to face stiff competition from other transport modes.

Table 12   Railway employment: index of reductions in employment
on state and/or main line railways, by countries, 1963–1973

(1963 = 100; the figure gives the 1973 index in each case)

U.S.A.	77·1
France	81·0
Belgium	92·6
Sweden	70·2
Netherlands	92·1
Spain	61·5
Eire	87·0

The proviso 'in their present form' is an important one. For just as
the modern motorway offers the road user what is virtually a new means
of movement compared with old-fashioned streets and roads, so there is
a new generation of railways either built or in plan, which should
restore some of the advantages the old railways once possessed and have
long since lost, particularly that of competitively high speed. Japan has
constructed railways on an entirely new railbed, on the latest sections of
which speeds of 260 km an hour are reached. Italy is following suit with
a Rome–Florence *direttissima* and France with a high-speed line from
Paris to Lyons. The alternative to making the huge capital investment
involved in the new generation of lines is to invest in faster vehicles for
the old routes, a thrifty policy of rather limited objectives which is
being followed in Great Britain.

But the fact is that the railway in either traditional or modern form
has a weakness, which is shares with the canal: it is tied to its tracks, and
the further it spreads its network the heavier the track maintenance
costs become. With any type of decentralized economic activity, there
comes a point where it is uneconomical to extend the tracks—or canal—
further, and trans-shipment becomes necessary. In the early years of the
Industrial Revolution and on the frontiers of settlement overseas, the
railways could create their own patterns of service, by drawing activity
towards themselves: that is why the railway played so important a role
in the nineteenth-century Revolution. But the very success of the early
lines encouraged the builders to extend the tracks still further; to bring
the benefits of rail service to remoter areas; in short, to try to make the
railway as universal as the road and telephone are today. But the railway

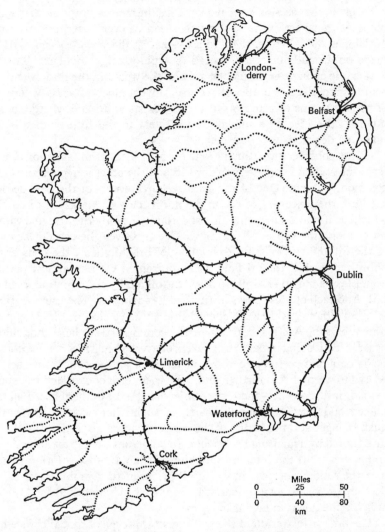

Figure 14: The dissolution of a railway network: the railways of Ireland. The map shows those lines remaining open to passenger traffic in the winter timetables of 1970–71. All other lines have ceased to carry passengers, and in most cases track has been lifted. It should, however, be added that some lines shown, particularly in the west, were narrow-gauge or light railways which were in reality little more than tramways.

is not and never was that kind of carrier, and all the pioneers did was to sow the seeds of future weakness by over-extension.

So far in this section we have been making the assumption that some mode of transport exists to meet the need of every user, and that the decision about which of them to use—that is, the *modal choice*—will be made on grounds of cost or speed or type of cargo involved. This is reasonable enough in developed areas of the world in the mid-twentieth century but there are also, of course, any number of areas where no organized means of transport at present exists at all and where, consequently, the idea of a modal choice refers to the future; that is, to planning decisions yet to be taken.

Let us consider two illustrations of this aspect of modal choice, one from the real and contemporary world and the other a hypothetical but common problem. One of the great resource events of the past decade has been the discovery of oil on the north coast of Alaska—a discovery which, as it now seems, will almost certainly be only the first in a whole series along the shores of the Arctic Ocean. Given the coastal location of the oil and the existing technology of oil shipment, the companies hoping to exploit the oil field were confronted with an almost perfect example of a modal choice—to move the oil out by sea, pipeline, road or rail. And each of these possibilities had its advocates. The usual instinct of oil men is to get their oil aboard ship at the earliest available opportunity. But the Arctic Ocean is hardly a commercial sea lane, though the possibility of using tanker ice-breakers or even submarines was explored. So it became necessary to think in terms of an overland route across Alaska to warmer seas further south. To each form of overland transport —road, rail and pipe—there were objections, most of them based on the climate and its effects, but also partly on such other factors as the earthquake danger and the habits of the caribou, whose migrations might be interrupted by a man-made obstacle. So numerous were these objections, and so powerful the interests lobbying for one or other solution that it took the sudden increase in world oil prices in 1973 to force a decision on the American government, which almost overnight, in face of the crisis, came down in favour of a pipeline.

The other illustration of the working of this type of modal choice has become common enough in the era of international technical aid since 1945. Let us suppose that conditions in the interior of some African state offer good prospects for commercial production of groundnuts, or lumber, or beef cattle. Development aid is available for building a transport route, but only for *one* such route. What mode of transport should be provided? Whatever the choice, it must be appropriate to the type of commodity to be moved (is it a mineral source concentrated at a single point, or an agricultural product diffused over a whole region?), and to the climatic conditions in an area where roads may be washed away by the rains, or railway maintenance may be costly. It must be appropriate, too, to the level of skills available to the operating company: the more sophisticated the mode, the more important does the maintenance aspect become.

Modal choice in today's world is a problem, therefore, not merely for the transport *user* but also and very importantly for the transport *planner*, and for governments wherever capital resources are limited. This leads us directly on to our next topic—that of transport policy.

TRANSPORT POLICY

We have already seen how uncontrolled competition in the provision of transport services had the effect of bringing on the industry government intervention. But it quickly became clear that a government which intervened to prevent abuses could equally well intervene with the positive objective of shaping the transport industry to a nation's needs. If this is once accepted, then there are two ways in which transport policy can evolve: by a government influencing the *provision* of transport and the *price* of the service.

Time and again, the construction of a road or railway or canal has been used by a government to carry out a particular policy. The Roman roads, over which the legions could be moved rapidly from one corner of the empire to another, are an obvious early example in Europe: comparable networks criss-crossed empires in China and the southern Americas. Wade's roads in Scotland were an eighteenth-century equivalent and then, with the coming of the railway, our examples multiply. The confederation of Canada in 1867 was strung together on a railway line: the Maritime Provinces at one end and British Columbia at the other refused to enter the federation without a specific guarantee that it would be built. Although the federal government did not build the line itself, it did what the United States government was also doing, and gave huge grants of land to finance the construction companies. A few decades later, the 'Berlin–Baghdad' railway became one of the most serious issues in European diplomacy; although it did not actually reach Baghdad until fifty years later it was—or rather, was thought to be—an instrument of German imperialism in the Middle East. Certainly there was no doubt about the political implications of another German transport project—the Kiel Canal, widened and deepened on the eve of the first world war to accommodate ships as large as those of the German High Seas Fleet.

After the first world war had altered the whole political structure of central Europe, a flurry of railway construction took place, to integrate new territories into national units within the postwar boundaries. In Poland, for example, where there had previously been no national rail focus (because since 1792 there had been no Poland), it was necessary to link the newly-acquired Silesian coalfield to the coast at Gdynia and the Wilno Corridor to the body of the nation. In each of these cases, and others mentioned in the next section, the existence of efficient communications was held to be vital to national development policy; indeed, to the very existence of the nation as a coherent unit.

The intervention of governments in the field of transport *pricing* may take a number of different forms. In most of these, the object is to benefit a particular sector of the economy or a particular region, providing some cost advantage for economic activity taking place within it. Examples of such arrangements are:

(a) A low level of transport charges may be granted to a region on goods shipped either into it or out of it, in order to compensate for its isolation or to open it up. Examples of both types of arrangements can be found in Canada. In 1927, the Maritime Provinces were given a 20 per cent reduction in freight rates on all goods shipped by rail out of the provinces to the rest of Canada. They had argued that their remoteness from the main Canadian markets placed their shippers at a disadvantage. The federal government accepted the argument and, by itself paying the carriers the 20 per cent lost by them, provided the Maritimes with a valuable subsidy. Several decades earlier, the Canadian government had come to the aid of the western wheat farmers in the same way: it had arranged with the Canadian Pacific Railway—at that date (1897) the west's only link with the east—that freight rates on wheat should be kept at an artificially low level, to encourage farmers to settle and plant. In exchange for the revenue forfeited, the railway received a grant of land.

(b) An alternative version of the same type of local or regional subsidy is the much more common situation in which the carrier is required to maintain *uniform* rates over a whole system, despite the fact that, in a particular region, his real costs may be higher than this prescribed rate level. In this way, one section of the system can be 'carried' financially by the others. In practice, this usually means that regions with sparse population and little traffic, or regions with difficult terrain and high maintenance costs, are carried by areas of dense population which generate abundant traffic. A case in point is offered by the railways of the Scottish Highlands, in their relationship with those of lowland Britain: the real costs of operating the Highland services are badly out of line with the revenue they produce, but the maintenance of uniform mileage rates acts as a kind of concealed subsidy to the high-cost section.[10]

(c) Since almost all freight charges depend on the class of goods carried as well as on distance, it is possible to graduate the class rates in such a way as to make it relatively expensive to move a particular class of goods and so discourage its shipment. The classic case of this type of manipulation took place, so it is claimed, between the northern and southern states of the U.S.A. in the years following the Civil War of 1861–1865. Since the railways were controlled by northern interests, the freight rates were set in such a way that it was cheap to ship the raw materials of the southern states northwards, but relatively expensive to ship manufactured goods. The South would therefore be encouraged to supply raw materials, like cotton or timber, to northern mills, but would be handicapped in developing its own industries—which, claimed the South, was the object of the whole manoeuvre.

Obviously, the opposite effect could be obtained by resetting the class differentials in an appropriate pattern and that, as we have already seen, is what the Canadian Pacific did when it fixed its low freight rate on export wheat in the 1890s to encourage western development.

(d) Where traffic is moving across national frontiers, it is possible to use transport charges as a particularly effective weapon in international competition—in fact, to use them as a kind of concealed tariff barrier to keep out foreign goods. When the European Coal and Steel Community began its work of creating a common market in western Europe, international through-rates were among the first subjects to which it turned its attention. The situation revealed was a remarkable one. It is illustrated by figure 15, which is taken from the Community's 1955 report. In pre-Community western Europe, each time a consignment of freight crossed an international boundary, a charge was made as if the goods had been unloaded from one wagon and loaded into another, whereas in reality they were never handled at all. This double handling-charge acted as a concealed tariff. Nor was this all. It is normal for freight rates to 'taper'

---

[10] Not, of course, that this subsidy solves all the problems of such an area: very far from it. The major transport concerns operating wholly *within* northern Scotland (i.e. having no lowland services to pay for the highland routes) receive additional, direct subsidies from the government of several hundred thousand pounds. Without these, they would have to raise their rates by at least one-third. Then again, it can be argued that the maintenance of uniform rates may help exporters shipping *out of* the region but also exposes producers within the region to competition from outsiders shipping *in*, against whom high-cost transport would otherwise protect them. But whether it helps or not, it happens.

as distance increases; that is, the charge per km is less for longer distances. But whenever goods crossed a frontier, they were regarded as

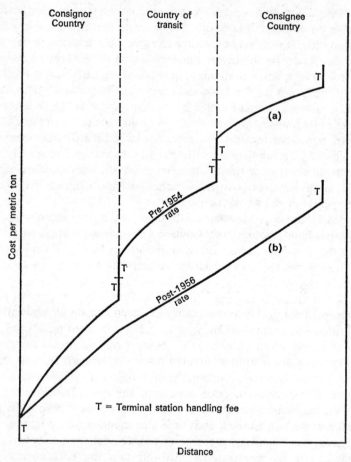

Figure 15: International freight rates: the effect of crossing west European frontiers, exemplified by the rates on fuels and ores, (a) before the European Coal and Steel Community began its work and (b) after the adjustments of May, 1956. Note the 'concealed tariff' effect of crossing each frontier. (Source: E.C.S.C. *Third General Report*, Luxembourg, 1955, p. 107.)

having started from that point, so that the benefit of the taper was lost each time. By these perfectly accepted means, therefore, each country was placing the goods of all its neighbours at a marked disadvantage in competition with its native freight the moment the foreign freight crossed its borders. This disadvantage the international through-rates are now designed to remove.

(e) Although the arrangements which we have been considering apply mainly to freight traffic, it is also possible to manipulate passenger fares to produce particular effects, especially around centres where traffic is heavy. One of the best examples of manipulation is to be found in Belgium where, over the years, the state-controlled railways have maintained very low workmen's (i.e. early morning) fares. The effect of these is to make it feasible for even low-income Belgian workers to travel 50 to 60 km to their work each day, which in turn makes it possible for the cities to draw their labour force from a very wide hinterland. In essence, the low fares act as a kind of indirect subsidy to the employers in the large cities, while at the same time they tend to draw labour away from the land (and, incidentally, affect the structure of agriculture by doing so). In Britain, on the other hand, workmen's fares were abolished some time ago. To replace them, or their effects, there have been proposals that the fares of season-ticket holders to and from British cities, especially London with its huge commuting range, should be subsidized in some way. These proposals are, however, understandably opposed by people interested in regional development outside the metropolitan areas of the country.

TRANSPORT NETWORKS

The motives behind the construction of transport lines fall under three main heads:

1   Lines of communication are built for strategic reasons, to make possible movement to or through an area for political or military purposes.
2   Roads and railways are built to open up to economic use an area or a particular resource, such as a body of mineral ore.
3   Communications are developed between existing settlements to make possible general interchange.

In any given area, it is likely that the first developments of the period of modern transport—from, say, the canal and turnpike onwards—took place for one or both of the first two of these three reasons, and that a true *network* of transport lines only came into being with the third. But it is also generally true that, in areas where modern transport was introduced for reasons of strategy or of economic development, the passing of time will see a gradual thickening of the original sparse framework of lines into a genuine network, so that it is possible to estimate the extent to which this later, developed phase of transport service has been reached in any particular region.

The interest of this development lies not only in its story, stirring though this has often been, but in the different patterns which are created on the map. For the pattern betrays the motive behind construction, just as it may reveal, too, the character of the terrain or the distribution of population within the region.

Let us briefly consider some of these patterns, and firstly those created where strategic considerations have been uppermost in the mind of the planner. Strategic lines of communication are often conspicuous on the map because they run through areas of sparse population, or because they show an apparent indifference to relief and areas of settlement. These routes were not constructed for the benefit of the local population but in the interests of whatever power occupied, or wished to occupy, their terminal points—so that troops could be moved swiftly or political pressure brought to bear at a distance from the centre of power. They occur both as single lines and as networks. The longest of all the world's railways, the Trans-Siberian, was of course an example; it was built to bring metropolitan Russia into some degree of contact with her Siberian and Far Eastern territories, and most of the present settlements along it owe their existence to the railway, although it was originally built for military purposes.

Similar in concept were the original transcontinental routes in Canada. As we have already noted, it was in a real sense the railway which made the Canadian federation possible, and not even the rails themselves, but simply the promise of their coming. That the North Americans on both sides of the 49th parallel were well aware of the strategic purpose that might be served by a single railway line is suggested by a pair of quotations from the period. The first is from a committee report of the United States Senate and refers to plans for a Northern Pacific Railway (actually opened in 1883) running, of course, within United States territory:

The opening by the United States of a Northern Pacific Railway seals the destiny of the British possessions west of the ninety-first meridian. [The western Canadians] will become so Americanized in interests and feelings that they will be in effect severed from the new Dominion and . . . their annexation will be but a question of time.

The second is from the first paragraph of the agreement of 1870 whereby British Columbia undertook to adhere to the Canadian federation, provided that:

The Government of the Dominion undertake to secure the commencement simultaneously, within two years from the date of union, of the construction of a railway, from the Pacific towards the Rocky Mountains, and from such point as may be selected east of the Rocky Mountains towards the Pacific, to connect the seaboard of British Columbia with the railway system of Canada . . .[11]

Almost a century later came the Trans-Canada Highway, as the first all-weather, all-Canadian motor route from east to west across the nation. Previously, most Canadians had simply crossed into the U.S.A. and used their neighbours' road network as a means of getting from one end of their own country to the other.

In network form, strategic routes are represented by Wade's and Roy's roads in Scotland, by the new Chinese roads in Tibet or by the railway network in India—the densest in mainland Asia—which, while it certainly had a basis in economic policy, owes much to the fears aroused by the Indian Mutiny. Strategic considerations have certainly weighed heavily enough, also, to influence the planning of the United States' own network of Interstate Highways, the 70,000 km of freeway which should be completed in the 1970s.

When we come to consider the patterns created by transport routes where economic development has been the primary motive, we should begin by recollecting the fact that the great economic events of the nineteenth century—the Industrial Revolution and the European exploitation of the world's new lands—involved from the outset the movement of goods in bulk on an entirely new scale. By sea, this presented no special problem; the difficulty was to transport these bulky goods—and in the first place among them, coal—to the waterside. So in Britain first, and subsequently in Europe, crude wagon-ways (later rail-ways) were built, and they ran, almost without exception, from mine or mill to port of shipment. They were not laid for the convenience of the local population, but for the sake of the single economic development to which they were vital.

When European traders, miners or planters entered the new lands of Africa and Asia, the same problem faced them. Here were fertile lands and rich ore bodies. There were fortunes to be made if only produce could be exported. The solution was the 'export line'—the overseas equivalent of the coal wagon-way in Durham or Fife. A line of rail or water routes was opened up from the coastal port into the potentially rich interior. Such lines were built from a score of ports on the coast of west Africa and south-east Asia 'up-country'. Railways were built round breaks in navigation on the Congo or between the river highways of the Parana–Paraguay system. These routes did not always arrive at any particular destination; their role was rather to open to European commerce the area adjacent to the line, and the railhead or river terminus was moved further inland as new development proceeded. Some of them linked with the coast a

[11] The two quotations are to be found, together with related discussion, in Leslie Roberts, *Canada: The Golden Hinge*, Harrap, London, 1953, pp. 255, 260.

specific mineral field or plantation zone, and very few of the lines were connected with each other.[12]

But the breadth of territory which a single line could 'tap' in this way was, of course, limited. In particular, it was found that, on the great temperate grasslands, it was impossible to grow cereals competitively at a distance of more than 25–30 km from a railway: the cost of haulage *to* the railhead was too high. Yet these lands were too fertile to waste, and too cheap to ignore. As a result there grew up, in certain of these grassland areas, a specialized and sophisticated version of the 'export line' pattern of transport. It is the pattern seen in its fullest development on the Pampas (figure 2, p. 8). Instead of a single export line there are a dozen, running out from Rosario, Buenos Aires and Bahia Blanca like the ribs of a fan. It is a layout designed to bring every part of the humid Pampas within economic reach of a port. As a layout it does little to cater for the convenience of the Argentinians, and nothing to ease north–south communication, but then it was a railway system laid out not by Argentinian but by British engineers, and they had a clear objective in view—to deliver the meat and grain of the Pampas at Liverpool with the least possible delay.

The Pampas pattern is found repeated in two others areas. One is the North American Spring Wheat Belt, where, however, the shape of the fan is distorted by the transverse line of the United States–Canada border, which cuts it into two. The other is a part of the Murray River basin of southern Australia. All three of these are areas of extensive farming, grading off into ranching at the dry margins, and all are remarkable for their smooth relief, for such a regular pattern of railways can only be constructed in an area free from relief obstacles.

It would be misleading to pretend, however, that it is always possible to distinguish between routes created for strategic purposes and those that were economic in motivation, for in many areas the two considerations merged. What is, perhaps, the classic example of this mixture of motives is revealed by the map of the railways of southern Africa (figure 16) on the eve of war—in this case the Boer War of 1899. On the map can be seen most of the elements that made the conflict inevitable. These are (1) the lines thrusting inland from the four rival ports of Cape Town, Port Elizabeth, East London and Durban, the first three converging on the southern end of the High Veldt, where they were obliged to halt and wait

---

[12] This lack of interconnection between the export lines was dramatically revealed in 1942–3 when the Japanese, in order to supply their armies in Burma from bases in Thailand, had to *build* a railway line along which to do so—the notorious Death Railway. As a commentary on the role of the railway in southeast Asia, it is worth adding that no sooner was the war over and the army withdrawn than the railway was abandoned to the jungle once again.

until the Transvaal government reluctantly permitted a line to be carried north to Johannesburg and the goldfields in the 1890s. Then there is (2) the telltale line of railway which hugs the western frontiers of the two

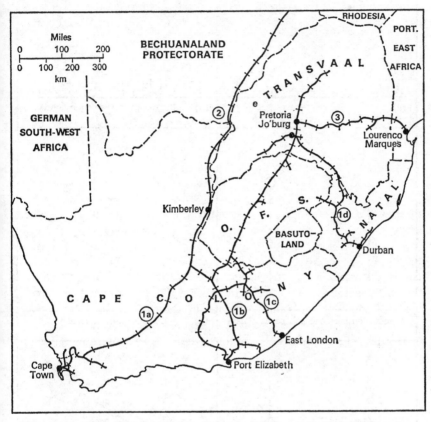

Figure 16: The railways of South Africa on the eve of the Boer War in 1899. The numbers identifying individual lines are referred to in the text.

Boer republics but never crosses them—the railway and the telegraph that marked the Road to the North and that played so important a part in Cecil Rhodes' project to get round behind the Boers and take Rhodesia ahead of them, as a long step forward in realizing his Cape-to-Cairo dream.[13] (3) There is the line to Lourenço Marques, the one line to the coast which was built not by the British but by a Dutch company for the Boers. It was their 'back door', their one route to the sea which did not cross British territory, and along it President Kruger of the

[13] Rhodes said 'The railway is my right hand and the telegraph my voice.' (Quoted by J. R. Day, *Railways of South Africa*, Barker, London, 1963.)

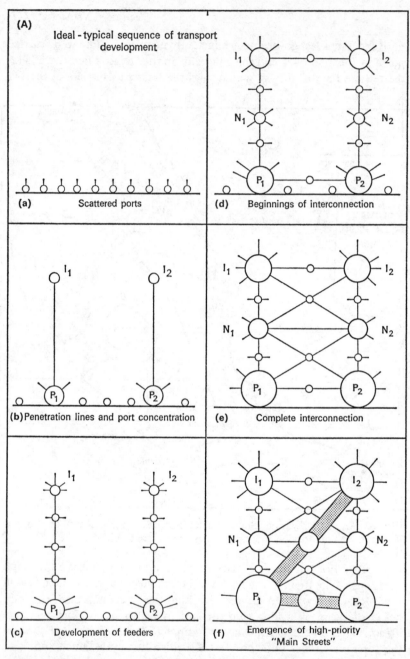

Figure 17A: Transport network development in west Africa: a model developed for Ghana and Nigeria which identifies six stages in network development. (Reproduced by permission from E. J. Taaffe and others, 'Transport Expansion in Underdeveloped Countries', *Geographical Review* 53 (1963), New York: © American Geographical Society, p. 504.)

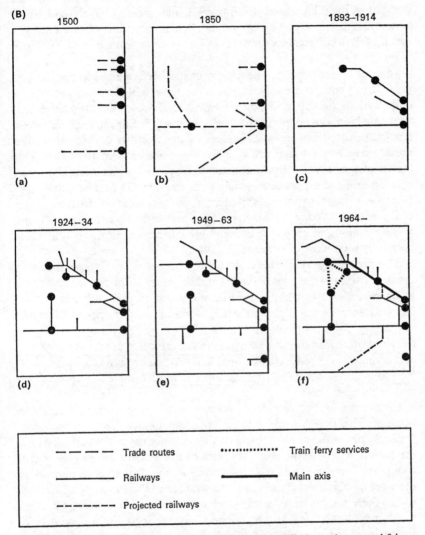

Figure 17B: The Taaffe-Morrill-Gould model applied to the east African situation. B. S. Hoyle has identified six phases to correspond with those described in west Africa: these are (**a**) historical antecedents of the modern network, (**b**) the zenith of the Arab trading period, (**c**) the coming of the first railways and (**d–f**) transport elaboration phases. (Reproduced by permission from B. S. Hoyle, 'Transport and Economic Growth in Developing Countries: The Case of East Africa', in *Geographical Essays in Honour of K. C. Edwards*, University of Nottingham: Department of Geography, 1970, p. 190.)

Transvaal fled into exile in the closing days of the war. That war had underlined the importance of railways—which seem to have exercised an almost magnetic attraction upon the British generals—and its course can be followed from a railway map better than from any other document.

In areas where economic development has been taking place for longer periods, a genuine network of transport lines will develop, the logical outgrowth of the web of footpaths or muletracks which links settlements in the more backward parts of the world. In western Europe such a network has long existed but in other regions of the world it is possible, at the present day, to see a network actually in process of formation. One such area is eastern Brazil. Here transport development began along the coast, where a series of export lines—mainly railways, but in part based on river routes—ran down to ports of shipment from the plantation areas and mines of the interior. Today these isolated lines are gradually being cross-linked and are coming to serve a genuinely *internal* communications role, reinforced by a network of super-highways.

The process by which this cross-linkage occurs has been analysed using the west African examples of Ghana and Nigeria.[14] The sequence of maps in figure 17a shows the stages of development in this case. Gradually, the existence of the original export line casts a transport 'shadow' over adjacent ports or centres that lie off the route. At the same time, the territory adjoining the line responds to the stimulus of access to market, and commercial production in turn leads to the growth of centres along the line, centres which in time generate sufficient traffic to require crossroutes between them.

How dense is the network of commercial transport routes likely to become? This depends on a number of factors. One of them—but not, surprisingly perhaps, the most important—is the density of population within the region. Many of the crowded lands of the east are virtually devoid of commercial transport. At the other extreme, the densest road network in the world, judged in relation to population, is in the Republic of Ireland, where there are 30 km of roads (and 20 km of surfaced roads) for every 1,000 inhabitants, against six in the United Kingdom, and only $3\frac{1}{2}$ in Bulgaria, at the opposite end of Europe.[15]

[14] E. J. Taaffe, R. L. Morrill and P. R. Gould, 'Transport Expansion in Underdeveloped Countries: A Comparative Analysis', *Geographical Review* 53 (1963), pp. 503–29.

[15] This interesting anomaly in Ireland can be explained in two ways: (1) The population of the Irish Republic is only a half of what it was in 1841, thanks to a century of emigration, so that many of these roads are the roads of a vanished generation. (2) Nineteenth-century Ireland suffered, as is well known, from repeated famines, and one of the standard ways of alleviating the distress these

Much more important than the density of population is the volume of circulation of goods and people within a region, although this is, of course, itself initially dependent on the provision of transport. But a subsistence economy within which each small community is virtually self-supporting generates little or no traffic. The amount generated varies with the degree of economic interdependence between communities or regions; or, alternatively, with the extent to which their production is geared to wider exchanges outside the region. Much of peasant Asia and Africa have no 'network' at all above the footpath level: India and the western U.S.S.R., by contrast, have a loosely-knit one, and western Europe and the eastern part of North America have a very dense network.

In practice, this means that there is a general correspondence between density of network and standard of living, for it is those nations which have advanced furthest that possess the densest network of communications. It is they who have the highest levels of production and consumption, and their citizens who have the surplus resources that form the basis for travel and trade. It is they who can afford the capital investment represented by roads or airlines, while the poorer members of the world community cannot.

But this correspondence is not complete, because in the process of opening up the new lands of the world in the nineteenth century, the European powers in effect extended their own transport networks overseas. They used their own capital resources to build roads and railways in areas whose development they wished to encourage and whose own population could never have afforded them. The British built railways and streetcar lines in Brazil and Argentina, Calcutta and Bombay. Perhaps the best example, however, of what might be called a 'superimposed' network of this kind was the one constructed by the Dutch in Java. While the rest of the Dutch East Indies—as they then were—had barely passed the stage of the canoe and jungle trail, Java possessed suburban electric trains running on four-track railways which were barely distinguishable from those in the Netherlands. The Dutch poured their capital investment into this one, densely-populated island, and produced a rail network rivalled before 1940 only by that of Japan in the eastern hemisphere.

So the density of the network is governed by

1   density of population
2   volume of circulation, which in turn is related fairly closely to standard of living

---

caused was to provide work on the roads. With famine occurring so frequently, it soon became difficult to find any more roads that needed building, and the new roads merely duplicated the old ones—and created extra headaches for the present-day local authorities which are responsible for their upkeep.

3   availability of capital resources.[16]

There is one other factor to be added to this list—the factor of competition which we considered earlier. Where all of the first three indices are high and where in addition private enterprise has been permitted free rein, there we find a kind of climax network of transport lines—a dense and wasteful mass, entwined on the map like some luxuriant creeper on a wall.

This kind of overdevelopment—as it must now be considered—took place in North America and in parts of western Europe. But nowhere else was it so marked, or so wasteful, as in Great Britain. By the time the canal era and the railway booms were over, Britain possessed transport facilities sufficient not only to handle her entire production at that date but to accommodate in addition all the increases that even mid-Victorian optimism could envisage.

In certain areas of central Britain this 'climax network' grew to its densest and one of these, perhaps the most remarkable of all, is mapped in figure 18—the Leeds–Sheffield area of southern Yorkshire. Here, all the network-forming factors were at work simultaneously: the exploitation of the Yorkshire coalfield led to the building of numerous colliery railways and the development of heavy industry; the growth of woollen manufacturing created a demand for fuel, raw materials and abundant labour; the worldwide character of the wool trade made access to a major port (in this case Hull) vital; the industrial towns vied with each other to get the benefit of transport links. All this took place adjacent to the main north–south routeway of eastern Britain, along which the railways competing to create an Anglo-Scottish chain were being laid, parallel with the major road to the north. Upon the transport facilities catering for more local needs there was thus superimposed a great crossroads of routes— England to Scotland, and the woollen towns to the sea. Here the old railway builders came closer, perhaps, than anywhere else in the world to making the railway the true universal of transport. Here, also, in the twentieth century, is growing Britain's first complex of intersecting motorways.

Today, there is not a great deal of railway construction going on in the world: so little, in fact, that the opening of a new line in Canada, or a project for a rail link in central Africa, have a news value that contains

---

[16] Readers who prefer a statistical presentation of this analysis will find it in K. J. Kansky, *Structure of Transportation Networks*, University of Chicago, 1963, where chapters III to VII are devoted to the subject. However, Kansky couches his analysis in terms of an index of 'technological scale' which is not created by or defined by him, but is borrowed from B. J. L. Berry, who evolved this composite index to express the effect upon network density of a large group of economic variables. This tends to limit the value of Kansky's analysis and he makes no explicit reference to the key factor of capital investment.

even an element of surprise that such a thing could happen.[17] Today, with the major air routes of the world firmly established, the important

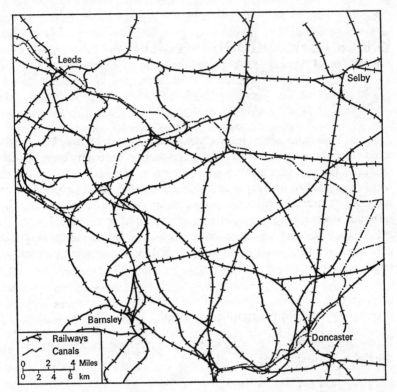

Figure 18: A network climax: railways and canals in central Yorkshire, where coalfield development, inter-company rivalry and transit traffic combined to produce one of the densest communications networks of the post-industrialization world. The map records the situation at the end of a century of railway building, prior to the second world war: many of the lines have now been abandoned.

developments in the field of transport are mainly occurring in the extension of road networks—of a primary network in Africa, Latin America and central Asia, or a 'second-generation' network of super-roads in Europe and North America. With the number of cars per head of the population everywhere rising, the road engineers are today recapturing some of the glamour which, a century ago, belonged to the pioneers who dug the canals and laid the rails for a world awakening to its resources and its opportunities.

[17] Canada has built about 5,000 km of new railway line since the second world war, mainly to link northern mining areas with the national rail net.

5

Bases of Economic Activity:
(3) Fuel and Power

The tremendous increases in productive capacity which have been registered since the start of the Industrial Revolution have only been possible
thanks to the application, through machinery, of a huge input of power,
which provides heat or pressure or motive force. The range of power
sources has steadily broadened in the meantime, so that almost the first
question a power user must settle is: what *kind* of power shall he use? In
this chapter we shall first consider some of the factors influencing such
choices, and then go on to consider individually the main possibilities
open.

CHOOSING A POWER SOURCE

Power users' decisions normally take into account four factors: availability,
suitability, cost and type of market.

I AVAILABILITY
The first and most obvious consideration is to discover what is available.
Availability, however, is not merely a matter of geography; it also involves technology. While it is obvious that some parts of the world possess
coal deposits or oil-bearing strata and others do not, it is also true that
centuries elapsed during which these minerals lay untouched because
no one had the technical capacity to exploit them; they only became
available, in this sense, when the techniques of deep-mining and well-
drilling reached a point of sufficient development to secure them.

Even so, a power source might be 'available' over only a limited area
because no satisfactory method had been evolved of transporting it to
market. The early oil industry in the U.S.A.[1] collected crude oil in wooden
barrels identical with those used for beer and spirits. Shortage of barrels
was the industry's first structural handicap: if a drilling crew brought in a

---

[1] The beginnings of the industry are usually dated from the oil strike at
Titusville in northwestern Pennsylvania in 1859.

'gusher', they could do nothing but stand and watch the oil go to waste because there was at that date no method of collecting it.

In the same way the electricity industry in its early days could transmit its product over only very limited distances: power was either generated close to the point of use or it was not generated at all, because the losses in transmission over distance were too large. Gradually, however, this economical transmission distance has increased. The grid has been followed by the super-grid and by international sales of electricity exactly like sales of coal or oil. Nowadays a transmission distance of 800 km is perfectly acceptable.

Availability must, however, be assessed by yet another criterion. We can distinguish between *primary* power sources, where the material itself—coal, oil or natural gas—provides the energy, and *secondary* power, which is manufactured from primary sources. The process of conversion may make power available where otherwise it would be either physically or financially impossible to exploit a source. Perhaps the best example of this situation is to be found in the Republic of Ireland. The traditional fuel of Ireland is turf, or peat. But this happens to be a fuel which is virtually useless in its natural form for any other industrial purpose than making whiskey; it is essentially a domestic fuel. The Irish Turf Board and Electricity Board have between them, however, made peat 'available' in the full sense to Irish manufacturers. They have constructed peat-burning power stations out on the bogs, to supply electricity to Irish industry, and they have developed a method of compressing powdered peat into briquettes which yields a solid type of fuel that resembles the briquetted brown coal of Germany and is no more difficult to use than bituminous coal, if rather more cumbersome.

2 SUITABILITY FOR THE TASK

The type of power source chosen must take account of the nature of the work to be performed, and the kind of equipment employed. Sometimes only a single source will do: in the smelting of aluminium, for example, there is no present substitute for a process using very large amounts of electricity. In the smelting of iron, by contrast, there is a wide range of choice; historically, this task has been variously carried out with charcoal, coal, gas and electricity, and each of these has its particular advantages. In the same way, the railways of the world today have an almost bewildering array of types of motive power: coal-steam, oil-steam, diesel, diesel-electric, gas-turbine and electric. Road vehicles, on the other hand, are restricted at present almost exclusively to the use of petrol and diesel fuel, despite continuous efforts to produce a workable electric vehicle.

Assessment of a suitable power source must take account of several factors. First and foremost is the nature of the operation. If it involves a moving vehicle, then all forms of fuel except electricity must be carried on board, and the bulk of this fuel must be considered. An old wood-burning railway engine had to stop every few kilometres to refuel, and a coal-burner rather less frequently, while a diesel engine can economically carry fuel for upwards of a thousand kilometres if need be. Electricity is not carried on the vehicle, but must usually be continuously supplied from a wire or rail, which implies that the vehicle must run on predetermined tracks; hence the difficulty of designing an electric motor car.

Within the operational pattern, it is also important to know at what point the heat or power is to be applied. One of the basic drawbacks to the use of coal, whether employed directly or as a steam-raiser, is that the burning coal cannot be far from the operational site; there is no method of remote application. A steam-driven mill was and is built around the boiler-house, the machine shops grouped as tightly as possible to reduce heat loss on the steam circuits. To spread the operations—and incidentally to improve the working conditions of the employees—is bound to be uneconomical; to do this one needs to use electrical drive.

A second consideration is the efficiency which can be achieved with a particular source of power. In processes involving heat, the significant index is the *thermal efficiency* of the machinery. In this respect, the ordinary coal-burning steam railway engine must be one of the most inefficient machines ever invented: it normally has a thermal efficiency of only 6–8 per cent, and but for the earlier lack of a suitable substitute would surely have been superseded long ago. The same is true of most other combinations of coal-and-steam power. A thermal power station, however, is likely today to have a thermal efficiency of 25–35 per cent. The best way to utilize coal as a fuel is therefore not to employ it directly in an inefficient furnace on wheels, where heat losses are enormous, but in generating electricity in a relatively efficient power station, from which the electricity can be fed, again efficiently, to an electric locomotive.

A third consideration is the degree of control required in the power source. Steel can be made with coke, gas or electricity, but where precise temperatures are needed, as in the making of special steels, the electric furnace is normally employed because it makes possible precision control of quality.

A fourth and final aspect of suitability can be described as the amenity factor. The Industrial Revolution established the automatic association in people's minds, of industry and transport with dirt. It was a revolution shrouded in smoke and steam, and its motive force was coal. It produced 'dark, satanic mills', and living conditions to match. To say that this was 'unsuitable' would be a gross understatement. Today, with smokeless zones and landscaped factories, we have relegated coal to a limited number of uses—of which the chief is power generation—where its residues can be controlled, even if it means building a chimney 250 m high to carry off the fumes.[2] We have become pollution-conscious, and have to view oil- and petrol-burning also with alarm, the smog in Los Angeles acting as a warning of what may be in store elsewhere in the future. From a pollution point of view, in fact, we are left with hydro-electricity and solar energy as the sole acceptable sources of power.

3 COST

Considerations of availability and suitability may still leave the power user with a choice of sources, and he will naturally assess comparative costs. Within the power industry itself, these fall under two heads, production and transport or distribution. Fuel and energy can be transported by so many different means—road, rail, water, pipeline, wire—that the assessment of relative advantage may not be easy. It may be simple enough to decide that, at a particular moment of time, oil delivered by canal barge or natural gas by pipeline offers a cost advantage. But a manufacturer equipping his plant to use one or other of these sources does not want to find, in a year or even ten years' time, that the fuel he has chosen to power his factory has lost its advantage, and left him wishing he had 'gone electric' instead.

It is necessary, therefore, to study the *trend* of costs in the competing branches of the power industry. In this connection we have to realize that we have just arrived at the end of an era—an era covering, in Western Europe, about two decades and in North America a rather longer period. During this period, the price of petroleum and natural gas in relation to other fuels has become progressively more favourable to the consumer. Both production costs and transport costs were held down (and in some cases reduced) in a period of generally rising prices, the first because the number of producers was increasing, the second because of the advent of the super-tanker and the spread of a pipeline network. Coal, by contrast, was being progressively priced out of its markets. This was not so much because it was an inefficient industry—output per man-shift, as Table 13 shows, has been steadily rising—as because in coal mining labour costs make up a large part of total costs,[3] and the cost of labour has tended to rise irrespectively of the efficiency of the industry. In practice, in Western Europe at least, if the price of other fuels could be held steady, it was only a matter of time before only the most efficient mines could compete, and their number was getting smaller year by year. At this point the Dutch government, reading the

[2] At the power station at Drax, on the Yorkshire Ouse, opened in 1969.
[3] 50 per cent, according to the National Coal Board accounts for 1973–4.

writing on the wall, decided to close down its Limburg coalfield altogether.

What then happened was that, within a single twelve-month period in 1973–4, the price of oil was suddenly raised between three and four times. The rise had nothing to do with the efficiency of production, or employment, or wages. It had something to do with supply and demand, but mostly it was produced by a simple unilateral decision on the part of exporting nations to increase the price and improve their returns. Suddenly, therefore, all the carefully calculated cost advantages of the past two decades were overthrown. Suddenly, too, the attractiveness of coal as a fuel source was restored. Henceforth, a new arithmetic has become necessary.

4 TYPE OF MARKET

Both the size and the nature of the market to be served are important. The size matters because a number of fuels yield big economies with increasing scale. As we shall see later on, the use of either large tankers or large-diameter pipelines can cut costs on oil and gas to a very striking degree; the question is therefore whether the market is large enough to warrant their use. The nature of the market matters because it affects distribution costs, particularly for electricity, where in rural areas of diffuse settlement distribution may account for as much as 90 per cent of total costs. It also matters whether or not the demand for power is stable and, if not, what the degree of demand fluctuation may be. The coal and oil industries can stockpile their product if demand falls off from season to season or hour to hour: the electricity industry cannot, and instead has to create stand-by capacity equal to the peak demand, keeping it idle for much of the time.

Consideration of all these factors produces what has been called the 'fuel mix'—the use of different fuels for particular purposes and in particular regions. But in present-day circumstances it is unlikely that the fuel mix will be the product of economic and technical factors alone. Even when the user has discovered what is, for his own time and place, the cheapest source of power, the price he is quoted is unlikely to be the 'natural' price. Rather, it is usually the product of *power policy*.

Government intervention in the power industries has become commonplace, even in such a temple of free enterprise as the United States petroleum industry, and there perhaps precisely because it was the industry which yielded the modern world's first billion-dollar fortune—that of the Rockefellers. There are two main reasons why governments control power sources. One is because the supply of power, like that of transport, is to some extent a public service, and it is felt that neither should be made a matter of private profit alone. The other is that, with the spread of ideas about resource conservation, national resource policies have become increasingly important, as we saw in chapter one, and these policies cover power supplies.

Power policies are introduced where

1   the present price advantage of one type of fuel or energy may lead to its over-use and consequent run-down
2   the price advantage of one type of fuel or energy may lead to the neglect of another type
3   a country may become too dependent on an imported fuel, so that in an emergency its home power reserves may be inadequate.

A clear example of the first case is offered by the oil commissions in the

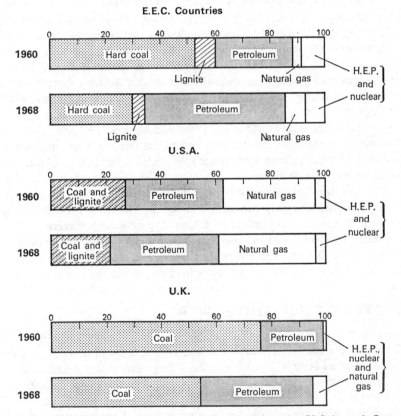

Figure 19: The fuel 'mix' in the E.E.C. countries, the U.S.A. and Great Britain, showing the percentage of total energy consumption (in hard-coal or thermal equivalents) provided by various fuel sources.

U.S.A., whose task is to set quotas on oil production within each of the petroleum states. The interest of the individual states is in seeing that their oil reserves are not squandered, during the present phase of fuel technology, for the benefit of other states which have alternative power sources; their job is to prevent mere bargain-hunting. An example of the second case can be seen in the work of the Irish government boards, which supplied the development funds necessary to make peat a commercial power source and give Ireland a native energy supply. An example of the third case can be found in the coal industries of the west European countries today. All through western Europe and Britain, as we have already seen, home-produced coal has been under very heavy competitive pressure (1) from petroleum products and (2) from imported (American and Polish) coal. From an economic point of view alone, it would probably have been cheapest to allow the coal industry to die a quiet, unhindered death and concentrate on imported fuel. But this was precisely what the west European governments could not afford to do, any more than they could afford to abandon their own agriculture and import their entire food supply (as some Britons had once believed), because in times of crisis they would risk being cut off from their overseas suppliers. What is more, while food can at least be produced between one harvest and the next, it would take a very much longer time to reactivate a coal industry, with its large labour force and necessary skills. However unfavourable the price situation of the home industry became, therefore, the European governments felt that they must nurse it along, in order to have some home fuel source at least available in case overseas supplies dried up.

In 1973, this precaution was seen to be justified, when the price of petroleum was abruptly raised. Coal, which had been steadily losing ground in cost terms, suddenly achieved a new attractiveness. With shortages and high prices in the petroleum market, it was some consolation at least to European countries that they still had coal supplies to fall back on, and a mining industry in being to extract those supplies.

TYPES OF FUEL AND POWER

I PETROLEUM AND NATURAL GAS

The first petroleum commercially marketed in the world was put on sale by one Samuel Kier of Pittsburgh, U.S.A., in 1847. It was called Seneca Oil because it was the Seneca Indians who introduced it to the white man, and it was sold as a medicine in half-pint bottles. After a time, however, dissatisfied with the rate of sales of his medicine, Kier began to experiment to find other uses for his surplus stocks, and in 1850 put on the market a lamp oil at a very reasonable 75 cents a barrel. With the discovery that distilled petroleum would ignite, the world's largest modern industry was born.

This brief tale seems to epitomize the development of the industry, which has evolved in a series of phases linked with new uses for its products. The first half-century of the industry, up to about the year 1900, was built on the demand for kerosene, an illuminant. Then came the petrol-driven engine, and a surge of demand for the new product. There then followed the growth of the petrochemical industries, using the by-products of the refining process; expanding during the second world war to include synthetic rubber, and culminating after the war in the present plastics revolution. Meanwhile, use was being made of the natural gas which the oil drills often released. Originally, this gas had been treated by the drilling crews as a nuisance and had been burned off. Only since the last war has it been treated as a prime source of energy in its own right, worth the trouble of drilling for from rigs anchored far offshore, amid the storm-driven waters of the North Sea. Naturally enough, the impact of these various product-phases on the character and location of the industry have not all been identical.

The petroleum industry basically has three phases—production, refining and transport. The production process is not complex: it can be undertaken by small operators and, where freedom exists to drill, as in the U.S.A., there are in practice plenty of such small men in the business. It is not the production which presents the problem, but the *disposal* of the product. This is especially true in the early stages of a well's life, when the oil is flowing under natural pressure: unless it can be disposed of into storage, the oil is simply wasted. The early drillers in Pennsylvania, following the 1859 strike, collected oil in earthenware pots, empty whiskey barrels or simply in holes in the ground.

What this means within the industry is, however, that the producer of oil is in a very weak position over against the carrier who transports the product away. The Rockefeller fortune in America was founded on this perception. The young Rockefeller visited the Pennsylvania oilfields from nearby Cleveland and, on his return, advised his partners to have nothing whatever to do with the production side of the business, but to concentrate on the transport of oil. Not only did this make immediate economic sense; it was not long before a sizeable share of the production business was under Rockefeller's control precisely *because* his pipelines were indispensable to the industry. Since his time it has become a commonplace that the big oil companies—the 'majors'—control the industry partly by their ownership of pipes and tanker fleets, and partly because of the rising expense of oil prospecting by modern methods in out of the way places like northern Alaska and the floor of the continental shelf.

The transport of oil and gas is normally by tanker at sea and by pipeline on land, with lesser quantities moving locally by road and rail. To transport gas, especially by tanker, is considerably more expensive than to transport petroleum fluids, and the latter therefore move greater distances. In the U.S.S.R., for example, policy is generally to use natural gas at home and to export oil. Movement by tanker and pipeline is cheaper than by either road or rail, but the relative cost as between the two depends on the size of tanker and the diameter of the pipe, and these in turn depend on the size of the market.

The way in which tanker costs vary with size of vessel is indicated by figure 20. It shows that the trend towards super-tankers is soundly based on the economics of the situation and that the layout of the industry as a

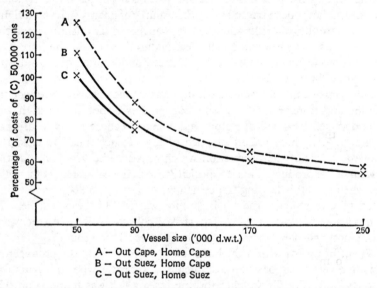

A — Out Cape, Home Cape
B — Out Suez, Home Cape
C — Out Suez, Home Suez

Figure 20: The transport of petroleum: the figure shows the relationship between cost of transport and size of tanker. Even when it is open, the depth of the Suez Canal limits the size of the *loaded* tankers which can pass through it; hence the need to calculate costs on the three separate bases shown in the figure. (Reproduced by permission of Esso Petroleum Co. Ltd.)

whole is consequently coming to depend to an ever-increasing degree on the whereabouts of deep-water terminals. The economies of size are even more pronounced for pipelines.[4] However, these economies can only

[4] G. Manners, *The Geography of Energy*, Hutchinson, London, 1964, p. 73. No one can write on this subject without in some degree being indebted to Manners, and this is perhaps the appropriate point for the present writer gladly to acknowledge his own debt.

be profitably obtained up to the capacity of the market. Super-tankers represent a huge capital investment, and a day's idleness for such a vessel may represent thousands of pounds in lost revenue; it must be kept fully employed. With pipelines, the capital cost (i.e. cost of installation) may make up 65 or 75 per cent of total costs, and the assurance of a large market at the delivery end is essential to justify the capital input involved.

The third phase of the industry is refining. This may, in principle, occur either before or after transport of the crude oil. In the industry's early days, up to one quarter of the refinery products was lost, and it was customary to refine at the oilfield, to avoid transporting the one gallon in four which was later going to be wasted. Nowadays, however, refinery location is usually planned to take account of two factors: (1) it is cheapest to refine at a point of trans-shipment, where the oil has in any case to be handled, and (2) it is easier and cheaper to transport the crude oil and refine it near the market, where the various by-products can more easily be distributed, than to refine at the field and then carry separately all the different refinery products to market. But the latter course is feasible if the throughput of the refinery is sufficiently large.

Since a very high proportion of the world's oil production—probably over 80 per cent—moves by ocean tanker at *some* stage or other of its delivery, the characteristic refinery location today is at tidewater, at either point of shipment or of delivery. The Gulf Coast of the U.S.A. and the shore of the Persian Gulf are examples of the former; the river estuaries of western Europe of the latter. As a relative newcomer among industries, one which occupies a great deal of space and may have unpleasant local effects, the oil refinery is normally situated well outside the main port complex, and sometimes in complete isolation. As tankers grow larger, the provision of deep-water terminals takes on increasing importance. To meet this trend, the oil companies have taken two kinds of action. One is to build new refineries in deeper water than the old; that is, nearer the open sea, as has been the case at Rotterdam, where the movement of the industry can be traced along the New Waterway from the outskirts of the city to the very tip of the Europoort complex (figure 21). The other is to create a terminal on deep water, and to carry the oil by pipeline to the refinery. This arrangement exists in Scotland between the deep west coast anchorage at Finnart on Loch Long and the refinery at Grangemouth on the Forth.

Unlike oil production, refining is essentially a large-scale operation. The more numerous the refinery products, of course, the more definitely is this the case: the investment called for, not only in plant but in terms of research, is too great for any but the 'majors' to undertake. Ownership of pipelines, super-tankers and refineries are all critical in this industry,

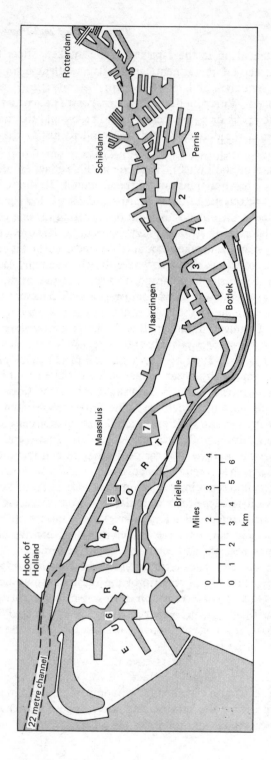

Figure 21: The port of Rotterdam and its oil terminals: the map shows the port's seven oil terminals (numbered 1 to 7) and the way in which the increasing size of the loaded tanker has made it necessary to move the discharging point down-stream from the original Petroleumhaven near the old docks to the deep-water channel of Europort.

and it is no wonder, therefore, that the industry accounts for some of the largest companies in the world—or that when competition between the majors takes place over a new field, such as that in northern Alaska, it is, like a battle between dinosaurs, very much larger than life.

Although oil and gas are fossil fuels like coal, they do not normally produce the same undesirable side-effects on the landscape when they are being worked—subsidence and slag heaps are not found on the fields. On a Middle Eastern oilfield, in fact, there may be only the most occasional evidence that anything is going on at all. Here the critical factor is the size of concession, which in turn is a resultant of the mining law. In this respect, there is a contrast between country and country which is very striking. At one extreme is the U.S.A. Under American mining law, the owner of the mineral rights on any piece of land (he may or may not be identical with the owner of the land itself; that is irrelevant) is entitled to anything he can extract from it. This structure of law works well enough for static minerals, but is much less satisfactory for a mineral which can in fact be 'poached'. If several different operators share the drilling rights for a single oil dome, it is obviously to the advantage of each to put down the maximum number of wells and pump out the oil ahead of his competitors. The result is seen in the forest of derricks which normally marks the location of an American field.

But the forest is not an indication of rational resource use; rather the reverse. By pumping competitively, the oilmen simply exhaust the field more quickly and have to move on. Besides this, they soon lose the natural pressure under which oil will generally flow for a time at least, and have to start pumping sooner. All this adds to the capital cost of the wells, and discourages the rational exploitation of the field.

At the opposite extreme can be grouped most oil producing countries of the Middle East. Here a single concession covers thousands of square miles, and in some cases a whole country. There is no private drilling, but a single long-term programme agreed between the oil company and the government, with the former providing the technical inputs and the latter receiving a share of the revenues. These arrangements ensure the maximum economic life-span (and minimum capital cost) for wells, pumps and pipelines. Each well in the Middle East therefore pumps, on average, many times more oil per day than does a well in the U.S.A., at a smaller capital cost.[5]

---

[5] Writing on the basis of data from the 1960s, Manners, *op. cit.*, p.28, gives figures as follows: yearly production per well in the U.S.A. is 550 tons on average, in Venuezela 15,000 tons and in the Middle East 275,000 tons. The cost of raising the oil in the same three regions was: U.S.A. $11·50 per ton; Venezuela, a little over $6·00; the Middle East, less than $1·00.

In between the Middle Eastern and the United States cases is the situation in most other producing areas, such as Canada and the North Sea floor. The Canadian oil strikes came sufficiently late in the industry's history (effectively, after 1947) for the federal and provincial governments to profit from lessons learned south of the border and obtain a fairly successful blend of competition and control, with concessions of intermediate size. Much the same balance has been achieved in the development of drilling operations within the British share of the North Sea gasfield (figure 22). In 1964 the British government divided the sea area into

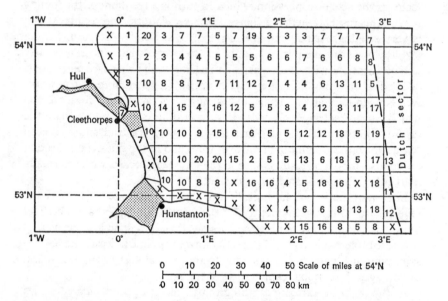

Figure 22: The North Sea gasfield: the original allocation of concessions in a part of the British sector. 25 companies obtained concessions, 20 of them (indicated by the numbers 1 to 20) in the area mapped here.

blocks of about 200 km^2, and some 20 companies or groups were granted licenses for exclusive drilling rights within the blocks. Considering the difficulty and expense of establishing a new rig on the sea bed, the last thing which either the government or the companies wanted was competitive drilling in the American sense and the concession size was chosen accordingly.

Even where planned long-term development has been the order of the day, however, it is not usual to find industry attracted to an oilfield in the same way that nineteenth-century industry was drawn to the coalfield. The *field* itself is too impermanent a feature, even though the oil-producing *region* may have a history going back over half a century or more, and the oil has in any case to be collected and refined before use. What we usually find, therefore, is that oil- or gas-using industries are attracted not to the field itself but to some point near by where another factor gives added strength to the locational influences. Thus a pre-existing urban centre—say Dallas or Edmonton—may benefit greatly by the development of oilfields within its hinterland. Similarly, the United States coast on the Gulf of Mexico is one of the fastest-growing industrial areas in the nation, and one reason is that a large part of the oil production of the southern states passes through its ports and refineries. Around these refineries, rather than on the fields, there grows up a complex of plants using the refinery products for further manufacture.

World production of petroleum and international trade in its products now form the greatest commodity turnover in man's history. Although world coal production has been in excess of 2,000 million tons a year in the past decade the figure is now tending to fall, while world trade in coal has seldom exceeded 100 million tons. The 1972 figure for petroleum production was over 2,800 million tons and tending to rise, and no less than 1,600 million entered international trade. Not only are these figures likely to increase in the future, but the market for natural gas is susceptible of much greater development than at present since gas is to be found in some areas, like north-western Europe, even where oil is absent or beyond recovery.

Yet even while we note the magnitude of these figures, and the dependence on petroleum and gas which they imply, we must also notice a corollary: that a world depending so heavily on one type of power source is a world susceptible to profound economic shocks whenever the supply of that power is altered even slightly, in volume or in price. In 1973 there was a slight restriction on volume of supply and a big increase in price, and very rapidly there developed a world energy crisis. There were the same coal supplies underground as in 1972, and no less water power in rivers and reservoirs. But world dependence on petroleum products had become so pronounced that, in the moment of crisis, none of this counted; the only thing that mattered was whether or not oil supplies could be maintained. Thereafter, two other questions had to be answered: (1) could new oil fields be found? (2) could the trend towards this dependence on petroleum products be reversed, by changing to other types of power supply? In the aftermath of 1973, it is to these questions that the nations most severely hit by the events of 1973 have turned their attention.

2 ELECTRICITY
The electric power industry is peculiar in that it is really two quite separate industries with a common end product. This product, in turn, is unlike

most other commodities produced by industry, since the demand for it varies from hour to hour and yet it cannot be satisfactorily stored. The industry's capacity to produce it must therefore be equal to the peak demand, even though that demand may only continue for a fraction of the operating period. Utilization of generating plant is therefore far below the 100 per cent of full use; in the U.S.A., in 1971, the figure was 50 per cent, while in Great Britain it averages 40 per cent.

If electricity cannot be stored, however,[6] it can at least be transmitted. It is therefore not necessary to have on the spot capacity sufficient to meet peak demand, so long as capacity *within transmission distance* is equal to demand. As we have already seen in this chapter, the distance over which electricity can be transmitted is now of the order of 800 km, and within a region as large as this there is a good chance that different demand curves will balance each other to some extent. How to reduce the proportion of time during which generating plant stands idle is one of the permanent problems of the engineer, and it is a problem which calls for ingenuity. A few years ago, for example, a cross-channel link was put in to take advantage of the fact that the French go to work earlier than the British and therefore this loading pattern is offset from the British peak. The French could buy electricity in the morning and sell it back in the evening.

Electricity may be generated either by water power (hydro-electricity) or by fuel-driven generators (thermal electricity). The normal thermal power station uses its fuel to produce steam, which in turn drives the generators; the fuel may be coal, oil, peat or nuclear pile. Of the two types of generation, it may perhaps seem self-evident that water-power is preferable, since the water is free. But the actual balance of advantage between the two is a good deal more difficult to strike than at first appears.

The relative advantages of hydro and thermal power depend, firstly, on the cost structure of the industry. The major cost elements in the electricity supply industry are

1   capital charges on the installations
2   distribution costs
3   in thermal stations, the cost of fuel.

Where the market is diffuse, as it is in rural areas where every customer lives on the end of a separate power line, distribution is likely to be by far the largest item. The first head of costs, capital charges, is likely to be as

---

[6] Various experiments in energy storage have, in fact, been made as, for example, by using off-peak electricity to create heat and storing the heat instead. But these efforts do not seriously restrict the truth of the statement above.

large for hydro-electric schemes as thermal power stations, and may well be larger. The second head is also likely to be larger for water-power schemes, because they have to be constructed where the power is to be found, however remote the site, whereas the thermal station can be sited in the centre of the market area, where distribution costs are at a minimum. The only advantage, therefore, which a hydro-electric generator has over a thermal station is that it requires no fuel: on the other two counts it is likely to be more expensive to run, at least over a 30 to 40 year period.

The relative advantages of the two types of generating depend, secondly, on the nature of the water supply involved. Water for power, like water for irrigation, must be available during the period of need as a regular supply. It is not the peak flow of the river that counts, but the assured flow, and the only way to increase the latter is to build regulating works—dams and reservoirs. The more variable the supply, the larger these works must be. Again, there is an advantage to the thermal station which can be built as close to its fuel source as a site can be found.[7]

A region possessing both water power potential and fuel supplies, however, is likely to use both to generate electricity. The proportions of the two may vary as between Canada, where three quarters of the nation's capacity is water-powered, and Great Britain, where hydro capacity is a mere two to three per cent of the national total. In most regions there is a certain amount of 'stand-by' capacity held in reserve for peak demand, and this is usually thermal, since it is more versatile and the capital charges on idle plant are likely to be lower than in the case of hydro-electric plant. Mixture of the two types is common in many areas: on the Tennessee River, for example—a river whose very name has become a synonym for water power—the Tennessee Valley Authority now generates three quarters of its electricity output by thermal means.

With thermal electricity production increasing at over nine per cent per annum over the past 20 years (the figure for hydro-electricity was about seven per cent), the construction of new thermal power stations has become one of the world's major growth industries. The post-war generation of power stations is of two kinds—the conventional, coal-burning type (although some of these have been designed to burn a particular, often low-grade fuel such as peat, brown coal or slurry), and the nuclear type. Both of them are now being built in large units: the newest stations on the Trent, for example, are in the 1,000–2,000 MW size range, while the nuclear-powered stations in Britain range from 300 to 1,250 MW. Simply to find a site for such a structure is a problem in itself,

[7] Most estimates of hydro-electric potential at power sites so far untapped are given in terms of 'assured six month flow' or some similar phrase; that is, the flow assumption must be stated, otherwise the estimate is likely to be misleading.

a problem which is particularly serious for a large coal-fired station, built on a coalfield and liable to subsidence. But the major locational factor is not fuel but water—for cooling purposes, and in very large quantities. Although the introduction of 'closed circuit' water use is intended to reduce these requirements, a coal-burning station will require several hundred million litres of water a day. Even if the water is returned to the river after use, its temperature has been raised, and this creates its own problems. A nuclear station will require still more water—100 to 150 million litres *per hour*, a quantity which, in Britain, almost certainly involves a site on an estuary, if not on the coast. Compared with these water requirements even the problem of supplying a coal-burning station with the 10–20,000 tons of fuel which it requires each day is relatively slight.

In Great Britain, these locational considerations have made the Trent Valley a focus for post-war development of coal-fired stations. In 1961, the Trent was described as 'the largest underdeveloped reserve of cooling water in eastern England, with a minimum recorded flow in 1959 at Colwick, just below Nottingham, of 470 million gallons (2,100 million litres) per day.'[8] Since that time, this state of 'underdevelopment' has been remedied by further construction, not only on the Trent but also on other rivers flowing into the Humber estuary, where the new stations stand on or near the still-developing eastern edge of the Yorkshire coalfield. In the U.S.A., in the same way, when the Tennessee Valley Authority had developed all the readily-available water power on the river and found electricity consumption still rising, it was able to build its thermal stations beside the river and so obtain both cooling water and barge transport for coal.

The British nuclear stations, by contrast, have all been sited on estuaries or coasts except one, which is beside a lake in Wales. We have already seen that the over-riding consideration is the huge quantity of cooling water required, but in the planning stages at least there were also the factors (1) of public confidence in the safety of a nuclear plant (which should therefore be situated at a distance from major settlements) and (2) even more than with conventional stations, the problem of finding a site which would support the weight of the plant.

Hydro-electricity is produced by the force of falling or flowing water on the turbine blades of the generators. This force varies according to the height of the fall, or 'head', and the volume of flow. If the volume is large, the fall need not be great; one of the most recent and ingenious of the world's water-power schemes—that on the Rance, in Brittany—is

[8] J. R. James and others, 'Land Use and the Changing Power Industry in England and Wales', *Geographical Journal* 127 (1961), p. 298.

based simply on the movement of the tide. Lack of volume is much more often a handicap than lack of head. Even in a country as wet and mountainous as Scotland (where virtually all Britain's hydro-electricity is

Figure 23: Great Britain: nuclear power stations in operation or nearing completion, 1971.

generated) the Hydro Board has to *collect* water to pass through its generators, rather as a miser collects coins, tapping a stream here and boring a tunnel there until it has a worthwhile volume to deal with. Some of these collecting systems are quite complex, as figure 24 shows. But it is cheaper to collect the water at a single generator than to generate on every small stream and collect the electricity. Even so, after years of work in the glens of Scotland, during which the Board has had to overcome the opposition of landlords, fishermen and nature-lovers, the system produces a mere two per cent of the total British output.

In some areas, the size of the impounding structures built for hydroelectric purposes is limited not by lack of water but by physical factors, in particular the danger of earthquake or volcanic activity, the result of which might be a catastrophic dam burst. This is a problem with which the Japanese, for example, have had to contend. The world's greatest

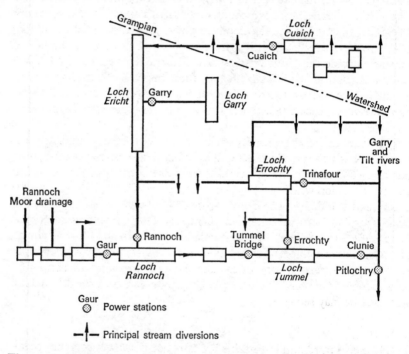

Figure 24: Scotland: topological map of one of the schemes of the North of Scotland Hydro-electricity Board. Even in a country whose climate is as humid as that of Scotland, the volume of water needed to produce power at economic rates must be painstakingly assembled at the power site by means of multiple stream diversions and pipelines.

H.E.P. producers are not, in fact, to be found in the mountains; they are nearly all rivers of the plain—the St Lawrence and the lower Columbia in North America; the rivers of southern Russia and the great basins of Siberia. One day in the future the list may well include the Amazon, the Zaire and the Yangtze, the world's largest rivers joining the group (which already includes the Nile and the Indus) whose power development is the key item in a whole programme of national and even international economic planning. The capital expenditures required are enormous, and they cannot be recouped in the short term by big sales of electricity; in most cases there is no market within transmission distance and there will be one only when the power is already flowing.

But the example of the Tennessee Valley is one which has attracted worldwide attention, and to which developing nations look—the example of a region transformed simply by harnessing the available water power. Simple, of course, it certainly was not. It is open to serious question, actually, how far the example of the Tennessee is relevant to the life and future of the underdeveloped countries of Africa and Asia. Nevertheless the vision of an integrated development powered, and eventually paid for, by hydro-electricity is a highly attractive one, and there are a number of schemes outside the United States to which the local name of 'T.V.A.' is optimistically applied. Realization of these hopes in the capital-starved countries that cherish them will depend largely on the goodwill of the more advanced societies in making available the necessary finance and technical skills.

The introduction of electricity as a prime power source for industry and transport has had the effect not only of making life cleaner and brighter but also of liberating the power user from the restricting ties upon his choice of location which were imposed in the era of coal. To revert to the example of the T.V.A., the main feature of industrialization in the valley since 1933 has been its dispersed character. There are no large manufacturing centres: there is no particular need for them. Electric power gives maximum flexibility of location, especially to the large user, and enables him to select the site which suits him best on grounds of manpower or materials, confident that the power supply can be brought to him wherever he may settle.

3 COAL

To place coal third and last in this list of major power sources may seem historically careless: its importance has been so great, its landscape impact has been so profound and its world production has recently been at an all-time peak. Yet there are good grounds for thinking that this is a proper place in our list for coal. Figure 19 (p. 123) suggests diagrammatically that the era of coal has passed. In countries where it once held an unchallenged position it is now called on mainly to fulfil the tasks not assigned to some other power source: it has become a kind of residuary legatee. In the U.S.A., where in 1930 coal accounted for 61 per cent of the thermal units consumed, the figure had fallen by 1971 to 18 per cent.

It is necessary, however, to be more precise about the status of coal today in the world as a whole. Consumption has fallen off sharply in the old industrialized countries of western Europe and is about stationary in the U.S.A. It is rising in countries whose industrialization is taking place at the present day—in South Africa and Australia, India and mainland China—and in the U.S.S.R. In other words coal is fulfilling its nineteenth-century role once again, in the mid-twentieth century, in countries which are undergoing a present process of industrialization. In those where the process of industrialization began earliest, it has yielded pride of place to newer forms of power.

The drawbacks to the exploitation of coal seams are obvious—the dirt, the subsidence problem, the destructive occupance of the surface by slag heaps or tailings, the fact that there is no remote method of obtaining coal as there is of obtaining petroleum; the miners must be where the coal is. Apart, perhaps, from whaling and fishing there is no form of resource exploitation which has made such demands on its labour force, or whose story is grimmer. If the era of coal is passing, it leaves little cause for regret.

At least the number of men engaged in the industry is falling, and falling more rapidly than coal production is declining, in western Europe. In the six original countries of the E.E.C. there has been an out-flow of 30,000 men a year from the industry. In Great Britain, the figure was 34,000 a year from 1963 to 1969. In the U.S.A., the labour force fell from 415,000 in 1950 to 138,000 in 1971, while the output in the later year was higher by 60 million tons. Thanks to the closure of inefficient mines and the mechanization of those which are larger or more modern, output per man/shift has been improving, as table 13 illustrates.

While, therefore, the world as a whole and especially the 'second generation' of industrial countries is far from dispensing with coal alto-gether, the uses to which it is put in the present era are far fewer and more specific than in the past. A small minority of the world's railway loco-motives are still coal-burning: in the U.S.A. alone, during peak traffic years of the 1940s, the railways consumed as much as 100 million tons a year, while today this figure is zero. Mills have converted from coal-steam power to electricity, and domestic consumers to gas- or oil-fired central heating.

Today, coal serves two major industries. One is smelting, a traditional market for coal or coke which has held up well, and the other is the pro-duction of secondary power, especially electricity. 58 per cent of the coal consumed in Great Britain is now used by the power industry. For the U.S.A., the figure is over 60 per cent. Such an arrangement, as we have already noted, has clear advantages. It represents a use of coal under fairly closely controlled conditions, in a small number of locations where pollution can be checked. It is a way of using low-grade coal economically, and of improving the energy output per ton consumed. In most cases it becomes unnecessary to haul large amounts of coal across country—electricity cables carry the product instead.

Table 13   European Economic Community prior to enlargement: underground output per man/shift in hard-coal mines, 1938–1972

(Note: all figures in kg)

Coalfield/Country	1938	1957	1964	1972
Ruhr	1970	1614	2680	4355
Aachen	1409	1314	1989	3663
Lower Saxony	1380	1264	2115	3805
Saar	1570	1800	2616	3945
Germany, Federal Republic	1877	1606	2613	4249
Campine	1523	1583	1980	3076
Sambre-Meuse	1004	1125	1603	1985
Belgium	1085	1253	1763	2638
Nord-Pas de Calais	1136	1506	1709	2024
Lorraine	2014	2310	3113	4445
Centre-Midi	1176	1634	2016	2706
Other	—	1219	1761	2331
France	1226	1682	2046	2046
Italy	—	957	2524	2801
Limburg, Netherlands	2371	1499	2140	3276
Community, 6 countries	1590	1560	2333	3663

It seems likely that this tendency towards concentration on a few large customers will increasingly mark the coal industry in the future—and that in those countries where coal output is still rising the same process of concentration will become apparent. In Britain the whole power supply is coming to depend on a small number of production points. Half a century ago, every town had its gasworks and its power station, both of them fed by coal brought in by rail or water. Small works of this kind could never hope to rival in efficiency the huge generating stations which are now being built, or the gas plants erected at mine sites from which household gas is now distributed by pipeline. One by one the local plants have closed and the electricity and gas industries have become centralized in the same way as, say, iron and steel making, in locations specially suited to the industries' structure and needs.

In Britain, the hold of coal even upon the gas supply industry was challenged by the import of gas from abroad and even more by the start of natural gas pumping from the new North Sea fields. While the discovery of this gas is of enormous potential value to the country as a whole, to the coal industry it simply represents the loss of another market for, probably, 20 million tons of coal a year.

What has taken place during man's technical advance and, in particular, during the past two centuries of industrialization could be called a process of power substitution—the replacement of an energy source by a more recently developed, or more suitable, alternative. This process has taken place time and again, and there is no reason to suppose that it will not do so in the future, or that a fuel mix consisting of coal, oil, gas and electricity represents some kind of ultimate in energy forms. The two most obvious, and virtually unlimited, forms of energy available to man are those of the sun and the tide, yet only the most minute part of this energy has so far been brought into service; these sources are to all intents and purposes untapped. They are likely to be needed in the future; however vast the reserves of fossil fuels they will ultimately be exhausted and, in economic terms, they may quite rapidly become too expensive to work. Then power users will have to look elsewhere for supplies—and the process of substitution will advance another step.

6

Primary Activity: (1) Production

Technical progress depends, as we saw in chapter two, on a society possessing an adequate productive base. This proposition is self-evident to a population living on the verge of starvation, where the slightest relaxation of effort is at once felt in the onset of hunger or famine. It is probably less evident in an advanced society where more than half the working population are not producers at all in any obvious sense of the term; where, in fact, society accords only a very lowly status to farmers, fishermen or miners, compared with that which it gives to such non-producers as lawyers, entertainers and sales managers.

Yet production, or primary activity, is primary in all senses of the term; not only because historically it has come first, but also because it is necessary to the support of a population developing at the secondary and tertiary levels of activity, and having to be fed and warmed while it does so. It forms the base which alone allows for technical experiment, and the consequent diversion and wastage of resources which that may involve. Only an adequate productive base can give a society the freedom to allocate its resources in new and, often, experimental ways. It is this margin of freedom which has played a large part in shaping the way of life of advanced societies in today's world. It is this which makes it possible, for example, for millions of people to live in the deserts of south-western America—by choice, and simply because they enjoy life in a dry climate— where they certainly produce nothing, but are amply supported by the productive base of the nation as a whole. On a larger scale, the industrial 'take-off' of the European nations in the eighteenth and nineteenth centuries depended on the ability of those nations' farmers to produce enough food both for themselves and for the non-farming population in the new factories and towns.

By the same token, a government today may decide to freeze the resources of a region by declaring it a national park or recreation area, in which strictly productive activity is actually forbidden (see p. 17). Only a wealthy society with an adequate productive base can afford this kind of luxury, the luxury of foregoing the exploitable resources of one area while supporting itself on the produce of another. When such a base exists, the possibilities of manipulating resources in this way are greatly enlarged: choices can be made which are not open to those who live on the margins of subsistence.

Originally, 'production' meant simply gathering natural objects that had a use within a particular community—plants or wood or wild animals. But at an early stage in the process of advance, 'production' also came to mean *cultivation,* the increase of the harvest by orderly management of the resource. Wild grasses and wild animals were domesticated. Only much later in the sequence came the parallel concepts of tree-farming and fish-farming. But the replacement of gathering by cultivation has, of course, been an essential step in the advance of every society and in the increase of its numbers for without cultivation, as the figures quoted in chapter two (p. 30) showed, the capacity of each unit of the earth's surface to support population is very low indeed.

Although the term 'primary production' covers agricultural raw materials, timber and minerals, it is the production of *food* which is the critical element; the rest is useless otherwise. This chapter on production therefore concentrates on food, although much of what follows is applicable to forest products, and some of it to minerals. And the starting point of our consideration must be the question: what kinds of food, and how much of them, are needed to support human life? We can then consider the factors which govern their production.

DIET AND ITS COMPONENTS

Food is needed for two purposes. One is for providing energy, and the other is for the upkeep of the human fabric. For the first of these purposes a diet should include either carbohydrates or fats; for the second, the body needs protein, either animal or vegetable, and minerals and vitamins. Most estimates of a 'balanced' diet call for an intake of 60 to 65 per cent carbohydrates, 20 to 25 per cent fats and 15 per cent protein, with small amounts of the other diet elements.

But food supplies in nature are not distributed in these convenient proportions. Both fats and protein are relatively scarce in relation to carbohydrates in their basic form of vegetable starch. In a resource-deficient situation, therefore, people are likely to be able to obtain energy-giving food, but to find that supplies of body-maintenance food are lacking. And just as one can neglect the maintenance of a car while still filling it with petrol and running it on the roads for a time, so it is possible to survive after a fashion on a diet of almost pure carbohydrate, each day's rations giving the energy to drag through another period of work. But the lack of maintenance is bound to make itself felt sooner or later. It may show itself in diseases due to lack of specific diet ingredients, as with rickets or goitre. It may be reflected in general debility and low work capacity (which doubtless formed the basis for many a tale of 'lazy' natives in imperial days). It may simply show itself in short life expectancy; the fabric wears out very rapidly. It will certainly reveal itself in the physique of all members of the community, and there is some evidence that it affects the birth rate, too: there is a degree of correlation between high birth rate and low intake of protein.

All diets do, of course, contain *some* vegetable staple—historically, wheat in the Mediterranean world, maize in central America (where both culture and religion were focused to a remarkable degree on the maize crop[1]), and rice in much of Asia. But besides these well-known and widely-used staples there are many others. Murdock recognized and mapped sixteen in the continent of Africa,[2] ranging from wheat and dates to little-known millets like eleusine and fonio which, although distributed over only a small part of the continent, play a vital role in local diets. As time goes by and standards of living rise, however, there is a tendency for the old staple to be replaced by another, more nutritious food. The most familiar example of this process is the substitution of white wheat bread for black rye bread across northern Europe, starting in the west and cotinuing eastwards. On the other hand, where pressure of population on resources is severe, the staple may be changed for a different reason: quantity may become more important than quality, so that a community is obliged to give up a varied diet based on a number of low-yielding plants, to concentrate on the one which offers the highest yield. The risk of diet deficiency is, of course, correspondingly increased.

A diet limited to vegetable starch is therefore a sign of resource shortage and is most undesirable on grounds of health. Nevertheless, it is all that much of the world's population can obtain. Specifically, it has been estimated that over 60 per cent of the world's people eat a diet which comprises 80 per cent or more of vegetable starch. The first sign of a rising standard of living will probably be a rise in consumption of the staple, as supplies become more plentiful, but the longer-term indicator of rising dietary standards is a lessening of this dependence on cereals or starchy roots. Insofar as statistics are available, it is possible to observe all stages

[1] A sixteenth-century Spanish chronicler reported of the Mayas: 'When one looks into the matter closely, one finds that all they do and say is bound up with maize. In fact they have almost made it their god. And so great is the joy and satisfaction which they derive from their maize fields that they seem to forget all about their wives and families, as if the cultivation of maize was their life's work and highest good.' (From the *Chronica de la Santa Provincia del Santissimo Nombre de Jesus de Guattemala.*)

[2] G. P. Murdock,' Staple Subsistence Crops of Africa', *Geographical Review* 50 (1960), pp. 523–40.

in this dietary progression among the nations of the world at the present time. Table 14, which is based on F.A.O. estimates, offers some examples

Table 14   Per caput food supplies available for human consumption in selected countries, 1930s and 1960s

(In gm per day)

	Period	Cereals	Potatoes & other roots	Vegetables	Meat	Fish
Argentina	1935/9	291	180	67	293	6
	1966	268	202	124	309	8
Canada	1935/9	254	165	154	170	15
	1967	186	210	228	250	17
France	1934/8	339	392	392	151	16
	1966	235	277	350	221	23
Greece	1935/8	446	57	74	53	15
	1967	331	161	382	111	28
India	1934/8	377	21	68	8	4
	1965/6	346	39	n.a.	4	3
Japan	1934/8	432	127	193	8	26
	1967	380	188	362	37	84
Pakistan	1934/8	377	21	68	8	4
	1966/7	429	38	43	11	5
Turkey	1934/8	520	16	87	41	1
	1960/1	611	105	288	37	6
U.K.	1934/8	261	226	149	184	33
	1967/8	200	283	173	204	26

of national diet levels, although all such figures are bound to be crude. Over the period of about three decades covered by the table we can notice several different tendencies:

(a) In the wealthiest countries—Canada, France, the United Kingdom —the consumption of cereals has fallen considerably, while that of meat has risen by a comparable amount. (In the U.S.A., which is not included in the table, consumption of cereals-plus-potatoes fell by more than one third over the same period, and of meat rose by two thirds.) Diet is becoming more diversified and the dependence on the old staples is diminishing. Argentina, Greece and Japan are all moving in the same direction, although the Japanese diet is still very largely vegetarian.

(b) In Pakistan and Turkey, there has been a general increase in basic food supply available, and this shows itself in increased per caput consumption of staples. But the improvement has not yet gone far enough to be converted into an increase in the consumption of livestock products.

(c) In India, where there was a rapid increase in population and only a very slow progress in agriculture, the food supplies available per person actually diminished over the 30 year period, while the diet remained almost entirely vegetarian.[3]

The inclusion of livestock products in the diet, which is most desirable on grounds of health, only becomes possible at the point where a community can *afford* the resource 'conversion' which livestock products represent. For a kg of pork is the equivalent of four or five kg of cereals; the question is therefore whether cereals are plentiful enough to be used in this way. Only a community rich in cereals can afford to be so lavish with them as to convert them to livestock before using them. Whereas in the U.S.A. it has become a commonplace to speak about 'marketing corn on the hoof' (i.e. after conversion), there are any number of other areas where cereals are eaten almost entirely by people, not animals, and where, if there is livestock on the farms, it is used for work purposes and not for the luxury of the protein it can supply.

An opposite substitution took place in Europe, including Great Britain, during the two world wars. As food imports dwindled, grassland which had been supporting livestock was ploughed up and planted to cereals; meat was rationed, and the area under potatoes was greatly increased, because in European conditions potatoes yield more calories per ha—crudely, therefore, more simple energy—than any other crop.[4]

There is, as might be expected, an upper limit to the consumption even of high-value foods in a wealthy society. In the U.S.A., the consumption of milk fell away by 20 per cent between 1940 and 1970, while that of butter fell much more steeply—from 7·7 kg per person in 1940 to 2·4 kg in 1970, under the double impact of competition from margarine at half the price and fears about the effect of animal fat on heart condition. But this trend is of purely academic interest to a large part of the condition. But this trend is of purely academic interest to a large part of the world's population. Table 14 goes some way towards suggesting the amount of leeway, in dietary terms, which has to be made up.

[3] Margaret Anderson, in her small but valuable book *Geography of Living Things*, E.U.P., London, 1951, p. 110, described how peasants in various rice-eating areas of India consumed over 1½ pounds (0·75kg) of rice per day, as well as millet and starchy vegetables and added a neat, housewifely note to place this in perspective: 'For comparison, my cookery book gives, as the quantity of rice needed for the English version of curry, 4 ounces of rice for three people, or 1·3 ounces each, one twentieth of the Kashmiri's daily rice consumption.'
[4] On a world scale, it appears that they come third—to bananas and manioc.

The problem of deficiency is compounded by the fact that total consumption is rising all the time. There are three main reasons for this. The first and most obvious is that total world population is increasing by two per cent a year, so that an annual increase in world food production of that order is necessary even to give everybody what they already consume, let alone increase the amounts in deficiency areas. Over the past decade and a half, the 'developed' countries of the world[5] have succeeded in increasing their production faster than their population: per caput production increased by about 1·6 per cent per year. But the 'developing' countries (where, of course, the need is immensely greater) achieved an average increase per caput of only 0·1 per cent a year, and for the continent of Africa the figure was actually negative—food production fell by 0·3 per cent per person.

The second reason is that life expectancy is everywhere increasing. However welcome this may be from the personal or social point of view, it is from the economic viewpoint merely one more contributing factor in the problem of consumption: crudely, one generation, instead of dying off and leaving the available food supply for the next generation, lingers on and claims its share. With life expectancy rising even in the healthiest societies (where it is now generally over 70 years) the potential for further increases, in countries where it is still only about 40 years, is obviously very great.

The third reason is that everywhere standards of living are rising or, if they are not, higher standards are being demanded or promised as part of political programmes. Consumption does not, therefore, increase in proportion to numbers of people but more rapidly; furthermore, it does not stop rising when the obvious deficiencies in diet have been overcome. Those who have the food eat more than they need and there is nothing but their own conscience, or income limit, or weight-consciousness, to stop them.

Between 1955 and 1968, world population increased by a little under 30 per cent. During this same period, the production of most major agricultural commodities increased by a good deal more than this amount (table 15). The shortfall was therefore in the sector of agricultural production where its effects are most serious and the need is most urgent— the subsistence crops of underdeveloped areas, which do not enter into trade on any large scale, but upon which the local population is obliged to depend for survival.

Given a situation of this kind, in which it is manifest that there is not now, and is unlikely to be in the immediate future, enough primary pro-

---

[5] 'Developed' and 'developing' in this connection are terms arbitrarily chosen and tactfully defined by the Food and Agriculture Organization, whose statistics these are, to separate the nations of the world into two groups.

duction on the global scale to meet everybody's needs, we are brought to
the obvious enquiry: what governs the volume of primary production?
If there are known to be shortages, why cannot they be overcome? In
attempting to answer these questions, we must consider two kinds of
control. For convenience, we can call them the physical and the institutional.

Table 15   Percentage increase in volume of world crop production,
1955–1968

Cotton	20	Maize	56
Coffee	32	Sugar	64
Rice	46	Wheat	67
Eggs	49	Marine fish	137
Vegetable oils	54	Soybeans	174
Meat	56		

THE PHYSICAL CONTROLS

The physical controls over agricultural production are temperature,
moisture, relief and soil quality. Of the 150 million km² of the earth's
land surface, at least 60 per cent can immediately be eliminated from
serious consideration for agricultural use, because one or more of these
four controls exerts a critical influence on the area—temperature in
the polar regions, relief in the mountains or lack of soil on areas scraped
bare by the passage of ice. Where the physical controls are less decisive,
on the other 35–40 per cent of the land surface, these physical factors of
course combine to make some regions much more favourable to agriculture than others. On a small scale, temperature deficiency can be made
good by the use of glasshouses. On a larger scale, aridity can be overcome
by irrigation, and relief by terracing hillsides. But over the greater part
of the world's agricultural surface the farmer simply adapts his operations to the natural circumstances; he produces within the framework
of the natural limitations, rather than try to modify them.

I THE TEMPERATURE CONTROL

None of these four controls is a single or unitary force: temperature
controls agriculture in at least three ways.

Since plant growth normally requires a temperature above a definite
base (which may vary from 0°C [32°F] for temperate latitude crops to
15°C or 18°C [59–65°F] for tropical crops), the first aspect of the temperature control is the aggregate period during which such temperature
conditions are available. At or near the minimum growing temperature of
a plant, growth is very slow; above the minimum, the rate of growth

approximately doubles for every 10°C [18°F] rise in temperature. If, during the warm season, insufficient heat accumulates above the base or threshold temperature of growth (which for a number of important crops may be taken as 6°C or 43°F) then the crop will not mature.

In low and middle latitudes, the number of days with a mean temperature above 6°C is often taken, therefore, as a guide to growth prospects, and referred to as the *growing season*. But to use a length expressed merely in days for high-latitude agriculture may be misleading: a 'day' in the Mackenzie Valley of Canada or in Siberia may contain 16 hours of sunshine, so that crops will ripen even between a late spring and an early autumn.

This brings us to the second aspect of temperature control. The period over which the accumulated heat of the warm season is available is important in lower latitudes as determining whether it will be possible to grow one crop or two. Double-cropping has almost the same effect as doubling the area of arable land, and is often decisive in tipping the balance between starvation and survival, but it does require a long growing season and not merely a short, hot peak period.

This is the low-latitude counterpart of the third aspect of temperature control, which concerns the extra-tropical environments—the effect of frost. Freezing temperatures critically affect the physiology of plants, and the period between the average date of the last killing frost of spring and the first killing frost of autumn is known as the *frost-free season*. It varies in length from 365 days in the lowland tropics to 40 days in inhabited regions of northern Quebec and northern British Columbia. Under the latter conditions, one of the major campaigns fought by European and American agronomists has been to produce new strains of crops with maturing periods short enough to be completed within the frost-free season. The wheat strains used by the earliest settlers on the Canadian Prairies required 130 days from seeding to maturity. Gradually, this figure was reduced, as Red Fife wheat was replaced by Marquis (110–20 days) and Reward (100–110 days), until now strains are available which will mature in under 100 days.

But the threat of frost damage to crops is not, of course, limited to particular dates in the year: the frost-free season merely defines the *average* situation. Far more of a threat to the cultivator is the *variation* in the frost-free period—the unusually late spring frost which sends the fruit grower hurrying round his smudge pots, or the early cold snap in autumn which makes harvesting a race against time. On the northern fringes of cultivation, where the frost-free period is 40 days, there may well be no month of the year in which frost has not been recorded at some time or other. On the southern fringes of the temperate zone, there may be an average frost-free period of 364 days—but still that one day of frost in the year, so capricious in its occurrence, may do a million pounds' worth of damage, or require a million pounds' worth of precautions.

2 THE MOISTURE CONTROL

This second type of physical control is the widest-ranging of all in its effects. Almost the least important aspect of moisture supply is the absolute figure of mean annual rainfall, a figure which may well conceal more than it reveals. To give the annual amount any relevance, we need to know at least three other things: what is the evaporation rate, what is the reliability of the rainfall and what is its seasonal distribution. And there are half a dozen other aspects which may be significant in particular areas or in individual climatic regimes.

For the majority of the world's farmers, moisture supply depends directly on precipitation and on the *effectiveness* of that precipitation for the particular purpose of growing crops. For the farmer, the optimum situation would be one in which the same amount of rain fell every year, concentrated in the growing season (when crop demand for water is at its highest) but falling at night (when evaporation rates are lower than by day). No such optimum exists in nature, of course. In the first place, precipitation everywhere varies from year to year, and it is often true that the smaller the mean annual figure, the larger is the mean deviation from the mean. In a dry area like central Australia, a mean deviation of 50 per cent or more may occur, whereas in the British Isles, with their notoriously unreliable weather, but higher total, the deviation is nowhere more than 15–16 per cent. Variability in total amount of rainfall directly affects yields on the farm (i.e. it is a factor in *quantity* of output, whereas frost tends to affect *quality*). In the Medicine Hat area of the Canadian Prairies, for example, a district where the variability in growing season rainfall is 25 per cent or more, an early generation of wheat growers had to survive, between 1910 and 1920, eleven harvests which produced average wheat yields as follows: 7, 18, 15, 11, 3, 37, 23, 20, 3, 2, 7 bushels per acre.[6]

Nor is there any statistical guarantee that a dry year in such an area will be followed by a correspondingly wet one: rather, the dry years and the wet years tend to arrive in clusters. It is this phenomenon, occurring on the dry margins of cultivation, which has produced the advance and retreat of the agricultural frontier so familiar in the settlement record of the North American grasslands or the Australian interior. A series of wetter-than-average seasons encourages advance and plough-up; then, no sooner are the newcomers committed to the area than the dry series begins—the early 1880s in South Australia[7] or the early 1890s in western

[6] 1 bushel per acre = $67 \cdot 25 \text{kg ha}^{-1}$.

[7] See D. W. Meinig, *On the Margins of the Good Earth*, Murray, London, 1962, chapter five.

Kansas and Nebraska. A single dry year the farmer may survive; it is the incidence of, say, three in a row that destroys him.

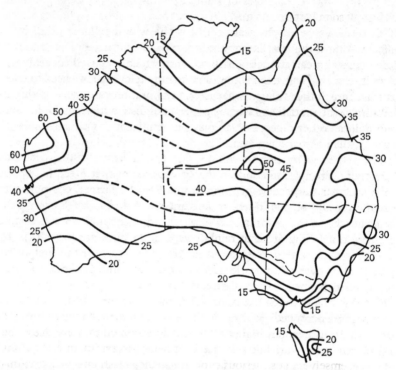

Figure 25: Australia: rainfall variability. The isolines show the average deviation above and below the normal as a percentage of the normal annual rainfall. (Reproduced by permission from the *Atlas of Australian Resources,* Canberra: Division of Regional Development, Australian Government copyright.)

Annual rainfall figures are also misleading unless they are broken down to tell us the seasonal incidence. The peak water demand in the field is normally early in the growing season, i.e. the spring and early summer. Heavy rains falling at the end of the season may well hinder the harvest, even if they do not actually damage the crop. Winter rainfall, while it may recharge groundwater supplies, may also involve the farmer in costly waterworks before he can obtain a supply at the time he actually needs it. Some regions of the world are permanently disadvantaged by the seasonal regime of their rainfall, the most obvious being the northern Mediterranean lands, where rain falls in the autumn and early spring, but the winters are not warm enough to permit much winter cropping. In the opposite situation, it is possible to cultivate the North American grasslands because, even where the annual rainfall is only 500 mm and evaporation rates are high, there is an early summer seasonal maximum (70 per cent of the annual total) well suited to the farmer's need.

The best-known examples of rainfall seasonality, probably, are those of the monsoon lands of Asia. While discussion continues about the physical factors involved in the onset of the monsoonal rains, there can be no question of the importance of the phenomenon which, in the case of India, brings three quarters or more of the annual precipitation at stations on both the east and the west sides of the subcontinent (Calcutta 75 per cent, Delhi 85 per cent, Bombay 93 per cent), and bursts each year within a few days of the same date in June; nor can the disaster of failure of the monsoon easily be exaggerated. In practice, the danger of failure is serious, especially over the Indus Basin.[8] The rhythm of life of the subcontinent is geared to the seasonality of rainfall.

As with temperature controls over agriculture, so one aspect of the moisture control is the length of the season. This is of particular relevance where temperature conditions make possible double-cropping—if only the water supply will hold out. In south-east Asia are to be found various cropping patterns adapted to rainfall seasonality: for example, one wet-season crop and one dry-season crop; one wet-season crop watered by rainfall and one crop under irrigation or, in exceptional circumstances, two crops of paddy rice and one dry-season crop.[9]

From seasonality of rainfall we move on to the form of precipitation which an area receives. There is little resemblance between the monsoonal rainfall of India just described and the fine, year-round rain that keeps the grass green in Ireland. The side effects of heavy, intermittent rain storms may in themselves cause serious problems—the splash effect of the raindrops, the alternate baking and beating of hot sun and heavy rain on bare earth, the damage to crops. In some crop areas farmers insure themselves against losses from hailstorms. In others, elaborate waterworks are necessary to trap the heavy rains which fall over a short period and otherwise run off too rapidly to be useful.

Snow is a form of precipitation which, although it represents a hazard to the pastoral farmer, may serve the cultivator very well. Snow in the mountains acts as a natural reservoir of summer water, holding back run-off during the unproductive season of the year and releasing it in the spring, at the moment of maximum demand. In the lowlands, on the other hand, it provides an insulating blanket against extremes of winter cold.

There is yet another aspect of the moisture control—humidity levels. Atmospheric moisture, apart from rainfall, plays a significant part in the

[8] See the maps in O. H. K. Spate and A. T. A. Learmonth, *India and Pakistan*, Methuen, London, third edition, 1967, pp. 64–5.

[9] R. Dumont, *Types of Rural Economy*, Methuen, London, 1957, has an interesting chapter (five) on these variants in Indo-China.

calculations of some farmers. The parching effects of hot, dry winds blowing off the desert in northern Africa, or from the southern plains into the edges of the North American Corn Belt, may seriously affect crop weights in those areas. Conversely, the Middle East knows not only the parching effect of low humidity but also the beneficial effect of the dew. On the coasts of the Red Sea and the Levant, as much as one quarter of the annual atmospheric moisture is received in this form, and certainly some such figure is needed to account for the great prominence attached to the dew in the Middle Eastern biblical record.[10] The heavy dew freshens the dried-up pasturage: on occasion, it has even kept stranded travellers alive.

3 THE RELIEF CONTROL

Relief affects agriculture through slope, altitude and drainage. Any of these may make agriculture either impossible or economically pointless, the first two because they are excessive and the third because it is inadequate.

Slope is associated with increased speed of run-off, with soil creep and with erosion. The cultivation of steep slopes may consequently not only do long-term damage to the land itself but also lead to immediate catastrophe through landslide and flood. To avert this danger and to give a surface on which it is physically possible to cultivate, the normal response has been that of terracing, a response found in Asia and Europe and Latin America alike. But the *absence* of terracing in North America or Australia suggests that, as a remedy for the problems posed by slope, it is a sign of resource poverty; it is only when pressure of population in the gently-sloping lowlands becomes excessive that it is necessary to climb the hillsides looking for cultivable land.[11] Few crops actually grow better on steep slopes than on gentle ones and where rural population pressure is relieved by other means—such as the growth of towns and industries—the terraces are soon abandoned (for example, at the southern edge of the Massif Central in France), leaving behind the ruined evidence of former herculean labours. In a situation of resource affluence, the slopes may be avoided altogether, unless valley drainage is a problem: it may be recalled that a major element of the restoration programme for the Tennessee

[10] For example, 'And he blessed him, and said . . . "God give thee of the dew of heaven, and the fatness of the earth" ' (*Genesis* 27: 27–8), or 'Elijah said unto Ahab . . . "there shall not be dew or rain these years, but according to my word" ' (*I Kings* 17: 1).

[11] This statement should probably be qualified to read that *high* terracing is a sign of poverty. Paddy rice, which is grown under standing water, involves levelling and banking for purely technical reasons, even in lowland areas. It is the staircase of terraces, rising almost to summit levels in the mountains, which is the clearest sign of resource shortage.

Valley was to replant with trees and shrubs fields which had, for several generations, been recklessly planted with row crops.

Altitude affects farming through its associated characteristics of low temperatures, wetness and ecological instability. We have already seen that temperature affects rate of growth and, in general, excluding the influence of local factors like exposure, the flowering of a species of plant is retarded by about four days for every 150 metres increase in altitude. Cool, moist conditions favour only a limited range of crops and there is, consequently, an upper limit of cultivation which can generally be traced north or south from the equator: in Ecuador, potatoes grow at over 3,000 metres, while in the Grampian Mountains of Scotland (56–57°N.Lat.) the limit can be observed to lie at about 400 metres.

But if slope and height are hindrances to the spread of areas of primary production so, too, are absence of slope and lack of drainage. For these are often associated with flooding or waterlogging and only by costly schemes of artificial drainage can such areas be brought into use. However natural may appear the dense concentrations of people on the fertile delta lands of southern Asia, it is necessary to remember that the lands themselves are almost wholly artificial, shaped in their present form by a centuries-long process of draining and dyking begun by the Chinese in remote antiquity.

As we shall see in a later section, in fact, the world's wet lands offer one of the major prospects for future reclamation. But they will need to be treated with care, for waterlogging or persistence of a high water table can be among the farmer's worst enemies. Especially is this the case in irrigated valleys, where the flat bottom makes water distribution deceptively easy. Absence of drainage in this case is liable to lead to the deposition at the surface of an alkaline crust, which might in time be flushed away but which is usually left and the ground abandoned: the fields are white but not unto harvest. Optimum conditions for irrigation are found not on the valley floor but on the evenly-sloping and gently-inclined alluvial fans which are a common feature of valley sides in arid zones.

4 THE CONTROL OF SOIL QUALITY

Soil quality is always a factor in agricultural yield and, left to himself, the farmer will usually discover where the most fertile soils are to be found, and concentrate on them. But on a world scale the question is rather: in what ways, or what particular regions, is soil quality acting as a brake on agricultural production?

In temperate latitudes, there are certainly 'problem' soils, such as the light, sandy soils of western Europe which are gradually being brought into use with the aid of fertilizers and research funds. But these are negligible in area, compared with the problem soils of the tropics, both the soils of the areas already in use and the half billion ha or so of potentially cultivable land. In the temperate zone the limitations imposed by soil quality are, to a large extent, accepted by the population because it does not actually *need* to cultivate a larger area: the light, sandy soil areas are turned into nature reserves or artillery ranges and the great areas of northern podsols are left to grow trees. But in the tropics, the shortage of cultivated land is general rather than exceptional. The problems of using tropical soils really need to be overcome.

Some idea of the magnitude of these problems was brought home to Europeans by the failure of the post-war groundnuts scheme in east Africa—a scheme for producing vegetable oils quickly, by the use of the most up-to-date techniques, at a time of acute shortage in Great Britain. It was a scheme which cost roughly £1 per head of the British population, but produced very few groundnuts and should probably have created a healthy respect for the native peoples who, with nothing more than a stick and hoe, succeed in obtaining some kind of livelihood from tropical soils.

These soils are developed in conditions of (1) torrential, periodic rains. In between the rains they are baked hard and the raindrops tend to bounce off them rather than sink in. They are produced (2) in high temperatures, which speed up soil processes so that humus formation is minimal. The combination of these factors means (3) that they are heavily leached and that hard pan forms; the hard pan then breaks the plough share. With all this, they tend to erode as soon as the natural vegetation cover is removed, in token of which the cultivators who work many parts of them practise a shifting agriculture which appears absurdly uneconomical but is a simple adaptation to all these difficulties.

On a world scale, therefore, there is every reason for considering soil quality a limiting factor in agricultural production, just as it is on a local or regional scale. It appears that the only alternative to low-productivity native cultivation in the areas of greatest food shortage is a massive input of capital in the form of fertilizers, earthworks and machinery and, even so, it is by no means certain that all the problems involved in intensive use of these tropical soils have yet been appreciated, let alone solved.

THE INSTITUTIONAL HINDRANCES

The physical controls which we have just been considering eliminate from primary production a large part of the earth's land surface, and severely restrict the possible output of a good deal of the area which remains. Yet even in areas where climate, relief and soil all favour agriculture, there may exist other barriers to increased production. These we shall call *institutional*, using the word to cover a group of factors which are social, economic and even legal in their nature. Of these factors the four principal ones are:

1   the ignorance or prejudice of the cultivator
2   the law of property as reflected in the pattern of land tenure
3   the lack of organization of either the farmers' production or farmers' marketing
4   the lack of capital.

1 IGNORANCE AND PREJUDICE

Since most of the world's agriculture—at least outside communist lands—is carried on at the discretion of the individual cultivator, the standards of operation and efficiency vary enormously, both between individuals and between regions. Inefficient practices are normally the result of either conservatism on the farmer's part or ignorance of any alternative, and for neither of these characteristics is he necessarily to blame. He may be conservative, and cling to old-fashioned methods, simply because he cannot afford to take the slightest risk: by the old method he knows that he will have *something* with which to feed his family, whereas if he adopts a new, and to him untried, method he may be left at harvest time with nothing. Only when he has a reserve to fall back on can he afford to innovate. Should the new method involve any fresh purchase of equipment, his hesitation will be even more understandable.

Nor should he be blamed for 'unscientific' farming methods if he is ignorant of the possible alternatives. It is impossible to assess ignorance precisely, but there must be many areas where a single crop, or combination of crops, is grown year in and year out simply because the cultivators do not know what else to grow. Even in an advanced agricultural community like that formed by British farmers, innovation is not easy to bring about, as witness the problems of introducing during wartime a crop like linseed, which the Ministry of Agriculture wanted to encourage, but which was unfamiliar to most farmers. It is not enough to develop 'scientific' methods on well-financed research stations: they must be geared to capital-deficient peasants' needs and the scale of their individual finances. Information about them must then be disseminated, a task which may well prove to be the hardest part of the whole operation.

2 THE PATTERN OF LAND TENURE

The size and shape of farm units have an important bearing on their efficient operation. A holding which is too small to allow the operator to make effective use of available machinery is inefficient, and so is a large holding which is undercapitalized because the owner cannot or will not make the necessary inputs. A farm which is in ten, or fifty, fragments instead of a single block is inefficient whether the fragments are scattered strips in a single open field or fields fifteen km apart. And where there are social or legal obstacles to the purchase of land for farm enlargement, or where the level of rents for the extra land is exorbitantly high, there is a clear case for reorganization.

Such a reorganization reached its climax in England during the eighteenth and nineteenth centuries; it is known as the Enclosure Movement, and some of its social side-effects were deplorable. Nevertheless, there can be little question that it created an agriculture which was more efficient than that carried on previously on the open fields it eliminated. It was capable, as the old system would not have been, of expanding production to meet the demands of the new industrial era. It enabled go-ahead farmers to improve crop strains and raise pedigree stock within their own fences, and it got rid of a whole class of inefficiently small holdings (which was an economic advantage to set against the individual plight of those displaced).

Outside Great Britain and Scandinavia, however, minute holdings and scattered parcels have continued to be commonplace in western Europe, as they are throughout much of non-communist Asia, Africa and Latin America. This applies not only to communities of peasant cultivators whose subsistence depends on their land; this we might expect. It applies also to an advanced economy like that of Belgium, a country which entered the 1950s with 90 per cent of its holdings measuring less than 5 hectares and had, before 1965, little official machinery for amalgamating them into economic units.

Small size and fragmented layout are the result of several factors: most obviously, but not exclusively, of population pressure. Division of the community's land into parcels was rational enough in a period when each member grew his own food and was entitled to a share of each type of land—slope, valley floor or peat-cutting. But what brought about a survival into the modern era of this sub-division was not so much utility as the law of inheritance. Under Roman law, property in land was divided equally between all the children of the owner on his death, and the Mediterranean world generally has retained this principle. In France, where it had fallen into disuse, it was revived in Napoleon's *code civil*, and applied by him to the Low Countries and other parts of his empire: the law actually forbade the property owner to will his land to a single heir. By contrast, northern Europe held for the most part to the principle of inheritance by a single child, usually the eldest.

A law of inheritance which assumed the subdivision of land holdings, and even barns and buildings, down to the ultimate degree ceased to be appropriate when agriculture passed from the subsistence to the commercial phase. Yet by that time it had its supporters, chiefly the small peasant farmers themselves, who found the fragmentation well suited to the scale of their transactions: they had no hope of raising capital to buy a whole farm, but a quarter or a half of a hectare was within their means. As we shall see in the next chapter, the task of convincing a man that his holding should be consolidated, even when he walks a thousand kilometres a year around his scattered strips (which is by no means uncommon) is not an easy one, but it has become very necessary in the 1970s.

3 LACK OF ORGANIZATION

In the non-communist world, the primary producer is, typically, a small operator and one who, however bound by group or tribal custom, ultimately makes his own production decisions. In a subsistence economy, those decisions are governed by the needs of his own family and affect no one else. But to the extent that he produces a surplus for disposal elsewhere, his individuality tells against him. To the extent that he produces for a commodity market of world dimensions, he as an individual is virtually helpless. And this helplessness acts as a powerful disincentive to increase production beyond the limit set by the needs of his dependents.

Conversely, the appearance on the market of particular commodities, and the emergence of commercially-producing areas, can often be correlated with particular steps taken to *organize* individual producers. Some of the ways in which this can be done are reviewed in the next chapter. Organization has sometimes been necessary at the production end. More commonly, the critical point has been the organization of marketing. In either case, the problem has been to coordinate the efforts of a thousand primary producers so that together they may achieve a secure position in commodity exchanges. Lacking security they may well not be, in a commercial sense, producers at all; that is, there is a vicious circle which can be represented simply as follows:

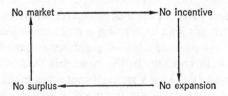

The problem is where and how to break the circle.

4 LACK OF CAPITAL

But lack of organization, the last hindrance we have been considering, is really only a special case of the fourth obstacle to increased production— a general shortage of capital to finance that increase. In the real world, even giant industrial corporations may well experience difficulty in raising capital for expansion. In agriculture, we are not dealing with a 'giant' of any kind, but with millions of individuals each of whom separately needs expansion capital to apply to individual projects, and most of whom have no security to offer as collateral for a loan against increased output, for they possess nothing, not even the land they cultivate for their landlord.

Here we have another, more general, version of the vicious circle referred to in the previous section. If we again represent it diagrammatically, we have:

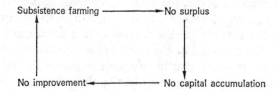

In this circle, there is little doubt where and how it must be broken—by an injection of capital into a system of production which is not, by its own nature, capital-accumulating. We saw earlier how ignorance of alternative techniques may restrict the farmer's range of production. But now it is necessary to go on and make the further, if obvious, point that knowledge alone will not necessarily result in increase of output, if the new knowledge involves fertilizers, fallows, new equipment or chemical sprays. All these have to be paid for, and it would be idle to suppose that, where the need for new inputs is greatest, there is any serious possibility of financing them out of the individual's current production. For this institutional roadblock an institutional bulldozer of larger size is needed.

THE PROBLEM OF DISTRIBUTION

There is one further aspect of the institutional problem: the fragmentation not now of the farmer's land or holding, but of human society as a whole. Because of this, it is possible for food surpluses to exist in one area and starvation to exist in another. In the past, this kind of tragic anomaly frequently occurred over a very short distance and within a single state, either because society was deeply fractured or simply through a lack of means of transport. It is well known that corn was being exported from the east of Ireland while the potato famine was causing the death of thousands in the west. This was because, in a society deeply divided between landlord and tenant, corn was not grown for food by the tenantry, but to pay the rent: food meant potatoes, and there were none. In India, the regional famine has been all too familiar both before and since independence: here, lack of transport and lack of disposable reserves have been equally to blame.

We may hope that, in an era of radio, helicopters and government-sponsored welfare, a strictly local famine can be avoided in the future. But the problem certainly still exists at an international level—the problem of *distribution* of available supplies. The areas of greatest need are remote from those of surplus. What is of more practical importance is that they are also separated from each other by political boundaries. There is therefore not only the problem of arranging the physical transfer from point to point, but the larger institutional problem of financing the transfer.

A nation which is short of food and raw materials can import supplies. But to do so involves spending foreign currency; the 'developing' countries are at present probably spending 4,000 million dollars a year on such imports. But they are almost all short of foreign exchange, and doing their utmost to cut down on these imports. They cannot afford to buy food from the surplus areas, which are virtually all in 'developed' nations—nations whose currencies are 'hard'.

This creates a situation in which the 'haves' appear to be hoarding their wealth while the 'have-nots' starve. The obvious remedy is for the wealthy nations to share their surpluses with the poor, by giving away what the poor cannot buy. Since the second world war a great deal has, in fact, been given away: altogether the U.S.A., as the largest giver, has placed about $80,000 million worth of assorted non-military grants and credits at the disposal of other nations since 1945.

But this merely creates new problems. In the world in which we live, trade between nations is vital to their economies. But this trade is based, as we saw in chapter three, on the assumption of *exchange*; in other words, that goods are bought and sold on the basis of an established value. If, however, in the market for wheat, or cotton, or rice, some quantity of these commodities is being offered at the market price and at the same time other deliveries of the same goods are free, chaos results. When the U.S.A., in order to reduce the huge stocks it was holding, began to dispose of wheat surpluses to India, the Canadians, who were doing their best to *sell* wheat to the Indians, were understandably put out. When the U.S.A. took the same kind of action with cotton, it was the turn of Brazil and Egypt to object. Commerce and charity do not mix. The livelihood of the Brazilian and Egyptian growers depended on obtaining a fair price for their cotton, failing which they, in turn, would be in need of charity.

This problem of international distribution is one of the most intractable that we face. Short of dismantling the whole structure of international trade as we know it, it cannot be solved frontally at all. The only possibility is to approach it from the other direction—to increase the productive powers of the 'have-nots' to the point where charity is not needed. It is to this subject that we turn in the next chapter.

7

Primary Activity: (2) Increasing Production and Income

In the last chapter, we have briefly analysed the various types of controls which limit production from the land. We now go on to make the assumptions that since (1) world population is increasing by roughly 70 millions a year, and (2) present production allows some of the existing population only a dismally low standard of living, there is a clear need for efforts to overcome the limitations and increase the output. Since, as we have seen, the controls on production are both physical and institutional, the efforts to overcome them must be grouped in the same way.

OVERCOMING THE PHYSICAL LIMITATIONS

There are two ways of overcoming the limitations set by climate, soil quality and the processes of natural growth. One is to bring new lands into production and the other is to increase the yield from each unit of the area already in use. We must therefore turn directly to consider the various means by which these objects can be achieved.

The creation of new lands for cultivation simply implies, of course, a continuation of a process which has been going on since the first planters and improvers began their efforts. The present world total of improved land, which is approximately 3,880 million hectares, represents the point reached after several millennia of reclamation of those lands from their natural state by the processes of forest clearance, drainage, irrigation or the removal of peat. What is being done today, and needs to be done in the future, is simply a continuation of the work of Neolithic cultivators burning a thin forest or heath cover off the loess lands of central Europe; of peasants clearing lands for cultivation under the direction of their overlord during the great European *Rodungszeit* of the twelfth and thirteenth centuries, or of Dutchmen laboriously recapturing coastland and fen from the empire of the sea.

I THE CLEARANCE OF FOREST

The forest cover of our planet has a present area of about 3,900 million hectares; that is, almost exactly the same as the area of improved land,

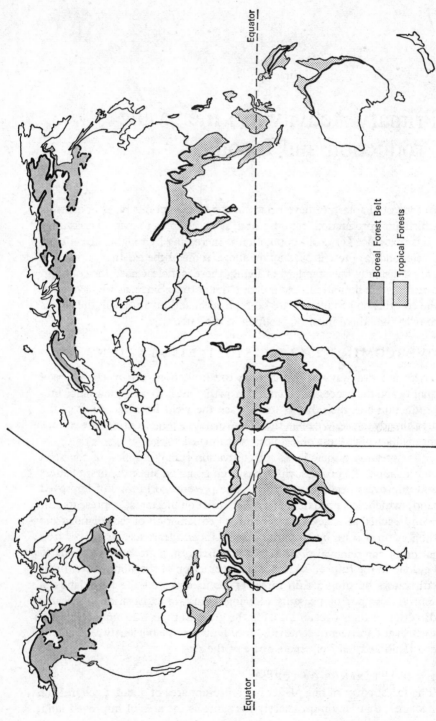

Figure 26: *see opposite.*

although there are obvious difficulties of definition. It is supposed that this represents a reduction in area of between one third and one half during the period of man's occupance, and much of this reduction can be attributed to clearance for agriculture. While a high proportion of the total forest remaining must comprise mountain-forest or swamp-forest, and so be ruled out of account for agricultural purposes, there is nevertheless a great reserve of potentially useful lands at present covered by the temperate and tropical forest belts of the world.

May we expect, then, to see the forest falling before the advance of the cultivator in the future? Is deforestation and plough-up one of the solutions to the problem of increasing production? Does continuation of the historic clearance process hold the key to the food cupboard of the future? Almost certainly, the answer to all these questions is: No. On balance, it is probable that the forest is at present *gaining* on agricultural land rather than diminishing.   Only locally is clearance for farming making progress.

There are, in fact, several good reasons for supposing that future net additions to the world's farmlands from this source will be small, even although the possibility of such additions remains open. One of these is that we face an increase in demand for forest products at least equal to foreseeable increases in demand for food or in population. The areas of forest into which agriculture might spread are precisely the areas of accessible forest on which the wood-based industries depend: inaccessible forest is useless for either purpose.

A second reason for discounting the conversion of much forest land to food-producing land in the future is found in the location of the major forest belts, the northern coniferous belt and the tropical forests. The first of these is, admittedly, a reserve; its southern boundary has been rolled back and penetrated by farming, and it is therefore adjacent to lands already cultivated. But if it is close to areas of present food production, it is *not* close to areas of present shortage. Nowhere along its present boundary does the population *need* to clear forest in order to survive. Its generally poor and acid podsols will yield only a meagre return for the labour of clearance. The value of the timber on each hectare is greater than the foreseeable value of agricultural produce: for that matter, so is the value of the tourist traffic which can be attracted to an area of untouched forest,

Figure 26: Boreal and tropical forests of the world. The boreal forest belt represents the main 'reserve' resource of the economically-advanced nations: its southern boundary is marked by a broken line because for much of its length it merges without interruption into the temperate forest belt. Its northern boundary with the tundra is much more clearly marked. The tropical forests generally give way either to savanna or to mountain forest. (Oxford projection used by permission of Oxford University Press.)

but not to an area of marginal farming. In such regions as Finland or the Atlantic Provinces of Canada, the former limited agricultural land use in forested areas is generally being halted in favour of more scientific forestry practices.

This leaves the tropical forest belt. It is, of course, in these latitudes that major food shortages occur. Here, if anywhere, there is a clear case for increasing the area under cultivation by all possible means.

Forest clearance is already the basis of much of the existing agricultural activity; in particular, of the shifting cultivation which involves burning or cutting the forest, temporary cultivation—two or three seasons—and then abandonment. It may be argued that this is an essentially wasteful method of land use and that if the temporary clearances were made permanent and the cultivators became sedentary, the area under cultivation could be stabilized at four or five times the area in use in any one year. But this is to reckon without the tropical climate, and especially the tropical soils, whose qualities have already been referred to. If we take these factors into account, then it may well be true that shifting cultivation, far from being a wasteful form of land use, is actually the *only* way to farm the tropical forest lands:

The forest is the fallow and cover crop that restores fertility and maintains the soil properties, and it may well be that in the long run this method is the only sure way of producing food from the poorer tropical soils.[1]

If the large-scale clearance of temperate forest for food production seems unlikely, therefore, on economic grounds, clearance of the tropical forests seems equally improbable on physical or ecological grounds.

2 IRRIGATION OF DRY LANDS

Rather more than 160 million ha of the world's agricultural lands at present receive irrigation water.[2] A quarter of this area is in mainland China, and the other leading irrigation users are India, the U.S.A. and Pakistan. It seems reasonable to suppose that a part, at least, of future food requirements will be obtained by enlarging the irrigated area: one estimate (admittedly made in the 1950s) foresaw the hydraulic engineer as providing up to, but not more than, one fifth of the new food requirements in the second half of the twentieth century.[3]

But the word 'irrigation' has too broad a range of meanings to be used

[1] *A World Geography of Forest Resources* edited by S. Haden-Guest and others, American Geographical Society, N.Y., 1956, p. 645.

[2] R. M. Highsmith, 'Irrigated Lands of the World', *Geographical Review* 55 (1965), pp. 382–9, quotes two estimates, of 405 and 431 million acres (162 and 175 million ha.)

[3] H. Addison, *Land, Water and Food*, Chapman and Hall, London 1955, p. 232.

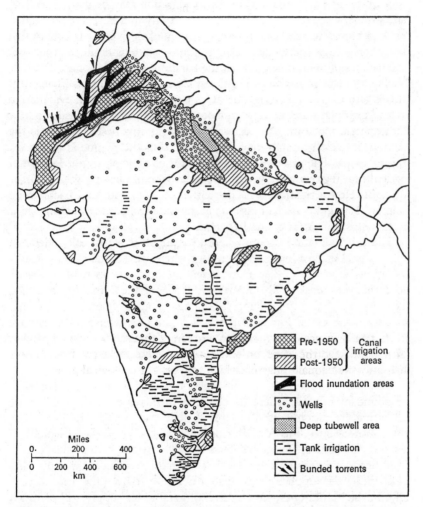

Figure 27: Irrigation (1): the national scale. The map shows the distribution of irrigation agriculture in the Indian sub-continent and emphasizes not only its widespread distribution but also the variety of types of irrigation practised by the cultivator in agricultural lands of great antiquity. (Reproduced by permission from O. K. H. Spate and A. T. A. Learmonth, *India and Pakistan*, London: Methuen, third edition, 1967, p. 231.)

without explanation. Not only are there a number of methods of bringing water to the crops—flooding, runnels, sprinklers—but there are at least four quite separate situations in which irrigation may be used. The first, and probably the one which comes most readily to mind, is the irrigation of desert areas which lack any water supply of their own. It is here that irrigation brings spectacular results—the desert blossoming as the rose; the patches of vivid green against the harsh brown background; the Nile Valley, the Imperial Valley, the Canal Colonies of the Indus Plains. But this is also likely to be irrigation at its most expensive, with evaporation rates from open water at 2,500 mm or more a year, and no assistance from atmospheric moisture. At least as common as this first situation is the second, in which rainfall may be plentiful, but the regime is wrong for raising crops. The principal areas where this is the case are the important agricultural regions with a Mediterranean type of climate, with summer drought. Here irrigation is needed either to store and hold back spring rain until it can be used, or else to tap the water released by melting snow in the Alps, the Atlas or the Lebanon.

The third situation occurs where the rainfall is statistically adequate for the type of farming carried on, but where the annual average masks variations from year to year. Here, irrigation serves mainly to offer *security* for farm operations already undertaken: it enables the farmer to make good any deficit in the natural supply. Among the areas where this situation exists are the Great Plains of the U.S.A., an area whose fortunes have been greatly improved by the introduction of thousands of small patches of irrigated fodder crops to lend security where formerly stock-raisers had only the natural range on which to rely.

The fourth situation in which irrigation is used is in areas of adequate or abundant rainfall, where its object is to increase yields. Under this definition, irrigation is used in Great Britain and in such humid areas as the south-eastern U.S.A.; Florida has 400,000 hectares irrigated. If we are considering the global food supply, in fact, rather than purely local needs, there is no question that the most economical way of using available water supplies for irrigation is not to irrigate the arid areas at all, but the humid ones, where the additional water supply will be much more efficiently used by the plant.

This rather broad statement leads us to consider the particular part that irrigation can or should play in increasing production of food and fibres. It has been employed for thousands of years and whole civilizations have been based on irrigation. But as a technique it has its limitations, being sometimes unwise and more often uneconomical. It cannot be used where soils are so light that water drains rapidly away below root level, or where drainage is inadequate and waterlogging may occur. Where competing water uses exist, it must also be borne in mind that irrigation is a very wasteful form of water use, and we need to enquire whether the waste is excusable. In the western U.S.A., it is estimated that 8–9 out of every ten litres of water withdrawn from natural supplies are used in irrigating part of the 14 million hectares of project lands which those states contain, leaving only the tenth litre for industry, domestic use, sewage control or wildlife. Even on the Columbia Basin Project, one of the most efficient, and certainly one of the most modern, irrigation schemes in the world, the overall efficiency in 1969 was only 62½ per cent; one litre out of every three diverted was lost en route by evaporation of seepage, and in many older schemes the figure is closer to two out of three. Under these circumstances the true cost of irrigation agriculture, if we take account of alternative water uses forfeited or of capital outlay on the engineering works, is likely to make it uneconomical; that is, irrigation is undertaken for the social or political values it confers, and not because it makes sense in cost accounting terms.

Nevertheless, there is no doubt that irrigation has a contribution to make to future increases in production. Four things should, however, be borne in mind. (1) It is likely that the benefits it brings can more cheaply and more efficiently be secured by using irrigation to *supplement* existing water supplies than by pouring water on a bare desert surface. (2) The next generation of extension projects are likely to be costly: they consist of projects too large for individuals, and even communities, to finance, and consequently the supply of capital is going to be the critical factor. (3) These large-scale projects afford an opportunity to do what undoubtedly needs doing in the future, and that is to plan and organize irrigation within the unit of the river basin. In practice, this has not proved easy, even in the U.S.A. whose basin-wide projects are by now famous—the Central Valley, the Missouri Valley, the Upper Colorado. And it was one of the unhappy aspects of independence in the Indian subcontinent that the international boundary of 1947 between India and Pakistan cut right across the natural drainage pattern of one of the most famous irrigated regions in the world, the Indus Basin. (4) While irrigation agriculture may secure the prosperity of a region of poor dry-farming, it may also mean an entirely new way of life for the inhabitants. In other words, it brings economic benefits but it also involves profound social changes, and allowance must be made for the necessary adaptation.

3 THE IMPROVEMENT OF SUBSTANDARD LANDS

Wherever agriculture is practised, there are areas which the cultivator initially avoided because of the difficulties they presented to him, but which are available for reclamation and improvement, if and when the need to use them arises. Probably the largest category of these substandard lands consist of poorly-drained areas, and most of those which remain

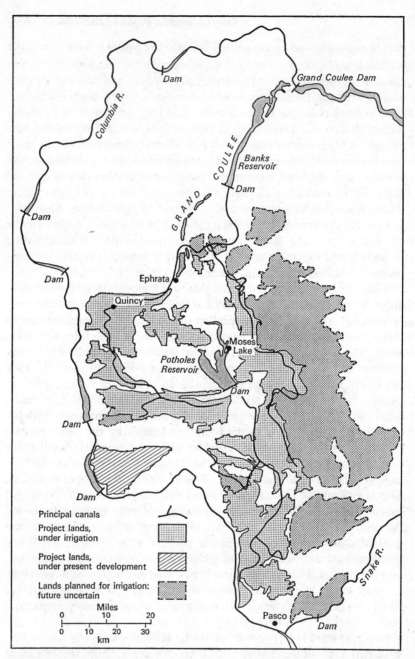

Figure 28: Irrigation (2): the individual project. The Columbia Basin Project in the state of Washington, U.S.A. The project at present waters some 200,000 ha by diversion from the Columbia into the former river bed known as the Grand Coulee, which acts as the scheme's storage reservoir. Irrigation at the fields is by runnel and also by sprinkler.

unimproved are in temperate latitudes, if only because in the tropics the limited lowland areas in, say, the Asian river valleys have long since been drained and now support a dense population. In Europe, drainage has been an on-going process for centuries, but some of the best-known projects of this kind belong to the last three or four decades—the Pontine Marshes, the Ebro Delta and the Camargue. In North America, recent activity has been concentrated, as it has for two centuries past, on reclamation of the Mississippi bottom-lands and the Gulf Coast, largely by increasing security from flood to the point where cultivation becomes a worthwhile proposition.

In northern latitudes, drainage may be the first step in reclaiming another category of potentially useful areas—the peat lands. The accumulation of peat may occur at any altitude where cool moist conditions exist and decomposition is slow and in Norway, for example, reclamation of peat lands has been essential in extending the cultivated acreage. In West Germany after the last war, when the farm population was abruptly increased by the arrival of several million refugees and expellees from the east, new farms were created by peeling the surface off the lowland peats of the North German Plain, leaving only 30 cm or so to form the new topsoil. The agriculture of the Clay Belts on the Canadian Shield owes its existence to the same procedure: the clays are overlain by a thick layer of peat. The procedure is, in fact, sufficiently widespread to focus attention on one area where, at least on the scale made possible by modern equipment, peat clearance for agriculture is almost unknown—Scotland.

A third category of substandard lands is formed by the light, sandy soils which, in Europe at least, were for so long covered by heath and scrub—the North German heaths, the Belgian Campine, the English Breckland, the Landes of south-west France. For most of these areas the first reclamation plan was to plant them over with forest, which was a rational enough use for them. But it has now been shown that, given capital, fertilizers and a careful choice of crops, even these light soils can support high yields under cultivation. Today, the once-famous Lüneburg Heath in Germany is reduced to the dimensions of a nature reserve, as a reminder of what, only a few decades ago, was a broad wasteland.

4 THE CREATION OF NEW LAND

There is one other means of enlarging the cultivable area, and that is by winning new land from the sea. With this particular technique we immediately associate the Dutch people, but this is only because they have employed it on a larger and more imaginative scale than others. Their near neighbours the Danes, Flemings and Germans have all made progress over the centuries against the attack of the North Sea, impounding the coastal flats a few metres at a time, and settling their dense populations further seaward, and the technique has been carried overseas to such areas as the Bay of Fundy.

But all these earlier efforts have been overshadowed by the scale and boldness of the most recent Dutch reclamation scheme, that of the Ijsselmeer, or Zuider Zee. Here, the nation which has the highest population density of any country in the world is well on the way to completing a scheme that adds 200,000 hectares to its farmland—an area, moreover, which apart from the space occupied by settlement and a few shelterbelts is one hundred per cent arable. The configuration of the Dutch coast was, of course, peculiarly favourable to such a scheme but there is no reason why, given capital and skill, the same technique could not be employed in other shallow coastal waters.

TECHNOLOGICAL ADVANCE AND INCREASED POPULATION

Some or all of the techniques we have reviewed will undoubtedly be used in the future to extend the food-producing area beyond its present 3,880 million hectares. But we must now confront the fact that, at any rate since the first world war and the end of the nineteenth-century frontier phase, the extra food production needed for a steadily increasing world population has generally come not from new lands but from increased yields. To double the output of an existing farm rather than establish a new farm on the periphery of an agricultural region has several obvious advantages: it does not involve the expense of providing a new infrastructure; it involves no shift of population to the harsh life of a frontier, and it ensures that new production is closer to areas of present demand than would be the case with a frontier farm. While there is still an agricultural frontier of the nineteenth-century type in a few areas such as southern Brazil, the bulk of today's efforts to increase production are concentrated on the scientific front.

Some of these efforts are actually designed to make available new lands at present barred to the farmer by plant or animal disease; for example, to force a way past what Ritchie Calder has referred to as the 'tsetse sentinel' in Africa. The remainder, however, fall under three main heads: the development of new plant strains and animal breeds; the improvement of chemical and biological defences, and the application of higher standards of farming.

I THE DEVELOPMENT OF NEW STRAINS AND BREEDS
There is little resemblance between the products of a British farm today and those same products as they were, say, three centuries ago: between

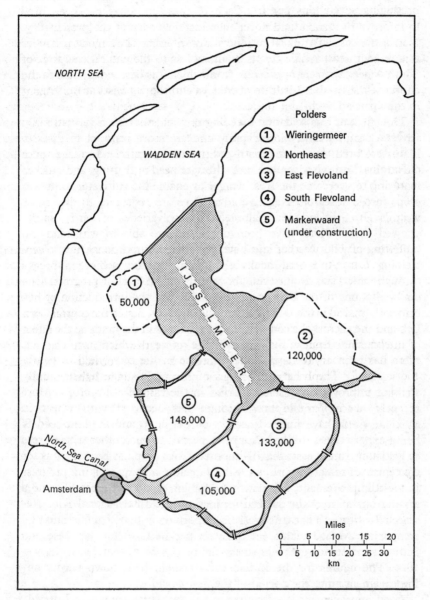

Figure 29: The Netherlands: the Ijsselmeer reclamation scheme, showing the polders in order of their creation.

an apple now and then, or a sheep, or between a field of the old Scottish
barley yielding only four grains for every one sown and the modern crop
producing seven tons per ha. Each of these products has been bred
to improve the strain, and never more actively than at the present day.
Nor is the case of tropical products any different. The modern rubber
tree in south-east Asia owes its qualities less to the natural character of
South America's *hevea brasiliensis*, from which it is descended, than to the
efforts of the Rubber Institute of Malaya and the botanists at Buitenzorg
in the former Dutch East Indies.

The effect of this scientific breeding on yields has been very striking.
Livestock gain weight more rapidly and are more resistant to disease.
Plants are bred which offer both positive and negative advantages over
old strains. Positive advantages are a heavier head or fruiting, and quicker
maturing to overcome the frost danger or enable the cultivator to fit two
crops into one season. Negative advantages are resistance to disease or
weather. In Scotland, for example, the new varieties of hardy, short-
strawed wheat which have been developed are able to withstand the
buffetting of wild weather and have replaced the traditional, but lower-
yielding oats. And occasionally the plant breeders achieve a breakthrough which stands out even above the general level of progress. Undoubtedly, one of the best examples of this was the introduction of hybrid corn (maize) in the U.S.A. from 1935 onwards, first in the central Corn
Belt and then across the country. Table 16 shows in the first line the effect
of introducing the new hybrid: over the 35 years which have elapsed,
there has been an average annual increase in the corn yield of nearly
100 kg ha^{-1}. The other three lines of the table suggest that equally
striking improvements have occurred in the case of other crops. More
recently, a comparable breakthrough has occurred with wheat in
Mexico: yields have jumped nearly 300 per cent, and the new seed is
being exported as rapidly as supplies permit to such other wheat areas
as Pakistan. In the east, the all-important rice crop has been a focus for
concentrated research work, with the Japanese making striking progress
in yield improvement, and new hope for low-yield rice areas like India
arising out of work in the Philippines by the International Rice Research Institute. That this work is important is best demonstrated by
comparing average yields (in quintals per hectare) for Japanese and
Indian rice. In 1973, the Japanese figure was 60·2; that for India was
18·3. The figures for the Indian subcontinent had shown hardly any
improvement since the period of the first world war.

Breed improvement is, of course, a process which cannot be hurried.
But it is a relatively cheap way of increasing food supplies and it has so far
hardly been brought to bear at all on the basic food crops of much of the
world's population. Moreover, if the yield of a staple can be doubled in

15 years, as was the case with corn in the U.S.A. between 1951 and 1967, we can best envisage the impact of this change by asking whether, if the *yield* had remained constant and the *cultivated area* had been increased, we could have expected the area to double in the same 15 year period. Obviously, we could not; certainly not in, say, India, where an absolute shortage of space makes even small increases in area difficult to obtain.

Table 16 U.S.A.: Yields of selected crops, 1931–1971 (national averages, in kilograms per hectare)

	1931–35 (av.)	1951–55 (av.)	1961–65 (av.)	1967	1971
Corn	1427	2445	4162	4912	5435
Wheat	879	1180	1691	1732	2268
Rice	2390	2862	4368	5055	5198
Potatoes	7170	17020	22350	23470	25680

2 CHEMICAL AND BIOLOGICAL DEFENCES

The Food and Agriculture Organization (F.A.O.) estimates, for what the figure is worth, that about 35 million tons of food or fodder products are destroyed each year by rats, insects, predators or fungi. To deal with a problem of this magnitude, such simple remedies as building granaries on stilts are clearly inadequate, and the last three or four decades have seen a remarkable growth in the range of defences available to the farmer. These include attacks on the breeding grounds of mosquitoes and tsetse fly, the locust patrols of the Middle East, the innoculation of cattle and the use of selective weed killers. The spraying of fruit crops has become commonplace; the refinements appear in such details as the use of insects introduced to fruit areas to eat the parasites which attack the trees.

So powerful have these defences become, at least in those areas where food producers can afford them, that we are already growing deaf to warnings about their effect on the ecological balance. By destroying insect pests we tend to break the food chains for all types of life further along the chain, and may simply end by replacing one pest by another. In any case, the 'normal' conditions of life for man as cultivator or as resident are themselves an alteration of natural conditions. When a field planted with a single crop covers 10 or 20 hectares, the possibility of a plant disease spreading is obviously far greater than in the mixed vegetation of a forest or heath; so, for that matter, is the possibility in a planted forest where spruce or pine grows unmixed with other species over hills and valleys. The re-arrangement of natural conditions which has allowed a single species—man—to construct an environment to suit

himself has involved disturbing the environments of other living things
as a consequence. The larger the human population becomes, the greater
the need for this 're-arrangement'.

3 HIGHER STANDARDS OF FARMING

Thanks to the efforts of technical specialists in numerous fields, therefore, it is possible today to modify, if not eliminate, all the physical
controls on production among the world's farmers. But shortages nevertheless remain: famine and poverty are still with us. One good reason
why this is so lies in the profound difference between achieving a technical advance and seeing that technique universally applied. The difference
is caused by two factors—the cost of application and the need for it to be
adopted by millions of individuals, one at a time.

Technical innovation of the kind which increases production has to be
paid for, either by the individual producer, or by his government, or by
some external agency. Since in the areas of greatest need it is usually the
case that the individual can afford nothing and his government not enough,
we find that seeds and fertilizers and agricultural advisers all figure pro-
minently in programmes of aid to underdeveloped areas. They represent
a capital investment in agriculture which the wealthy can afford and the
poor cannot. It is arguable that, in any small-scale aid programme to an
underdeveloped country, the first three items on the 'shopping-list'
should be a supply of chemical fertilizers, a fertilizer factory to keep up
the supply and the services of a plant geneticist and livestock expert.
These are the measures which would have the greatest immediate in-

Table 17   Prairie Provinces, Canada: sales of commercial fertilizers,
1960–1967 (thousand tons)

	1960	1961	1962	1963	1964	1965	1966	1967
Manitoba	22	30	35	47	60	75	153	181
Saskatchewan	35	39	48	72	119	137	215	266
Alberta	80	104	127	171	224	252	316	399
Prairies total	137	173	210	290	403	464	684	846

fluence on production. More elaborate schemes of land reclamation or
land reform could then follow.

This kind of assistance was available in most colonial areas in the pre-
war period, and since then it has been extended and increased within the
framework of such schemes as the Colombo Plan and the Development
Fund of the European Economic Community. But assistance paid for must
also be applied and in this respect the educational problems are enormous.

To form some impression of these problems in areas far removed from normal channels of technical information, we have only to recall, as in the previous chapter, how slowly farmers in the world's most advanced agricultural regions may take to innovations. A good example is provided by the figures for fertilizer consumption in Canada (table 17), where it is only since the second world war that the idea has been decisively accepted that money spent on fertilizers is money well spent. If this was not apparent to farmers in constant touch with world markets and disposing of the services of a network of experimental farms, it may well be difficult to convince farmers of whom neither of these things is true.[4]

Agricultural improvement may, therefore, require a programme of national education, not to speak of social incentives of a kind to be reviewed in the next section. One example of such an educational programme is that in Indonesia known as BIMAS (or 'mass guidance'). Its essential ingredients are the use of students from agricultural colleges to 'spread the word' as a part of their training, at a rate of one student to every 25–30 hectares of rice cultivated, and the input of fertilizers, pesticides and new strains of rice introduced from the international research centre in the Philippines. This combination of native and foreign inputs characterizes most of the successful educational efforts of our period; the developing country needs assistance to provide technical equipment, but there is no substitute for local effort when it comes to the point of involving individual farmers in the scheme. In their first three seasons in the field, the BIMAS students enlisted some $2\frac{1}{2}$ million Indonesian farmers.

It is, perhaps, worth pointing out that, among the numerous methods we have been considering for increasing the volume of production, no mention has been made of mechanization. In an extractive activity like forestry or mining, mechanization *does* increase production, but in very few forms of agriculture does it do so. The first impact of mechanization is on *labour inputs*, not on output. In the first stage of agricultural improvement, therefore, investment in machinery is unproductive. Certainly, it

---

[4] It is worthwhile adding the F.A.O. statistics for fertilizer consumption in the 'developed' and the 'developing' countries, in order to show how much progress remains to be made in the latter.

Consumption of Commercial Fertilizers
(Nutrient content of N, P_2O_5 and K_2O)

| | Consumption (million metric tons) | | Consumption per arable hectare (kilograms) |
	1952–57 (av.)	*1967–68*	*1967–68*
Developed countries	18·8	46·1	68
Developing countries	1·4	6·9	12
World total	20·2	53·0	46

may save the cultivator some part of his day-long work in the fields but it will not make two ears of rice grow in place of one and unless there are alternative occupations for the labourer, it merely increases his leisure while reducing his income by the amount of the depreciation on his investment. There is therefore little point in mechanizing farming where labour is abundant: this form of investment should occur in a *later* stage of development, when one or both of two conditions are fulfilled:

1   there is new land available for occupation, which will permit the farm labour force to be spread more sparsely than before; that is, when mechanization can increase the area cultivated per caput

2   there are alternative occupations open to those whom mechanization will make redundant on the land. In short, mechanization increases output per worker but does not necessarily have any effect at all on output per unit of area.

OVERCOMING THE INSTITUTIONAL LIMITATIONS

We saw in the last chapter that the institutional arrangements which surround farm production act as hindrances to greater output, and those hindrances are best summed up in one phrase: faulty organization. Something has already been said about shortcomings in the education of the farmers: the present section will deal with faulty organization (1) of the farm as a unit, and the measures of reform for which this calls, and (2) of farm supply to the market and the consumer.

1 LAND REFORM
Farms may be poorly organized with regard to size, shape or ownership. To the remedy for any or all of these faults, we commonly apply the term *land reform*, although it quickly becomes apparent that the three faults are largely independent of one another. Shape, or layout, of the farm may be improved without affecting either size or ownership. On the other hand, reform of ownership in most cases has resulted in a reduction in average farm size, often to an uneconomically small scale which in turn creates problems of its own.

The first measure of reform, then, is *the adjustment of farm size*. In a European context, this almost always implies an *enlargement* of the operating unit, to give economies of scale and to allow the operator to accumulate capital for necessary improvements. In South America, on the other hand, there is considerable evidence to show that, in relation to national average size (a rather meaningless conception in South America, however), output per hectare would be higher if farm size were *reduced*. We must consider each of these situations in turn.

In Europe, despite a migration from the farms which has been in full swing for a century or more, there are still far too many individual farm operators for optimum efficiency. This is, of course, a relic of a period when access to land was for most people the only possible way of securing their livelihood; when landless labourers were liable to starve. Although in Europe this has long ceased to be true, holders of land have clung to it and small holdings have become smaller as they were subdivided between heirs. Western Europe ended the 1950s with an average farm size of little more than medieval proportions: of 14 million holdings in the area (excluding Spain) in 1958, Lamartine Yates found[5] that more than 9 million were less than 5 hectares. Nearly 4 million were less than one hectare, a size which only in the most exceptional cases—such as vineyards and market gardens—can provide an adequate livelihood for the operator.

In areas like north-west Europe, where cities and towns offer plenty of non-agricultural employment, the smallest size of holding is nowadays farmed only on a part-time basis, if it is farmed at all. The operator derives his main income from other types of employment. In this way there has grown up, in the period of Europe's postwar labour shortage, a class of commuter-farmers: its members board trains at wayside stations in Belgium, to travel to jobs in Brussels and Antwerp, or are collected by company buses from crossroads in Germany to work for Mercedes or Opel. The effect of this trend on numbers and sizes of agricultural holdings is shown, in the case of France, in Table 18 (where, however, the number of holdings under 1 hectare was somewhat increased, in the 1970 census, by a more complete enumeration than previously. But the general trend is clear). But not even the competitive pressures of modern farming are reducing the number of small farms sufficiently rapidly. Several western European countries have therefore introduced *incentives* to farm enlargement by offering farmers a pension if they will retire in late middle-age and make their land available for amalgamation with that of a younger neighbour. So, too, the French have introduced the idea of voluntary collective operation of groups of small farms, the *Groupements Agricoles d'Exploitation en Commun* (G.A.E.C.'s), societies whose members are committed to working as a group for greater efficiency in using the factors of production. As a commentary on these facts it is interesting to notice that, on the Dutch polderlands of the former Ijsselmeer, where farms were laid out for the first time in the

[5] P. Lamartine Yates, *Food, Land and Manpower in Western Europe*, Macmillan, London and New York, 1960, pp. 169–71.

1950s and 1960s, the planners began by adopting a 12 hectare unit, but later raised this figure to 50 hectares, as being a more realistic size in the agricultural context of the period; subdivision of these units is forbidden.

Table 18   France: numbers of agricultural holdings, 1929, 1955, 1963 and 1970 (figures in thousands of holdings)

	1929	1955	1963	1970
Less than 1 hectare	1014·7	151·7	94·6	127·0
1–5 hectares	1146·3	648·8	454·0	328·9
Over 5 hectares	1805·4	1485·2	1351·8	1131·7
All holdings	3966·4	2285·7	1900·4	1587·6

But what if there is *no* alternative employment to draw off the land the operators of the smallest holdings—those whose lands cannot yield an acceptable livelihood and whose operations are too small to generate capital for improvement? This is still the case in some parts of western Europe: it was very generally the case in southern and eastern Europe at least up to the time of the second world war. Areas like southern Italy or Galicia were rural slums, in which the standard of living was forced down as the population density increased, but each family clung precariously to its small patch, often under threat of eviction and paying an exorbitant rent. Particularly acute was the problem in areas of the continent, east or south, where rainfall was too slight to allow the farmer to adopt any form of cultivation more intensive than growing cereals.[6]

In this situation, farm size becomes smaller, not larger, and a remedy involves some external force. Historically, war and famine have been 'remedies' reducing overcrowding. Today the main outside force is government intervention, to alter the balance of the economy, to draw population off the land, and to inject capital into farming. The methods used to achieve these effects have been more drastic in eastern than in western Europe, but then the need for action in the east was far greater. Whether the result is a gradual increase in farm size, as in the west, or an

[6] The condition of this European peasantry was illuminated in pre-war days by Doreen Warriner's *European Peasant Farming*, London, 1939; it is still worth reading. For the changes which occurred after 1945, see her *Revolution in Eastern Europe*, Turnstile, London, 1950. On the difficulty mentioned above of farming extensively on very small holdings she writes, in the latter book (p. 144), 'Eastern Europe in fact was practising prairie farming of the kind that is suitable for countries with very sparse population and big reserves of land, but not for countries with a very dense population and no land to spare. What was needed was more intensive farming.'

abrupt switch from peasant plots to 2,000 hectare collectives, as in the east, the object is to improve the efficiency and increase the output of the unit.

The case of South America is quite different. Here, field studies show that output per hectare bears a consistently inverse relationship to farm size (figure 30 and table 19). The largest holdings, the *latifundia*, are on the whole grossly under-capitalized and under-worked, despite the fact that their owners are usually the only people with any access whatever to capital resources. The *latifundia* lie waste or fallow while the holders of *minifundia* must cultivate intensively to survive, often on inferior soils. Quite apart, therefore, from social or political considerations of equity, there is a clear case on grounds of need for either breaking up the *latifundia* or obliging their owners to cultivate them. The population of South America is increasing more rapidly (3 per cent per annum) than that of any other continent, and agricultural production per caput is lower now than it was before the second world war.

If the recent experiences of Europe and Latin America are in some respects contradictory, is there an *optimum* size for the operating unit? Experience in North America (to take a third area neutral between the other two) suggests that there is, but that this size is steadily increasing and that it varies for different cropping patterns. For maximum output per unit of area, the family-farm operation is usually as efficient as a larger operation, and often more efficient, even although the latter may achieve higher output per worker or larger net income per hectare. A family farm in North America may vary in size from 25 ha of fruit to 400 ha of wheat, and with the advance of mechanization these figures tend to increase; the definition is not made in terms of area but of labour input. Beyond this size, enlargement seems to have little positive effect on output per hectare; it may well reduce it.

The second aspect of land reform concerns *the consolidation of fragmented holdings*. In recent years, students of European agriculture have become familiar with 'horror stories' of 5–8 hectare farms divided into 50 parcels, and with maps that show these scattered operations. (The map of *ownership* is likely to be more horrifying still, since in practice farmers often exchange parcels in order to save themselves a journey, and owners of isolated strips let them to neighbours.) Figures from other continents may be even more remarkable, like those for the Punjab village where 5,200 hectares were divided into 63,000 fields.[7] Outside Europe, too, custom is apt to assign ownership or usufruct of even a single tree, or a half-share in a tree, to a person living many miles away; in north Africa, land reformers had to contend with claims based on the right to the *shade*

[7] Reported by O. H. K. Spate and A. T. A. Learmonth, *India and Pakistan*, Methuen, London, third edition, 1967, p. 263.

of a tree. In underdeveloped lands with a surplus of labour—very commonly, female labour—the effect of such customary rights on output is probably not very great. What is, however, remarkable is that fragmentation should have persisted to the present time alongside modern,

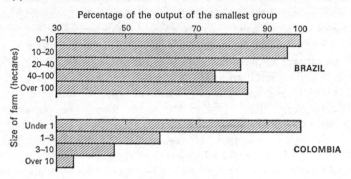

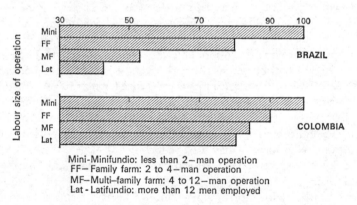

Mini-Minifundio: less than 2—man operation
FF—Family farm: 2 to 4—man operation
MF—Multi—family farm: 4 to 12—man operation
Lat - Latifundio: more than 12 men employed

Figure 30: South America: the relationship of farm size to productivity. The figure, which is based on case studies in Colombia and Brazil, shows the generally inverse relationship between size and productivity, whether the latter is measured in terms of output per unit area or output per unit input of labour. (*Source:* P. Dormer and others, 'Land Tenure and Reform', *Newsletter* 29, p. 6. Reproduced by permission of the Land Tenure Center, University of Wisconsin.)

mechanized, large-scale farming in the most technically-advanced areas of western Europe.

At the end of the second world war, in fact, some of Europe's worst fragmentation was to be found along the densely-settled axis formed by the

Rhine lowlands and their borders. It was a situation calling for action on a national scale and, of the governments concerned, it has been that of the Netherlands which has accomplished most. This may in part be because of the extra dimension of the fragmentation problem in the delta lands of the Rhine and Maas: it is serious enough where plots or strips are separated by earth baulks, but it is much worse where the strips are divided by water-filled ditches, the upkeep of which is an obligation on the farmer.

As early as 1924, the Dutch government began a programme which is a

Table 19 South America: Some examples of the relationship of unit size of holding to land use and investment

1 *Brazil, 1959–1960, sample districts*

| | | As a multiple of figures for minifundia | | |
| | Average size | Total investment per farm | Cropland per farm | Investment per unit area of cropland |
Class of holding				
Minifundia	1	1	1	1
Family farms	10	14	4	4
Medium multi-family farms	29	58	8	8
Latifundia	316	153	46	4

2 *Seven Latin American countries*

(a) Percentage of land under various uses

Class of holding	Cultivated	Natural pasture	Forest & scrub	Other, including barren
Minifundia	55	30	9	6
Family farms	29	52	14	5
Medium multi-family farms	33	42	18	7
Latifundia	16	52	23	8
All classes	24	49	20	7

(b) Percentage of the cultivated land in (a) above under various crops

Class of holding	Annual crops	Permanent crops	Improved pasture	Fallow
Minifundia	61	13	12	14
Family farms	42	7	28	23
Medium multi-family farms	26	7	25	42
Latifundia	17	6	29	48

Note: The definitions adopted for the four classes of holdings throughout the table are standardized on a basis of approximate labour input, as follows:

Minifundio: 2 man operation or smaller
Family farm: 2 to 4 man operation
Medium-sized multi-family farm: 4 to 12 man operation
Latifundio: operation employing more than 12 men

Source: U.N.O., *Economic Survey of Latin America, 1966,* pp. 340, 346.

good example of this type of land reform. The initiative for re-parcelling (Dutch: *ruilverkaveling*) must be taken by the local landholders. When a majority of them agree to apply to the government for action, surveyors are sent in; they replan boundaries, ditches and roads, consolidate holdings and allay the suspicions of the minority that, whatever the soil analyst may say, the new holding is inferior in quality to the parcels being exchanged. At the same time, the opportunity is taken to relocate not only fields but farm houses (so that they may be closer to new holdings) to break up overcrowded agricultural villages where there is no more room for new barns or tractor sheds, and to plan recreational and amenity space. The result is an entirely new landscape. For this, the government provides the capital and pays about two thirds of the cost; the farmer repays the other third by annual instalments. At the peak of the programme in the late 1950s and early 1960s, the Dutch government was devoting to *ruilverkaveling* as much as a half of its total expenditure on agriculture. In West Germany, the *Flurbereinigung* programme followed similar principles; so, too, did the *remembrement* in France.

The third aspect of land reform is *reform of ownership*. This aspect, although often treated as the only one meriting the name of reform, has been left until last precisely because it is so subject to political and emotional interpretation. Doctrinaire revolutionaries everywhere call for reform of ownership: most landowners everywhere defend the *status quo*. What concerns us, however, is the question: what effect does such a reform have on agricultural output? Given a case in equity for reform, what will happen to production? Fortunately, we now have available reports on a sufficient number of reform projects, in different political contexts, to be able to form some kind of non-political judgement on this question.[8]

The normal course of these land reforms has been that the government passes a law taking powers either to expropriate or to buy all land held in excess of a certain maximum by large landowners. This maximum, or exemption limit, depends both on the nature of the agriculture and on the complexion of the government; in Japan, the Americans ordered a reform in which the landowner might retain $7\frac{1}{2}$ acres (3 hectares) cultivated by himself and $2\frac{1}{2}$ acres (1 hectare) leased to a tenant, while at the other end of the scale the 1964 reform law in Ecuador allowed the owner to retain 3,500 hectares on the coast, or 1,800 hectares in the interior, which can hardly be described as a radical reform. The expropriated areas are then redistributed to small farmers or landless workers. This immediately creates two dangers. One is that the hunger for land among

---

[8] References given in the list of suggested reading for this chapter cover all or part of the Middle East and Latin America, together with Japan and India.

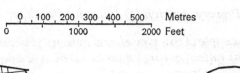

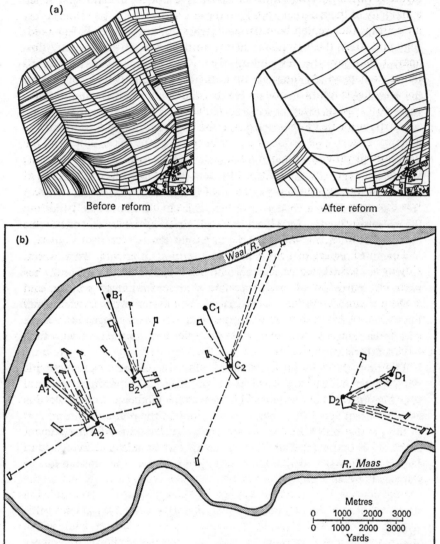

Figure 31: European land reform programmes: (**a**) Conversion of the old strip fields in a community where the average size of the 1,295 old parcels was 0·135 hectares and the new average is 0·61 hectares: a German example from the Kraichgau in Wurttemberg. (**b**) Consolidation of the scattered holdings and relocation of the farmsteads on newly allocated lands: a Dutch example from the region between the Waal (Rhine) and Mass rivers. (**b** reproduced by permission from F. de Soet, *Rural Development in the Netherlands,* The Hague: Ministry of Agriculture and Fisheries, 1959, p.17.)

the have-nots is likely to lead to an attempt to satisfy *too many* of them: the new unit size is too small for effective operation, and *minifundia* with their accompanying problems replace *latifundia*. The other is that production may fall because the new farmers are unused to independent decision-making and are either unskilled or ill-equipped. This happened with the break up of the slave-worked cotton plantations in the southern U.S.A. after the war of 1861–1865; it equally happened with the break-up of the Prussian estates under communist control after 1945 and in both cases, therefore, the initial grant of ownership to the newly-independent cultivator proved to be of only temporary benefit to him.

It may be, however, that the basic change brought about by land reform is simply to abolish the middleman—the landlord to whom many of the world's cultivators are paying a third share, or even a half, of their crops as rent. Where change is violent, this should immediately increase the operator's income by a third or a half. Freed of the burden of rent, he can raise his own standard of living in proportion—at least so long as the new regime does not substitute some new burden for the old rental. Where reform is gradual, rental paid formerly to the landlord is generally replaced by payments of smaller amount to the government, and these go to the purchase of the land over a period. This system whereby the farmer buys himself free, with the government holding his mortgage, has become widespread since it was introduced into Ireland under the land acts of the nineteenth century.

The first, and very understandable, effect of reform on production is not to increase it but to divert it to the producer. This producer had been handing one third to one half of his crop to the landlord. The landlord in turn had then acted as wholesaler; he supplied the non-agricultural part of the population. After the reform, the producer simply retains a larger share of his output, and uses it to raise his own standard of living. Thus Dore found in Japan[9] that the consumption levels were affected by the reforms there as follows:

	Whole Country	Urban Districts	Rural Districts
1934–6	100	100	100
1950	79·2	69·8	93·5
1954	110·7	94·1	136·4

The producer simply retained a larger share of his output. The output itself then began to rise, but on the question of how much of the credit for this should be given to the reform measures, Dore was guarded:

[9] R. P. Dore, *Land Reform in Japan*, R.I.I.A., London, 1959, p. 202.

'. . . the land reform is far from being the sole, or even the chief, factor.'[10]

It seems clear that the opportunity to work on his own account, as we might intuitively expect, is a stimulus to the individual farmer, sometimes in unexpected ways. In Uttar Pradesh, for example, Singh and Misra noted that, once the *zamindari* (landlord) system was abolished, the area under cultivation increased considerably, and that under old fallow or lying waste was correspondingly reduced.[11] However, the achievement of increased output depends on the farmer being supplied with the necessary technical, social and financial structures to support him in his new role. Doreen Warriner asserts that, in the Japanese case just referred to, the critical factor was the supply of *capital* to the farmer.[12] The independent cultivator is now financially 'on his own', bearing the full risk of his operations (a risk which the sharecropper divides with his landlord). If the landlord has disappeared, a new marketing system must also be developed for disposing of the crop. And since he is now making his own decisions, the farmer will require guidance. Almost certainly, too, where reform leads to the 'atomization' of holdings, it will not be long before the smallest group is eliminated as uneconomical, so that the reform should preferably provide from the start for the removal of some of the would-be farmers to other occupations.

Here is the point. Far from there being any satisfactory evidence that the abolition of the landlord class on doctrinaire grounds will automatically create Utopia, we can see that a reform of ownership must be planned with the greatest care if it is not to cause a whole series of problems worse than those it solves. In areas like Latin America, where it is calculated that 1·5 per cent of the holdings (those over 1,000 hectares) occupy 65 per cent of the land, there is a clear case for reform on grounds of equity. But:

the ideal land reform programme is an integrated programme of measures designed to eliminate obstacles to economic and social development arising out of defects in the agrarian structure. For many countries, the execution of such a programme will prove to be a continuing and many-sided process.[13]

---

[10] Dore, *op. cit.*, p. 218.

[11] B. Singh and S. Misra, *A Study of Land Reforms in Uttar Pradesh*, Oxford Book Co., Calcutta, 1964.

[12] D. Warriner, *Land Reform in Principle and Practice*, Oxford University Press, 1969, p. 47.

[13] U.N.O.–F.A.O., *Progress in Land Reform, Third Report*, New York, 1962, p. vi.

2 THE ORGANIZATION OF PRODUCTION AND MARKETING

Throughout this chapter so far we have been considering ways of increasing production. There is a good deal of evidence to suggest that one of the most powerful stimuli to production in the past has been the provision of a market and a means of transport to it. Given these facilities, the producer can see a clear incentive for increasing his output beyond the level of community demand—in short, for changing from subsistence to market-orientated agriculture or fishing. The kind of evidence we possess is, for example, the rapid rise in British milk production after the setting up of the Milk Marketing Board (the object of which was to ensure an outlet for every farmer's milk production), or the development of plantation agriculture along the railway routes of central Africa and south-eastern Asia, where the plantations appear after the railway line and within a limited distance on either side of it. On a much larger scale, agricultural exports—in this case, exports of plantation crops—showed a sharp increase after the opening of the Suez Canal provided a shortened route to European markets.

If we return for a moment to the vicious circle described on p. 157, and the question of where to break it, we find that the provision of a market has generally been the critical point. Certainly, we have some dismal examples to draw upon where production has been increased *ahead of* access to market, and piles of cotton, or cocoa beans, or groundnuts were left rotting in the backwoods. There then follows the further question as to how the farmers are going to confront the consumer in the market— one by one, as individuals sitting behind a basket of eggs and a barrow-load of vegetables, or as an organized group matching forces with the buyers.

This transition from subsistence to market-orientated production is taking place in many parts of the world at the present time. In Europe, it is virtually complete, and it is here that we can observe most clearly what happens. The transition did not occur in all parts of the continent at the same time. Its onset can be correlated with increases in population density and, especially, with the growth of towns, so that areas which early developed an urban network provided the first conditions for the change.[14] In general, therefore, it occurred first in western areas like the Low Countries or the Paris region, and later in non-urbanized eastern Europe. It occurred spontaneously with the progress of industrialization, and artificially when, from time to time, a government set out to induce higher production by forced levies of corn, or by tariff policies. Much of the early transport to market was performed by water traffic, and the rail-

[14] See B. H. Slicher van Bath, 'The Rise of Intensive Husbandry in the Low Countries', in *Britain and the Netherlands* edited by J. S. Bromley and E. H. Kossman, Chatto and Windus, London, 1960, pp. 130–53.

ways completed the process, linking even the remote north-western tentacles and mountain valleys of the continent with its commercial life.

But if production increases occurred spontaneously as individual farmers felt the stimulus of market opportunity, it still remained to make the market an outlet sufficiently assured to take some of the risk out of 'going commercial'. To confront the market successfully, farmers either organize themselves or are organized. In the non-communist world, they form co-operatives. In the communist world—or rather, according to communist doctrine, which is not quite the same thing—they are organized into collectives. These are simply two alternative solutions for the organizational problem.

The agricultural co-operative in its modern form was born in Scandinavia; specifically, the Danish dairy co-operative dates from the 1880s. In northern Europe it spread to other forms of production until, today, probably 90 per cent of Scandinavian farm output passes through co-operative channels. With its spread came numerous benefits for the farmer, including the one with which we are here concerned, increased production. Millward[15] comments:

The co-operative dairy led to the extension of scientific ideas to farming all over Demark . . . and there is no doubt that the co-operative movement quickened the life of the Danish countryside. Through their marketing organizations the co-operatives have obtained higher prices for better butter. As a result of widening markets and higher prices more cows were kept on medium-sized and small farms all over the country, and with the rising quantities of skim-milk and butter-milk, which the dairies returned to the farms, large numbers of pigs have been reared. In turn, these have contributed to the expansion of the bacon industry. To complete the cycle, the increasing numbers of animals on the farms have given more manure to the fields to improve the output of crops.

From Scandinavia, the co-operative idea has spread very widely—to wine producers in France, small dairy farmers in Ireland and coconut growers of the Pacific islands. Perhaps the most important development has been its spread into some of the poverty areas of the world: in this respect India, as the world's most populous non-communist state, is a critical area for testing the kind of voluntary organization implied by the term co-operation. Spate and Learmonth reported[16] that, in the decade of the 1950s membership of co-operative societies rose from 14 million to 34 million but, in India, the question of credit facilities rather than higher production has been behind much of this development:

[15] R. Millward, *Scandinavian Lands*, Macmillan, London and New York, 1964, pp. 227–8.

[16] Spate and Learmonth, *op. cit.*, pp. 274–5.

the main stimulus to joining a society has been the wish to escape from the grip of the moneylender rather than to increase output. Whatever the motivation, there can be little doubt that the political future of the Indian subcontinent will be powerfully influenced by the success or failure of this 'democratic' alternative to the collective.

The collective has become identified with communist ideology, although it is or was a common enough form of organization at the community and tribal level. It appeared in the U.S.S.R. soon after the revolution of 1917, and spread in stages (and against ferocious opposition, especially at the stage where livestock holdings were collectivized) throughout the 1920s and early 1930s. It appeared in eastern Europe after 1945 and in China after 1948. As a means of increasing output, how does it compare with the non-communist alternative of the voluntary co-operative?

The production record of collectives, at least in Europe, is indifferent. It is notorious that, area for area, where the individual is allowed to retain a garden plot and sell its produce, the yield from these plots eclipses that from the collective land. In Yugoslavia, where compulsory membership of the collectives was abandoned in 1953, production rose spectacularly. On the other hand, however, collective attack on formerly non-agricultural land, as for example in the Rumanian Dobruja, has met with considerable success.

The uneven production record of the collectives can be explained by two main factors: over-swift change and doctrinaire application. Given more time, the idea of the collective might have been more generally accepted and, given more flexibility, the same solution might not have been tried for the problems of so many diverse land-use types. In particular, the suppression of the more wealthy peasants (the *kulaks*) on purely dogmatic grounds should have been avoided for they were, in the main, the men of enterprise whose efforts would have initiated a general rise in output levels when allied to the new investment in agriculture which formed part of the new programme of the communist states.

The collective has produced best in areas

1   where some measure of private enterprise and of competition has been allowed to remain, as in Poland
2   where the rural population was not too dense.

Such areas have included regions of new settlement, like the Dobruja, and regions where an active programme of industrialization has thinned the rural population. In addition, collectivization can be said to have fared better in the U.S.S.R. generally than in eastern Europe, for in the latter the rural population density is on average twice as high as it is in the Soviet Union, and there is no question of thinning it by means of a 'new lands' programme on the Russian scale.

Despite this patchy record, however, we must not write off the collective as obviously inferior to other forms of farm organization—as the Americans, for example, are apt to do in extolling the virtues of the 'family farm'. If production levels and efficiency in the east are both low compared with the west, we must remember the relative starting levels, and acknowledge the improvement that has been registered. To quote Doreen Warriner again: 'No one who knew what east European farming was like before can doubt that it was necessary to reorganize the farm system', and to those who might argue that a co-operative solution on western lines would have been sufficient, she posed the question, 'Can the change really come on a voluntary basis?'[17] That question, in its various local contexts of ignorance, prejudice and fear, lies somewhere close to the heart of the problem.

The transition from a subsistence agriculture to commercial production can be observed in other continents besides Europe, and for a second example we may well take the case of plantation agriculture in the tropics. This example is one where it was necessary to organize both production and marketing of the commodities concerned. Thanks to the changes brought by industrialization and a rising standard of living, Europe found itself in the nineteenth century in need of a number of new products which, for climatic reasons, could not be grown within the continent. This had, of course, long been true of sugar and spices: what happened in the nineteenth century was that the demand for tropical produce expanded very rapidly—too rapidly to rely on ordinary processes of natural growth of these products, or on the native channels of commerce which might eventually place them on the world market. The problem therefore became one of organizing their production and delivery on the scale demanded.

But most of these products were either unknown and useless to the native cultivator, or else were grown by him as a mere sideline to his main interest—that of producing food for his family. To convert him into a commercial producer, it was first necessary to arrange three things:

(a) *An input of capital.* This was needed for research and development, to convert the natural product into a commercial product (see p. 172); for processing equipment such as drying plant, mills or extractors, and for transport to bring the commodity out of jungle or swamp, across the sea and into Antwerp or Hamburg.

(b) *A local food supply.* If the commercial product was to be cultivated (or, for that matter, mined), native labour was essential and that labour,

[17] *Revolution in Eastern Europe*, pp. 142, 148.

diverted from its previous business of growing food, would itself need to be fed. In practice, this often meant arranging food imports from elsewhere—for example, rice from Burma into Malaya, to feed labourers on the rubber plantations and in the tin mines. This, naturally, demanded further capital investment.

(c) *A reason for the change-over.* Left to himself, the native producer could never be relied upon—at least in European terms of reliability—to grow the necessary crops, and there was in the native system no inherent reason for making such a change. So, in practice, the organizing agency had two courses open—persuasion and coercion. 'Persuasion' in this context has usually taken the form of an offer of the frills of civilization; that is, the subsistence farmer has been enticed into the commercial economy by the desire to own beads or a bicycle, which he can only obtain in exchange for money or specified crops.

The forms of coercion have been rather more varied. The most open is slavery. Among its variants is the enforcement of new obligations on the native population. For example, a head-tax may be required, payable only in money, to obtain which the native must work within the framework of commercial production. A familiar alternative is the forced delivery, introduced in what was, perhaps, its most notorious form by the Dutch in the East Indies under their Culture System of 1830. This was a system whereby one fifth of the cultivated area and one fifth of the working year (66 days) were required to be set aside for the cultivation of specified crops—indigo, sugar, coffee, tea, tobacco, pepper and cotton. Since, after 1830, the Netherlands were financially in dire straits following the loss of Belgium, the terms of the system were gradually stiffened, to increase the state's revenue from these commodities. Stiffening the requirements of the Culture System led in due course to local famine; the cultivator had neither the time nor the energy to devote to his own food crops. This was a system which it is hard now to forgive, yet it lasted for over 30 years. It is small wonder that the term 'plantation agriculture' has acquired such strong overtones of forced labour and degraded standards of values. The creation of incentives in any case takes time; it is quicker to coerce than to persuade. This may explain, too, the part played by governments and chartered companies in European development of the tropics: whoever initiated the development had necessarily to possess the power to coerce. It comes as a relief to find that there is also a *post-plantation* phase of development in these regions, and that from an area such as Malaya today tropical products are exported which are grown by smallholders operating in the European manner and on a fully commercial basis; that is, the transition has not been forced upon this generation, but accepted by it.

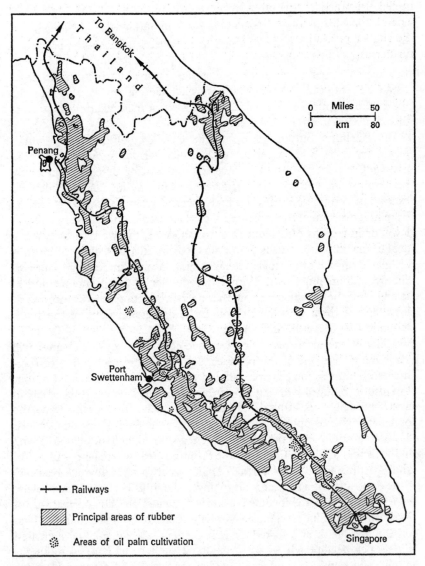

Within the map:

To Bangkok

Thailand

Miles
0   50
0   80
km

Penang

Port
Swettenham

┼─┼ Railways

▨ Principal areas of rubber

⠿ Areas of oil palm cultivation

Singapore

Figure 32: Malaya: plantation agriculture. The map shows the whereabouts of commercial production of rubber and oil palm in the peninsula, and stresses the dependence of the plantation everywhere in the tropics on transport facilities (see p. 186). (Reproduced by permission from P. P. Courtenay, *Plantation Agriculture*, London: G. Bell, 1965, p. 160.)

THE FACTORS OF PRODUCTION AND OTHER GOALS

At the start of this chapter, we made the assumption that any adjustment of the areas under cultivation or the practices of primary producers should have as its object the increase of total output, and in the body of the chapter we have considered the various means by which this increase could be achieved. In other words, we have chosen as objective the maximum output, and have considered ways of manipulating the factors of production to attain this goal.

But maximum output is not, of course, the *only* objective open to the producer. If he is an American or Brazilian farmer, he may well recall the sight of piles of unsold potatoes or coffee being destroyed, precisely because production had increased *too much* for the market to absorb the excess. In certain countries, he may cheerfully have pocketed payments from his government for agreeing *not* to plant crops. Only at the theoretical level, or in regions of evident resource shortage, can we assume that the goal of maximum output is being pursued; locally, it is likely to be subordinated to such other goals as maximizing income, increasing leisure or, simply, minimizing costs. Primary production is an economic undertaking, and the producers know that over-production *reduces* income; at least, any of them who lived through the depression years of the 1930s will find that lesson hard to forget.

Many of the measures which we have considered in this chapter will serve more than one of the producer's goals. The consolidation of fragmented holdings, for example, should not only lead to increased output but also to reduced working hours for the farmer, who no longer has to make the daily trek around his scattered parcels. In the same way, the organization of co-operatives should improve the farmer's income as well as his volume of production. But different goals call for a different ordering of the factors of production. In those favoured areas where land is plentiful and agricultural surplus is normal (Anglo-America is the obvious example) little or no attention may be paid to physical output per unit of area; what concerns the farmer is income per unit of production. The normal way of increasing individual income has for long been to acquire or rent new land on the one hand, and to reduce unit costs on the other. The increased yields per hectare which we considered earlier (table 16) are in the nature of a bonus to the farmer, rather than his chief concern.[18]

---

[18] In witness of this assertion, the American literature reviewed by the present writer contains almost no studies in which yield by area is the focus of attention, but a very large number devoted to costs by area and costs per unit of production. Ironically, American interest in yield levels (apart from the purely rustic delights of winning prizes at the county fair) may be said to stem from

Optimum income levels may be assessed either on a per-area basis or per unit of production. Since *net income* depends on the margin of gross income over costs, there is a very wide range of possible input levels, all of which yield a similar net income—low input–low output (or extensive) operations may yield the same income as high input–high output (or intensive) farming. Consequently, it would be extremely naïve to suppose that every primary producer was operating as intensively as possible. Characteristically, as a farmer grows older, he reduces his inputs to allow himself more leisure and to reduce his capital at risk: he is then farming less intensively than formerly. (In this connection, it cannot be overlooked that, in both North America and western Europe, the average age of farm operators is rising, since the farmers' sons and the younger generation of the rural population are increasingly looking to the cities for employment.) In bad times like the 1930s, farmers reduce their inputs because to incur *any* costs is a risk, and the man whose inputs are least stands to lose least. In some areas there is a tradition of low-input farming, even although natural conditions would favour intensification: it was in the 1940s that a writer on Irish farming described the Republic as possessing 'an agriculture of opening and shutting gates', which can be translated as the raising of beef store cattle on natural pasture, free from such costly refinements as planting fodder crops or getting rid of the rushes (*juncus spp.*) that choked hundreds of hectares of pasture.[19] And we have already noted how recent is the 'fertilizer habit' in some areas of highly commercialized farming, which means that farmers have only recently come to accept that to intensify their inputs in this way will benefit their net income.

Optimum returns on inputs vary not only with the type of operation and its intensity but also with the size of the operating unit. Studies made in the U.S.A. suggest that costs per unit of area and of production both reach a minimum within the scale of farm operated by one, or at the most two, men but this scale naturally depends on the nature of the farming. In the Red River Valley of Minnesota, minimum costs by area on the cash-grain farms studied occurred at about 400 ha (a one-man or two-

[19] In County Leitrim, as rush-choked as any in Ireland, it was confided to the writer that the rushes were actually good for the pasture—presumably because they kept the remaining grass away from hungry cows.

the depression, when the Roosevelt administration began the system of quotas, under which farmers receive financial supports so long as their *planted area* of the crops on quota does not exceed an agreed figure. Placing the quota on area rather than on output clearly encourages the farmer to accept the area quota and then produce a maximum from the given area. This is still the basis of the United States support price system.

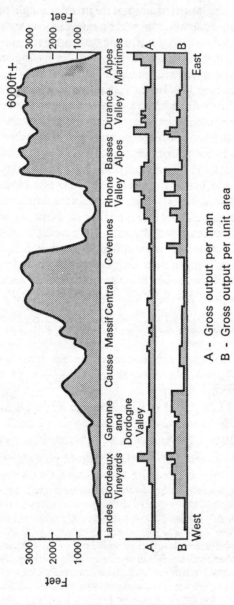

Figure 33: France: comparative agricultural output along a transect from west to east across the southern part of the country. The section illustrates the wide variations in productivity which may occur within a country through differences in physical conditions and agricultural systems. (Reproduced by permission after A. N. Duckham and G. B. Masefield, *Farming Systems of the World*, London: Chatto and Windus, New York: Frederick Praeger, 1970, figure 2.6.4.)

man unit), while in Oregon wheat country there was little change in these costs over 300 ha. In the western Corn Belt, in Iowa, costs per hectare showed little reduction beyond 100 ha, and costs per unit of production beyond 130–160 ha, leading Ottoson and Epp, in the neighbouring state of Nebraska, to suggest that in the Corn Belt it yields a higher return per dollar invested to intensify input on a farm below 100 ha than to increase acreage to a larger figure: 'our analysis appears to indicate that increases in size of farm measured in acres will be accompanied by less than proportionate increases in income.'[20]

We are, of course, dealing here with only a small number of case studies from one country, and they are introduced merely to illustrate the general problem of determining what is the most profitable form of primary production, given the local cost of inputs and the degree of input intensity which is either chosen by the operator or forced upon him by the general level of rents (see p. 32). This form may be largely determined by tradition, in which case it can be successfully changed by bold innovation (usually backed in practice by capital resources large enough to take most of the risk out of the change-over): it is one of the functions of state farms and research institutes to initiate such changes. Or it may be governed by the cultivator's individual evaluation of his needs, even in the 'hungry lands', where it seems that the law of diminishing returns is well understood, even if only empirically—Morgan writes of the peasant cultivator in tropical Africa:

. . . a closer examination of peasant agriculture than the mere measurement of holding sizes reveals that few peasants cultivate as much land as even their limited techniques would allow. They cultivate enough to satisfy their wants, and produce what surplus they estimate they can satisfactorily sell, exchange or give to friends or dependents. An important limitation is their own estimate of the value of the result of the labour expended . . . and, like many other peoples, they may put a high value on leisure and on the need to find time for other activities.[21]

Or again, forms of organization may be determined by the supply or shortage of a critical input—land, labour or capital. In many technically-advanced regions, for example, it is the cost or scarcity of farm labour which has been influencing operators' decisions in recent years. In Anglo-

[20] H. W. Ottoson and A. W. Epp, 'Size of Farm and Farming Efficiency in Northeastern Nebraska', *Journal of Farm Economics* 38 (1956), p. 811. See also J. V. McElveen, 'Farm Numbers, Farm Size and Farm Income', *idem.*, 45 (1963), 1–12, and J. P. Madden, *Economies of Size in Farming*, Agricultural Economics Report 107, U.S. Department of Agriculture, 1967.

[21] W. B. Morgan, 'Peasant Agriculture in Tropical Africa', in *Environment and Land Use in Africa* edited by M. F. Thomas and G. W. Whittington, Methuen, London, 1969, p. 244.

America, it is well known that the class of hired labourers on the farms has been rapidly declining in numbers (there remain only about one million of them, compared with over $2\frac{1}{2}$ million in the late forties), and this has increased the concentration of production units on the family farm, which augments its owner's labour with an array of machines. In Great Britain, where labour inputs are on average much larger per hectare than in Anglo-America (and in fact intermediate between these and the general level in continental Europe), the farmer's problem is to pay the ever-increasing wage bill and, on the smaller units, to employ even one man economically—on these units, labour costs can only be cut by enlarging the unit.

One effect of the cost and scarcity of farm labour which can be seen both in Britain and in some of the continental countries (Belgium is a good example) is that farmers have switched from livestock farming to simple arable operations. Not only does the former involve larger labour inputs, but the loss of experienced stockmen (who can earn more on routine jobs in a factory than they can exercising their acquired skills on the farm) is far more serious to the farmer than the comings and goings of, say, tractor drivers. In this way, land use tends to reflect cost of labour. It is one of the weaknesses of our contemporary economy that the wage structure does not take sufficient account of the kind of non-quantifiable skill which the stockman possesses.

Over much of the underdeveloped part of the world, it is not the labour factor which is critical; labour is abundant. It is capital which is in short supply, and the lack of capital limits the productivity of labour. As we saw in chapter two, labour and capital are largely interchangeable inputs in relation to final output but they are not, of course, in relation to the farmer's income. In the example we considered earlier (p. 28), in which both the Chinese and the American rice grower produced roughly the same amount of rice per hectare, the American cultivated 50 ha or more and obtained the gross income from the entire area, while the Chinese grower cultivated only a single hectare per crop season. Even allowing for the much higher level of costs to the American grower, his net income was many times greater than that of the Chinese grower. Furthermore, as table 16 showed, the American grower's yield is capable of being steadily increased through further capital inputs, while that of the capital-deficient Asian is likely to remain static (as we saw earlier in this chapter, yields in India have risen with desperate slowness in a period of recurrent regional famine). Some method of increasing capital availability is therefore essential if the general standard of living of the world's cultivators is to improve.

This standard of living is, of course, already maintained at an artificially high level in many countries. For a variety of reasons, governments support farmers and farm incomes. Originally, they did so for reasons of national security: a healthy peasantry was considered the backbone of the nation's army, and agricultural production the sinews of its war effort. In the great Corn Law controversy in Britain at the beginning of the nineteenth century, economic arguments were added to those concerned with security: the farm population accounted for a large proportion of the nation's total consumption and purchasing power, and must be kept in a prosperous state.[22] Most governments use incentives and controls in times of war and emergency to increase home production and reduce reliance on imported supplies. The question is then how much incentive is necessary or justified *in between* emergencies to keep the agricultural economy in a reasonable condition of readiness.

The answer to this last question depends in part on the structure of the national income. In a purely agricultural society it would obviously be impossible to subsidize agriculture other than by imposing a tax equal to the subsidy to be paid. In a country whose economy is mainly that of a primary producer, the amount of help the individual can be given is strictly limited, and it increases as the contribution of non-primary sources to national income grows larger. One place where this could be seen quite clearly was on the two sides of the border between the Irish Republic and Northern Ireland in the 1960s. In the republic, almost one quarter of the national income was derived from agriculture and fisheries, and subsidies for the farmer have until very recently been a luxury the nation could not afford: even now, they are minimal. Northern Ireland, on the other hand, enjoyed the benefit of all the subsidy and support schemes common to the rest of the United Kingdom, paid for by the tax-payers of a nation in which income from agriculture and fisheries represented in 1960 only four per cent of the total. Much the same contrast existed until recently between Canada and the U.S.A.—support for the Canadian farmer has become possible only as the secondary and tertiary sectors of the national economy have gained strength to the point where they can subsidize the primary sector.

But the level at which agricultural incomes are maintained also depends very significantly on political factors—on the power of the primary producers to influence legislation. If we wished to examine this subject in detail, we should have to go further and distinguish between separate agricultural interests—the interest of large landowners (which was dominant, for example, in eighteenth-century British politics) or of small-

---

[22] 'This was indeed an important and valid consideration, because at this time agriculture contributed a third or rather more of the national income and gave employment to about the same proportion of the employed population.' J. D. Chambers and G. E. Mingay, *The Agricultural Revolution 1750–1880*, Batsford, London, 1966, p. 122.

holders and tenants (as represented by the Peasant Party or Smallholders' Party in several east European states after 1918). But for present purposes it is sufficient to note that farmers everywhere watch price levels and bring to bear all kinds of pressure on price-controlling agencies, from blocking roads with tractors to lobbying their representatives in the legislature.

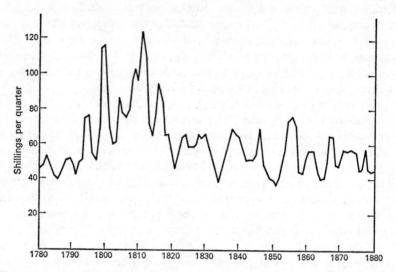

Figure 34: English wheat prices, 1780–1880. In considering these violent fluctuations it should be borne in mind that, for a considerable part of the period covered, there existed legislation designed to *control* these fluctuations—without which, of course, they would have been still more violent. (Reproduced by permission from J. D. Chambers and G. E. Mingay, *The Agricultural Revolution, 1750–1880*, London: G. Bell, 1966, figures 2 and 5.)

Non-agriculturalists who must pay for the support prices and subsidies then complain about 'feather-bedding'.

The farmers' case is built on memories of the way in which agricultural prices in the free market have fluctuated in the past. It is hard to imagine, for example, how rational plans of land use and farm management could be built up when wheat prices like those recorded in figure 34 were being registered year by year, in spite of the existence of various Corn Laws. During two world wars the farmer was wooed and pressed to increase his output. After the first of them he was almost immediately abandoned to his economic fate. After the second, he used his political influence to avoid being jettisoned again, a reflex which was entirely understandable, and reasonably successful.

We have seen, then, that the factors of production can be manipulated to serve any one of a number of aims, economic, social or political. The choice of these objectives is in some societies very powerfully influenced by government, assisted by its professional advisers in agricultural economics. Sometimes the influence is more doctrinaire than practical, and the objective is purely conceptual, whether it is expressed as 'the land for those who work it' or 'the family farm is the foundation of democracy'. In such cases, time usually betrays the weakness of mere dogma. But in primary production, whatever the political climate, it is still generally true that the individual producer counts; that it is he, short of capital, imperfectly informed, remote from his markets and harassed by weather and blight, who ultimately decides the pattern and volume of world output.

8

Secondary Activity: Manufacturing

The range of activities that fall within the secondary category is a very wide one, and it tails off at its extremities into a twilight zone where census takers and statisticians sometimes disagree over their definitions. But essentially this category covers the *activities of transformation*, or those operations in which materials are converted from one form to another. Such a transformation may involve several stages, each carried out in a separate plant, and not merely a single operation, and it may occur either in a craftsman's shop where hand processes are employed (as the origin of the word 'manufacture' suggests), or in an automated factory with computerized control. In the U.S.A., the world's largest industrial producer, the Census Bureau lists over 400 different kinds of manufacturing. When we multiply this variety of products by the variety of circumstances in which it is produced, we account for a very wide range of activity indeed. To use the word 'industry' without qualification, as if its content were predefined, is clearly to run the risk of gross over-simplification, and we must shortly attempt, in this chapter, to differentiate between industry and industry on the basis of the characteristics of each.

Secondary activity is, of course, very unevenly distributed across the world; much more unevenly than are primary or tertiary activities. Manufacturing can only exist where circumstances favour it. It is not a universal, but the result of conscious decision in a given place and at a particular time. It may be for this reason that it has attracted so much attention from geographers, for its presence presupposes a chain of reasoning and decision-making which, with an average amount of diligence or good fortune, the geographer may hope to unravel. Where there are people there must necessarily be primary production of some sort, but the presence of manufacturing activity can almost never be inferred from the population map; not even from the existence of a dense population or the presence of towns.

It is true that certain basic crafts, such as the making of clothes or ornaments, approach the universal. But the more complex forms of manufacturing occur with decreasing frequency until, at any particular moment of time, there is sure somewhere to be a factory advertising that it is 'the only plant in the world making this product by this process'. The most patent evidence in recent years of this specialization at the top has been the small size of the 'nuclear club'—the group of countries capable of producing their own nuclear power. But the size of the club is gradually growing while, at the lower end of the scale of manufacturers, the number of participating members has risen very significantly since the second world war.

Modern industry flourished first in Great Britain. During the two or three centuries before the Industrial Revolution Britain, like Spain and the other colonial powers of Europe, had done its best to *prevent* the simple industries of the day from springing up elsewhere—in the American empires, for example—so that Europe should act as the sole source of supply. Then in the nineteenth century came the great industrial advances and there were undoubtedly some short-lived hopes that, once again, Britain might achieve a monopoly of the production which her inventors had made possible. But there was, in practice, no way of doing more than delay the spread of the new techniques across national frontiers and soon, accepting the inevitable and adopting the converse doctrine of free trade, British engineers were installing machinery and building railways in a score of countries.

Nevertheless, up to the first world war, the number of countries which had independent manufactures of an advanced type was still small. Most of them were in Europe: overseas, there was the U.S.A. and, remote and unique in Asia, the emergent Japan (although the British had allowed some small measure of industrial growth in their Indian empire). There were the makings of a meat-packing industry in the Plate River region of South America and textile mills on the China coast, but even such a relatively advanced nation as Russia was industrializing only with the help of huge injections of capital provided by foreign investors.[1] Much of the world's cotton crop still moved from the growing areas to Lancashire and New England, to be returned later in the form of cotton cloth, while the countries which manufactured, say, railway engines could almost be counted on the fingers of one hand.

In the period between the two world wars a number of new members 'joined the club'. Among them were the newly-independent states in eastern Europe, but their progress had only been slight before they were engulfed in the General Depression. More threatening to the established club members was the rise of Japan, whose cheap manufactures in the twenties and thirties undermined the Lancashire cotton industry's hege-

[1] It is estimated that, in 1914, one third of all joint-stock capital in Russia was held by foreigners—mainly French, British, Belgian and German.

nomy and challenged a whole range of other British goods in the home market.[2] Other names began to appear on manufacturers' labels, and it is difficult now to recapture the shock of seeing them for the first time: shirts from India or Brazil; machinery from Canada; cars from Spain. Evidently, the club was enlarging, and the older manufacturing nations responded by abandoning production of the cheap and simple goods with which they had flooded the world markets, and by undertaking a sometimes painful search for products in which their superior technology enabled them to re-establish their industrial monopoly—motor cars, power-station equipment or electric trains.

Since the second world war the same processes have continued, but with different participants and different products. It is no longer the competition of Japanese textiles that Europe fears: the cheap textiles now come from Hong Kong and India. The impact of Japanese competition nowadays is felt at the most sophisticated levels of the world market— in the production of cameras, motor cycles, electronic and optical equipment. Japan, in turn, has become susceptible to the competitive pressure of newer arrivals, and the number of industrial nations has risen sharply. Indeed, there is probably not a state in the world today which does not have a programme that includes the creation or expansion of industry. Some of these programmes are, as we shall see later, wiser than others but, extravagant or sensible, they all stem from the same motives. One is the desire to become independent of foreign sources of manufactures (which many of the states in question in any case do not have the foreign exchange resources to buy), and the other is the desire to emulate those countries which are both wealthy and industrialized—and which therefore may give the impression that they are wealthy simply *because* they are industrialized.[3]

In practice, it has been rare for manufacturing to develop in a new area without help from an older one. We have already noted how, in the nineteenth century, British engineers could be found in many out of the way places, installing plant, training local labour and running railways. The twentieth century has seen this activity multiplied many times over, especially in the era of competitive international aid which has lasted from 1945 to the present day. There are Russian or American or Czech or Chinese engineers building factories and power plants throughout

---

[2] This was a period when British schoolchildren, like the author, were subjected to considerable propaganda at school to 'buy British' and, their own purchasing power being negligible, to harrass their parents into following this maxim, especially in refusing in the shops anything which bore the dreaded mark 'Made in Japan'.

[3] UNESCO lists manufacturing data for some 94 countries. See UNESCO, *The Growth of World Industry*, 1972 edition, New York, 1974.

much of Asia, Africa and Latin America. They are providing the technical base for an industrial society. The psychological base for such a society is, however, harder to create—that is, the acceptance of the new attitudes, skills and social groupings needed in a community whose previous organization has been rural and agricultural. That may prove, in the long run, the critical factor.

THE CHARACTER OF INDUSTRY

Among the numerous variables which distinguish one industry from another, the one which has been given most attention by geographers is the location variable. Geographers have a long-standing interest in the topic and there is a steadily growing volume of literature concerned with it, made up both of theoretical statements and of case studies. But before we come to consider this topic, it will be as well to review some of the factors which distinguish industry from industry and which consequently are responsible for the differences between industrial landscapes.

I SIZE OF UNIT

The first and most evident expression of the character of industry is the size of the industrial unit, the specialized premises where processing takes place. As we noted in chapter two, the development of such premises has been a necessary part of the growth of industry, because the processes involved could not be carried out in a home as spinning or weaving might be. The medieval craftsman in Europe, like the native craftsman in Africa or Asia today, could operate in a workroom in his own cottage or house. But the smith and the miller needed special premises, and when the transition began to the use of water or steam power, it brought with it the textile mill and the foundry.

The size of unit may vary a good deal from industry to industry, and even within the same industry.[4] Generally speaking, however, it varies with one or more of the following considerations:

(a) The volume of demand for the product.

(b) The economies of scale which can be achieved in the particular process involved.

(c) The number and complexity of processing techniques. It has become increasingly commonplace that processes which, formerly, would

[4] At Thiers, in central France, for example, where three quarters of the cutlery for French tables is produced, output is divided between a group of modern factories and a host of individual workshops in the ground-floor rooms and basements of the old town. The two produce cutlery side by side.

have been carried out in separate plants, perhaps many miles apart, are now carried out under a single roof. There is, for example, a clear cost advantage in organizing steel production on an integrated basis (see p. 224), so that the steel works handles the whole sequence from iron ore, through pig iron, to steel plate, without the heat losses involved in cooling, storing, shipping and reheating the intermediate products, the pig iron and crude steel.

(d) The size of the product. Large objects involve large plants. In the nineteenth century, some of the largest objects manufactured were railway locomotives and stock, and in that period the railway works at Swindon and Crewe and Springburn (Glasgow) were among the largest industrial units of the day. In the twentieth century, the obvious counterpart is the aircraft industry—an industry now manufacturing objects so large that, whenever possible, assembly and storage are carried out in the open, in the same way as in shipbuilding.

(e) The financial and managerial organization of the industry. Not only is there today a clear tendency towards concentration in industrial leadership, through mergers and take-overs, but there now exist communications sufficiently swift and flexible to make possible control of ten or twenty plants from a single headquarters. This centralized control results, in many cases, in the concentration in a single plant of work which had formerly been carried out in smaller, scattered units; that is, the reorganization may lead to an increase in the size of the individual plant. But in some cases the reverse is true; once sufficient central finance is available, manufacturers can plan the most rational size of unit, whatever it may be, under given market conditions so that instead, for example, of having the entire national output of their product concentrated in one place (a place where it may well be situated for historical reasons which bear no relation to modern markets), they can decentralize production into the various market areas. Whether or not centralized control leads to centralized operations depends in this case on company policy which, in turn, is likely to depend on distances involved and costs of transport for the manufactured article.

2 NUMBER AND TYPE OF EMPLOYEES

Assessments of industrial quality are very commonly, and understandably, made in terms of employment. The question 'How many people will be able to find work in the plant?' is one of obvious and immediate concern to the community in which it is located; it represents the social impact of the presence of secondary activity. The employment potential of industry has been a prime concern of governments and rural interests for a century and a half, since the factory era began to drain workers in large numbers off the land and force them into crowded urban slums; the farmer had to reckon with the flight of labour and the urban authorities had to grapple with the accommodation problem at the other end. More recently, employment potential has been the concern of local interests wishing to *attract* industries to areas where unemployment rates are high, and there is great local rejoicing when a new industrial plant is lured within the borough boundary.

But industries are no more alike in their employment potential than they are in other respects. According to the most recent Census of Manufactures, the U.S.A. has, in round figures, 300,000 industrial establishments and 19 million industrial employees, or an average of about 60 employees per establishment. In suburban Detroit, however, the Ford Motor Company employs a hundred thousand workers in its Dearborn-River Rouge complex. At the other end of the scale, there are around 50,000 industrial establishments in the U.S.A. recognized by the census which have no employed hands at all: they are simply family affairs. This is a measure of the range of size above and below the average of 60 workers. Even in a highly sophisticated industrial society like that of the U.S.A., only about one third of all establishments employ more than 20 workers.

The setting up of industry does not, therefore, involve or guarantee the provision of jobs for thousands of workers. And as time goes on, employment provided by industry forms a less and less reliable guide to development. Economics and human nature being what they are, manufacturers are constantly on the alert for ways of replacing employees by machines, which do not go on strike, fall sick or have personal problems. In other words, once an industry is established, *constant* output is likely to mean diminishing employment, and increased output will mean a less-than-proportional increase in employment. For the world as a whole (less the communist countries) if we take 1958 as index year ($=$ 100), industrial *production* rose from 42 in 1938 to 130 in 1962 but, during the same period, industrial *employment* rose only from 60 to 110.[5]

At least as important as total employment in industry, in fact, is the type of employment which is offered. Any community contains job-seekers of different kinds—male and female, middle-aged and school-leavers, more and less skilled or intelligent. An industry which offers only one type or level of employment does not provide that *balance* of jobs which the community needs. The early textile mills, for example, provided abundant employment for female labour at the lowest wage level, but almost nothing for male labour and little in the way of higher grades for

[5] UNESCO, *The Growth of World Industry, 1938–1961*, New York 1965, pp. 178, 188.

the ambitious. In this respect, one of the significant industrial phenomena of the present day is the way in which work in industry is tending to be 'upgraded'. The proportion of openings for unskilled workers offering little but brute strength has dwindled and, with it, the chance of gaining employment without proper education and training. A balance of employment is necessary if the unskilled are not to become a public burden or, on the other hand, the enterprising workers are not to be lost through frustration at unrewarding types of work.

But in economic terms the trend is clear: the replacement of men by machines which do the heavy work means that each labourer produces more, and this brings us to our next variable which serves to differentiate between types of industry.

3 VALUE ADDED BY MANUFACTURING

The benefit accruing to a community or nation from the operation of an industry is not best measured, then, by the number of workers employed, but by the sum total of extra incomes earned as a result of its presence. The transformation process adds to the value of the original materials, and it is the work expended on the transformation which results in wage payments. One common statistical index of the importance of a particular manufacture is therefore that known as Value Added by Manufacture (V.A.).[6] And the impact of this on the community at large is seen when we divide the V.A. by the number of employees, to arrive at the *Value Added per Employee*.

This figure varies greatly from industry to industry. If we again take the U.S.A. as an illustration, V.A. per employee in the various major groups of industries in 1970 was as shown in table 20. At the top of the table, the value is four times that at the foot. This does not mean, of course, that wages or profits are four times as high in the petroleum refining industry as they are in the clothing trade. It is necessary to bear in mind that the petroleum industry is one in which capital inputs are enormously high, so that interest charges and, in practice, tax demands are far greater than in the clothing trade, much of which is carried on in small back rooms and may involve little more capital input than a sewing machine. But this index doeś point to the wide differences between the structure of these industries. The top three groups on the list are industries in which a high degree of automation has been achieved: of the three, only the chemicals group in the U.S.A. has a large labour force

---

[6] The U.S. census definition of Value Added is: 'the sum arrived at by subtracting the cost of materials, supplies and containers, fuel, purchased electrical energy and contract work from the value of shipments for products manufactured plus receipts for services rendered.' This Value Added has then to cover wages and salaries, taxes, interest charges on capital, and profits.

(over 800,000 employees). The presence of this type of industry is likely to provide a few well-paid jobs.

Table 20   Manufacturing in the U.S.A.: value added per employee, by census groups, 1970

	$ (thousands)
Petroleum and coal products	37·2
Tobacco manufactures	34·9
Chemicals and allied products	31·9
Instruments and related products	19·6
Food and kindred products	19·5
Paper and allied products	17·5
Transportation equipment	17·1
Primary metal industries	16·9
Machinery excluding electrical	16·8
Stone, clay and glass products	16·6
Printing and publishing	16·0
Fabricated metal products	15·5
Rubber and plastic products, n.e.c.	15·4
Electrical equipment	15·1
Miscellaneous manufacturing	14·0
Furniture and fixtures	11·2
Lumber and wood products	10·7
Textile mill products	10·1
Leather and leather products	9·5
Apparel and related products	8·7
Average, all groups	15·5

At the bottom of the list are the industries whose low V.A. per employee means that $8,000–9,000 have to cover wages, all non-material charges *and* the profit to the owner, which makes them industries of low wage rates, part-time employment and small capital expenditures—in other words, hardly the type of industry to excite a community with an aggressive policy of attracting new employment. If, by coincidence, several industries with a low V.A. per employee are found in the same region, the situation is particularly serious. This was notoriously the case in New England before the second world war: its basic industrial employment (more than 40 per cent of the regional total in 1939) was in textiles and leather goods, two of the bottom three groups in the 'league table'. This meant that the region's industries were unable to renew adequately their old and wornout industrial equipment, despite a pressing need to do so in face of competition from better-equipped rivals; it also meant that the region lacked (though it has since been able to acquire) sufficient high-value industries to offset them.

If benefit to the local community is the criterion, then certain groups in table 20 stand out as most likely to have the desired effect; these are groups which *both* have a fairly high V.A. per employee *and* are themselves large employers of labour, so that the effect of their presence is as widespread as possible. Among these are certainly the food processing industries, and the manufacture of instruments and vehicles, and these groups have the additional advantage that they are, for the most part, inoffensive to their neighbours: they do not belch coloured smoke or keep nearby residents awake at nights. In a society which is economically and socially alert, all these factors are known and borne in mind. Industries are more or less welcome according to their characteristics, and this brings us to the next of our set of variables.

4 IMPACT ON THE ENVIRONMENT

Some industries are unpleasant neighbours. Because of fumes or noise or wastes generated in the transformation process, they create pollution or disturbance. They therefore tend to repel from their vicinity all but other industries like themselves and the poorest class of residential area and, in a period when zoning has become an accepted part of life and government, the range of locations open to them is severely restricted. Other types of industry, using electric power and a minimum of heat and pressure processes, are perfectly at home in residential areas and cause no more disturbance than, say, a school. This is an important consideration where the industry concerned is seeking labour supplies, particularly female labour, for a residential area is precisely where a labour reservoir is likely to be found.

The segregation of industries detrimental to the environment is now very largely taken for granted but this was not, unfortunately, the case in the early phases of industrial growth; it not only *was* not, but *could* not be taken for granted. The absence of any form of local transport made the plant and its workers interdependent. Smoke might shut out the sun and fumes might poison the air but the workers still had to be within walking distance of the factory. Today, it is not normally regarded as sufficient that a plant responsible for hazards to health or safety should be segregated from other land users. It goes without saying that an explosives works should be in open country, and it will be as well if the oil refinery is out there too, though on the opposite side of the town. But it is also expected nowadays that positive efforts will be made to cut down the emission of harmful wastes, whether they are fumes or liquids, and even when this adds a considerable cost burden to the manufacturers. In the past, the cleansing of waste has been left very largely to the conscience of the individual industrialist, but it is now clear that conscience is not enough, and that compulsion will be necessary. Lake Erie is a dead sea; poisons flow down the Rhine from Germany into the Netherlands; Chesapeake Bay oysters may well be off the menu because they are unsafe to eat.

Environmental impact is a factor, then, either in deciding the *location* of industry, by limiting the choice of sites available to it, or in the *costs* of industry, by adding to the normal costs the additional factor of purification.

5 THE COST STRUCTURE OF INDUSTRY

This brief survey of the ways in which industries differ from one another is best brought to a focus by considering one further variable; one which, in practice, plays a large part in influencing the location of industry. This is the *cost structure*. By this we mean the proportion of total costs contributed by each major factor in the transformation process—raw material, labour, power, transport, taxes and capital charges. In particular cases it may then be important to go further and determine the proportion of these costs which is *fixed*, or independent of the volume of the industry's output, and the proportion which is *variable*, in accordance with that volume. It may also be of importance to calculate the *timing* of costs incurred—for example, when an industry involves a large initial outlay of capital before production can begin. Analysis of these costs will influence both output and location: it will affect the choice of a site where total costs can be minimized and also suggest to the manufacturer departments in which useful economies can be made.

We have already encountered this idea of cost structure in other contexts—once when assessing the relative advantages of thermal- and hydroelectric power (p. 132) and once when reviewing the efforts of the railways to make their operations more competitive. In the latter case we saw that, contrary to what might be expected, the bulk of the year-to-year costs borne by railway do not arise out of its material holding of rails or stations or locomotives, or their upkeep, but out of labour costs: 60 per cent of railways costs were, until recently at least, accounted for in this way. No matter what economies are adopted in other departments— greater economy, say, in the use of coal or diesel fuel—three fifths of costs remain unaffected; the major source of future economies is to reduce labour inputs. In industry, the same kind of consideration applies, with the additional factor that a railway is tied geographically and an industry need not be; if necessary an industry can move to another location where its particular cost structure is better served.

The idea of cost structure is often presented these days visually by the mass media; perhaps the commonest example is the government's periodic diagram showing how the tax pound is divided among the various costs of government services. In industry, no two types of manufacturing have precisely the same cost structure. Table 21 illustrates this with reference

Table 21 Manufacturing in the U.S.A.: payroll as a percentage of value of shipment, by census groups, 1970

	Percent
Printing and publishing	33·9
Miscellaneous manufacturing	32·4
Electrical equipment	30·6
Machinery excluding electrical	29·7
Furniture and fixtures	28·9
Leather and leather products	28·3
Instruments and related products	28·2
Fabricated metal products	27·1
Stone, clay and glass products	26·6
Apparel and related products	
Rubber and plastic products, n.e.c.	26·0
Lumber and wood products	24·6
Textile mill products	22·8
Transportation equipment	22·3
Paper and allied products	21·6
Primary metal industries	21·1
Chemicals and allied products	16·1
Food and kindred products	12·0
Tobacco manufactures	8·3
Petroleum and coal products	6·0
Average, all groups	22·4

to a single variable: the proportion of value of shipment for each industry group in the U.S.A. which is accounted for by payroll. (This is the closest one can come, on a national scale, to finding the proportion of total *costs* represented by the cost of labour.) It is evident that the range of variation is even wider than in table 20; as we might expect, the two tables present the industry groups, measured by these criteria, in roughly inverse order. If similar calculations are made for the proportion of costs attributable to raw materials or power, they give a guide to the significance each of these factors is likely to be accorded in planning for the particular industry in question.

Cost analysis also plays a part in determining the geography of manufacturing in those countries or areas where it is decided, for reasons of policy, that industry should be introduced, and the question then arises: *what kind* of industry should be encouraged? Where labour is plentiful and cheap, as it is likely to be in an underdeveloped country, then a labour-intensive industry like textiles makes an obvious choice, rather than an industry in which a large amount of capital investment and outside technical aid are necessary before a single local labourer gets a day's work in the plant.

THE LOCATION OF INDUSTRY

The presence of industry presupposes

1   the collection of materials at a point where processing can take place
2   the processing itself, which implies inputs of labour and power
3   shipment of the finished product.

These three phases, assembly, processing and shipment, are found in virtually all industries. In a very few cases (such as the processing of mine products at the pithead) the assembly phase is eliminated, but normally the object of the manufacturer is to find a location in which the central function—processing—can be carried out between the other two.

This simple location decision is represented by figure 35a. But so far we have nothing to suggest *where*, between the source of the raw material and the market, the processing should take place. One way of deciding this would be to weight the various factors in our diagram according to the quantities they represent. But as we have already seen in chapter four, it is not the weight alone but the cost of moving this weight of material which is the decisive factor. Instead of a simple flow diagram, therefore, we now have a series of weights, each resistant to movement away from its source in proportion to the unit cost per km of moving it (figure 35b). Once we are operating in cost terms we can, of course, include in the calculation such factors as electric power, which do not involve physical movement as such at all. The greater the resistance, the greater the economic penalty for locating the processing plant at a distance from that particular input source or outlet.

Insofar as the raw material sources, the power supply and the market represent fixed locations, therefore, we can visualize each of them as surrounded by a series of concentric *isotims* or lines joining points with equal costs of each supply factor. (In a particular case, the labour input might be treated in the same way, but it is unusual for labour to be concentrated at a point or to be moved elsewhere as a part of a regular input sequence, since it possesses its own, built-in mobility.) We then have the situation represented by figure 35c. Given this situation, it is relatively straightforward to determine the point or points at which

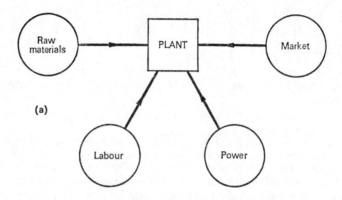

(a)

(b)

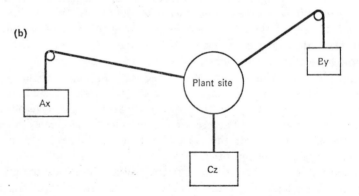

Figure 35: The location of industry: diagrams to illustrate the principles discussed in the adjoining text. The simple assembly diagram (**a**), which disregards quantities and distances, can be modified as in (**b**) to take account of assembly costs, where A, B and C are the quantities involved and x, y and z are the costs of movement per ton-km. An equilibrium or least-cost-of-assembly location can then be calculated.

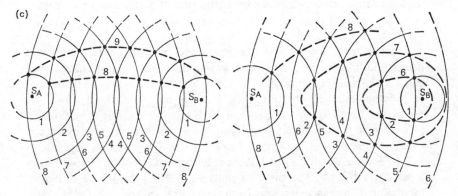

Figure 35c: Assembly costs can be conceived of as concentric circles centred upon source or destination points: they represent unit cost of movement to or from these points. Total cost of assembly is given by the sum of the unit costs at any given point, and lines (isovectures) can be drawn joining points of equal total cost, as shown in the left-hand diagram. Note, however, that with two sources, as soon as we make the assumption that the cost of movement to and from one point (S_B) increases more rapidly than for another point (S_A), then S_B becomes automatically the point with the lowest total assembly cost (right-hand diagram).

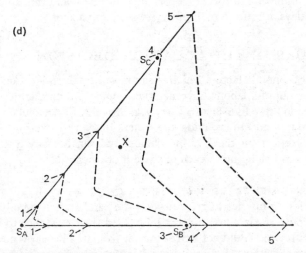

Figure 35d: The real isotims around a point are seldom if ever concentric circles as in (**c**); their spacing depends on the structure of freight rates, and is usually highly irregular, depending on the network of transport lines and on exceptions made for particular places, as with S_B and S_C on the diagram. The cost of movement to and from any point X which is *not* directly on a transport line depends in practice on the cost of trans-shipment and the type of carrier.

total costs of assembly and distribution are at a minimum. This can be done either empirically or by using one of the conceptual frameworks of location evolved by economists and geographers from Alfred Weber to August Lösch and their successors.[7]

Even while we are constructing figure 35c, of course, we know that it needs modifying to conform to reality. For one thing, only in a minority of cases is the market a single location; it is much more likely to be an area entirely surrounding the industrial location and, as such, it cannot be represented on this type of diagram at all, although it might be possible to represent it, say, as an underlying trend surface whose character is based on population density or income level. For another, the cost of movement is unlikely to be uniform outwards from a point. Freight rates taper with distance (p. 105), so that our isotims should be drawn at increasing distances apart away from the centre. In any case, freight rates apply along lines of transport and not to each and every point within a particular radius from the point of origin of the freight. The true figure of movement-cost away from a point is, if we bear in mind all that was said in chapter four about freight rates, much more like figure 35d than it is like the regularly-spaced pattern of isotims with which we began. These complications in fact make it difficult to construct a realistic general location model, but they do not of course hinder the individual manufacturer from carrying out an empirical study for his own plant before committing himself to a particular location, and this kind of study is, nowadays, a routine preliminary to selecting a site.

FACTORS IN THE LOCATION DECISION

The four economic factors which weigh most heavily in location decisions are power supply, labour, raw material sources and market. Only rarely, however, do these four factors carry *equal* weight. In particular cases, one of the four tends to override the other three, and exert a dominant, anchoring effect on the location choice. We can identify a number of industries as belonging to each of these four categories:

I POWER-ORIENTATED INDUSTRIES

The earliest industries to grow beyond the handicraft stage of technique were all power-orientated, in that they owed their existence to a specific power source and could not move far away from it. There was no means of applying water power far from the mill wheel, and the early iron industry seldom strayed far from its charcoal source in the forest. When in the late eighteenth century coal became the prime source of industrial power,

[7] The subject of locational analysis and references to the work of Weber, Lösch etc. are referred to again in the Postscript.

the concentration of manufacturing on the coalfields became virtually a law of nature. Proximity to coal supplies overrode almost all other considerations; certainly it overrode the amenity factor, as the industrial workers knew to their cost.

Power supplies today possess a flexibility which has greatly reduced this particular influence on location decisions. But it still exists for a few industries, whose power requirements are very large: the best-known group is made up of those using the electrolytic method of smelting metals, especially aluminium.[8] Whether in the west of Scotland or the St Lawrence Valley of Canada, the aluminium industry depends on an abundant supply of electric power, and the importance of this factor is seen in the location of the processing plants not merely far from the sources of bauxite (the ore of aluminium) and the plants producing alumina (the intermediate product), but far from all other settlement, in places as remote as Kitimat, on the west coast of Canada at 54°N.

2 LABOUR-ORIENTATED INDUSTRIES

There are two types of situation in which labour supply tends to dominate location assessment. One is where a very large plant requires a work force of, say, 20,000 labourers, as is often the case in the motor vehicle industry. It is obvious that in only a small number of locations can such a force be assembled and that a large labour reservoir is needed to provide the variety of skills and trades which the plant will require if it is to operate. A plant of this kind will, almost necessarily, have to be located close to a first-rank city, if it is to attain optimum economies of scale. This is, perhaps, most clearly seen in the case of the West German motor car industry, where the Opel works draw on the Frankfurt-Mainz conurbation and Mercedes-Benz draws its labour from Stuttgart—but even so has to send its buses out into the surrounding villages to reinforce the labour available in this city of 600,000 people. And the fact that the Volkswagen plant at Wolfsburg is *not* on the fringe of a city caused constant difficulties for the management, as the company increased in size so spectacularly in the post-war years.

The other situation in which labour supply is of paramount importance is where not the quantity but the quality of the supply is involved. There are still some trades in which the skills required are so specialized that the industry must be wherever the workers are. Probably the best example of this specialized locational hold is offered by the chinaware industry of the English Potteries. In its origins, this industry owed something to local coal supplies and something, too, to the canal system by which the china clay was brought to the potter. Today, the kilns may be fired by electricity

[8] It requires 20–22 kw hours of electricity to convert one kilogram of alumina into aluminium.

and the canal is unimportant, but the industry remains in its old location, because its labour force is, in the short term at least, irreplaceable in every

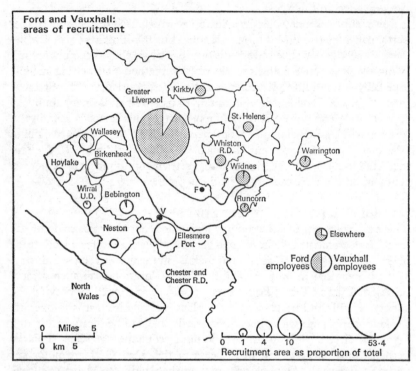

Figure 36: The labour hinterland of a major plant: the case of car production in the Merseyside region. The map shows the area from which two vehicle manufacturers, Ford and Vauxhall, draw their labour. (Reproduced by permission from J. Salt, 'The Impact of the Ford and Vauxhall Plants on the Employment Situation of Merseyside, 1962–1965', *Tijdscrift voor economische en sociale geografie* 58, Rotterdam, 1967, p. 257.)

sense of the word. Only if workers and plant are moved together can relocation occur. In the years after the second world war, this very thing happened as whole groups of workers made their way from East Germany into the west. Given the presence of the workers, it was no problem to re-establish the industry in a new location—in those days, often enough a barn or village hall—because the major asset, the work force, had been preserved intact.

3 RAW MATERIAL-ORIENTATED INDUSTRIES
There is a large group of industries in all of which the manufacturing

process is accompanied by a loss of weight or other reduction in the cost of movement. As a result, there is every incentive to carry out the processing as close as possible to the source of the raw materials, so as to waste as little transport space as possible on hauling valueless material.

Among the most important members of this group of industries are all those which convert bulky natural products into manufactures or semi-manufactures—the products of mines, forests and agriculture. There is no point in carrying a mineral ore containing 1 per cent or less of metal any further than is strictly necessary, before separating it from the 99 per cent of waste. A rich ore—say a 60 per cent iron ore—may stand the transport, but as the ore becomes leaner so its journey is likely to become shorter, and it may first undergo the intermediate step known in North America as 'benefication' to reduce the waste and enrich the ore before carrying it. Much the same is true of the forest products industry, which is typically deployed with even its most sophisticated units—the pulp and paper mills—only a short collecting journey from the logging frontier. What is true of trees is true also of agricultural produce like sugar,[9] and it is becoming increasingly true of livestock products, too, for the meat-packing industry has shown a tendency in recent years to move out from the big cities, nearer to the farms and ranches.

A rather more specialized example of an industry situated in relation to raw material supply is that of the 'linked' industry, which uses the by-product of some other plant and is therefore often to be found at its gates. The petroleum and chemical industries today contain many examples of these linkages, some of which are in lineal descent from the industries that grew up around the coal mines and produced coal-tar or dyes. The modern lumber industry is another case in point; beside a major mill there are likely to be a whole row of smaller plants using chips, sawdust or bark to turn out hardboard and other aggregates.

4 MARKET-ORIENTATED INDUSTRIES

If the last group of industries we have been considering are those in which there is a *loss* of weight in processing, this fourth group consists of those in which, by contrast, either there is a *gain* of weight in processing or the cost of transporting the finished product is much higher than that for the raw material.

This is a large and growing group. It contains, for example, all those

---

[9] It is normally true of cereals, too, which lose bulk by milling. However, in North America, as an exception to this general situation, the freight rates on milled and unmilled cereals are deliberately adjusted so that there is no cost advantage in milling at a particular point en route from the farmer to the market. This gives all the mill towns along the shipment axes an equal opportunity of sharing the business.

industries which market their product elaborately packaged. A gallon of fluid in a metal container is easily transported but, divided up into half-ounce bottles in fancy cartons and sold as expensive perfume it has become a cargo of quite a different character. The range of this type of goods is steadily increasing; it is a function of rising standards of living.

This being the case, it may seem strange that another member of this same market-orientated group is the steel industry. But today this is so: as we saw in chapter four, the cost of transporting the finished steel product is high in relation to the rates on coal and iron ore and as, in any case, technical changes in the industry are reducing the volume of inputs of the raw materials, their influence upon the location decision is lessening. At the same time, there is an increase in the number of steel mills which ship not simply crude steel in ingots or bars but strip, plate or fabricated forms, all of which carry a higher freight rate than the simple product.

One of the most elaborate products of the steel industry nowadays is the motor car. On the very broad scale provided by the North American continent we can see how there has been a tendency to market orientation in the motor vehicle industry too. Although its focus is still in Michigan, the industry has set up assembly plants in all the main regional markets. By this means it is possible to ship, relatively cheaply, the components of the vehicles (which are put together at the market) and so to avoid shipping for thousands of miles a product which, after all, involves a considerable amount of empty space in its 'packaging'.

Given the necessary data, it is possible to identify the point or points at which the combined assembly costs of these four factors of production either are at a minimum or will yield the greatest margin of profit. To the four major factors it may then be necessary to add such other considerations as local levels of rates and taxes, which may vary enough to affect costs at a choice of sites. But even when the least-cost location is known, it is by no means certain that it will be chosen by the manufacturer for there are, in practice, other factors beside these to affect his decision.

One of these is the legacy of past investment, which creates location inertia even when the original choice of site has ceased to be the least-cost location. Let us imagine that, under careful assessment of the assembly costs, a steel mill costing £50 million has been erected at the least-cost point. A change in transport or technology then alters the cost structure,[10] and the steel company faces the fact that its costs would now be diminished by £0·3 or £0·5 per ton if it moved to a fresh location and built a new mill for £60 million. But the chances of selling the old plant for even a fraction of its original cost are slight: buyers of secondhand

[10] For ways in which this may happen, see the next section.

steel mills at higher-than-least-cost locations are few and far between. The company must then calculate how many tons of steel it will have to produce in order to justify the new investment. At a saving of £0·3 per ton, the move will pay for itself only after the company has produced 180 million tons or so of steel; that is, it may take 75 to 100 years for the move to justify itself in cost savings and, long before then, *new* changes in cost structure will have occurred and the company will, like the Bedouin, have had to fold its tents and move on again. Unless there is some prospect of expanding sales and justifying the new plant in these terms alone, the company will simply stay where it is and absorb the higher costs.

The steel industry faces this problem in a particularly acute form, for there are few other industries which call for so large a fixed investment. But the fact is that very little of the steel industry in the main producing countries is ideally situated in today's circumstances: there are a few modern plants whose location approaches the optimum, but in due course they will join the other, older plants which have already lost the initial advantage they once had. It was the recognition of this reality which led the American steelmakers, in the early 1900s, to attempt to protect their investment by a remarkable kind of stage-managed industrial inertia which became known as Pittsburgh Plus. Led by the great U.S. Steel Corporation (which was founded in 1901), the steelmakers agreed that all steel sold in the U.S.A. would be priced at *cost plus transport from Pittsburgh,* even though it had actually been manufactured only a step from the customer's door. Pittsburgh was where the industry's major investment was centred and, by pricing on this basis, the steelmen made it pointless for anyone to erect a new plant, in a particular market area, which would compete with the rest of the industry still based at Pittsburgh. For two and a half decades, until the U.S. Supreme Court struck down the arrangement as illegal, Pittsburgh Plus worked well for the steel industry and protected its investment. And by operating efficiently within the framework they had created, the steelmen even managed to satisfy a reasonable number of their customers too.

A second situation which arises in practice when location decisions have to be made is that created by the existence of a wide range of site choices with equal costs. A number of industrial cost factors these days—the price of electricity, for example, or the level of wages—are constant over a whole region, if not a whole country. In this sense, they become a matter of indifference in the location decision, which is then taken on other grounds. There used to be cited examples of plants whose location was chosen because the owner was a keen golfer or fisherman and wanted to be near a favourite golf course or stream. These examples were not so wild as might at first appear: they simply meant that, within what might be called the circle of indifference one site is as good as another from the point of view of costs, and there is no reason why some other factor, such as golf courses, should not be used to tip the balance in favour of a particular choice of site.

The more common case, however, is that of the company choosing from among several equal-cost locations on the basis of social amenity for its workers and executives. In this respect, the whole business of plant location has changed for the better since the period when only a minority of enlightened manufacturers took into their accounting the social costs involved in their decisions. If the old philosophy was, approximately, 'where there's muck there's brass', the new attitude to plant location is much closer to that of the manufacturer who said, 'A city in order to be attractive to industry must first be attractive in itself.' In the competitive atmosphere and broad expanses of countries in the Americas or Australasia, there may be a dozen widely-separated locations where total costs are comparable, and the final choice among them is taken on such grounds as: 'What is the quality of the schooling available? Are the home-owners houseproud? What recreational facilities are there?' Some communities, in their anxiety to attract industry, may offer bargain levels of rates and local taxes, but these tend to act as a disincentive to a thoughtful manufacturer, since only by contributing a fair share to local revenues can he reasonably expect efficient services in return.

On a much larger scale, most governments nowadays pursue a policy of the same kind, the object of which is to obtain a distribution of industry suited to the needs of the country and its regions, whether these needs are economic or social; in either case, they are of political importance. At the local level, zoning restrictions are designed to protect the community against industrial intrusions which might damage the social environment. At the regional level, efforts may be made to get industry either to move to regions where unemployment is high or to stay out of regions which are becoming overcrowded. The first object is generally achieved by granting loans or suspension of national taxes for an initial period at central government expense. The second object can be achieved by withholding building permits from industry in the overcrowded areas, as in the case of the London region, or Paris, or the Ruhr. In principle, the higher costs to industry of being diverted away from the least-cost location are absorbed by central funds, and the manufacturer is compensated, at least in the short term, for modifying his choice.

At the national level, a government may pursue a policy of planned industrialization, usually behind a tariff wall, in order to free itself from dependence on external sources of manufactures. In this case, the location of its industries becomes a matter of political convenience rather than economics—at least as long as the tariff wall stands, and the uneconomically placed producers are not subjected to outside competition. In the same

way, a government may adopt a national policy of industrial decentraliza-
tion for strategic reasons, a policy which has been formulated, at various
times, by governments as dissimilar as those of the U.S.A., Nazi Germany and the U.S.S.R.

In all the cases we have been considering, there is the same refusal to
let economic conditions alone decide questions of industrial location. This
is, of course, all very well so long as the community is wealthy enough, and
agreeable enough, to absorb the higher costs involved. But if this policy
is carried to its logical conclusion, in a country hoping to export manufactures and keep its tariff barriers low, there comes a point where the
social costs built into industrial production price the manufacturer out
of the market. At home, industrial production is being subsidized by
the taxpayer: abroad, the industrial product is no longer competitive.[11]

This has led to some heated discussion among economists and planners
as to the extent to which it is sensible or useful to encourage industry to
locate in places which are not even approximately least-cost locations.
Usually, the alternative is to bring the labour—in this context, the unemployed—to the least-cost location rather than to move the plant to the
labour supply. In practice, of course, no one suggests that labour can be
shifted in the same way as coal or steel: most people, certainly most
people in Europe—the Americans being much less earth-bound in this
respect—are reluctant to leave their home territory, even for better
employment openings elsewhere. Short of direction of labour (an unacceptable solution in peace-time in most civilized societies) the result is
bound to be a compromise solution. *Some* workers will move, and *some*
will refuse to do so, and for these it may be possible to provide local
industrial employment by inducing manufacturers to enter the area. But
this should almost certainly be done sparingly.

LOCATION CHANGES

Even where a least-cost location has been carefully sought and adopted
by a manufacturer, it is liable to change in time. These changes may be
due either to alterations in the cost of assembling the factors of production,
i.e. in the transport costs, or to changes in the technology used by the

[11] This can happen *within* a country too, if there is considerable local freedom to set conditions for the manufacturer. In the U.S.A., for example, one of
the main factors contributing to the transfer of the cotton textile industry from
New England to the Carolinas after 1920 was the burden placed on manufacturers in the former by state legislation. Their costs were increased by such
factors as the refusal of some northern states to allow women to work on a night
shift, and property taxes up to five times the level in the southern states on
each spindle installed.

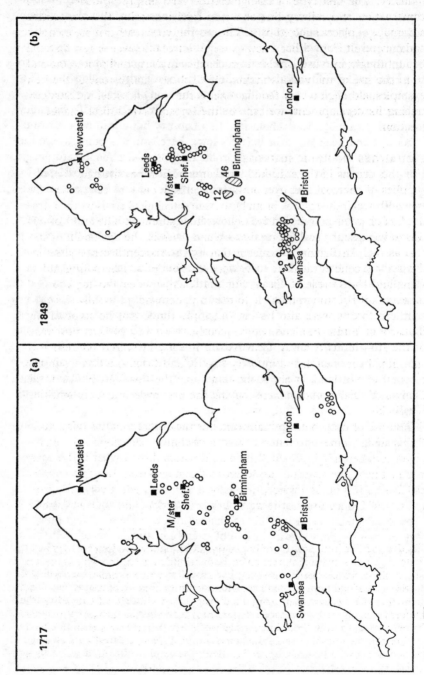

Figure 37: *see opposite.*

industry. The first type of change can be very simply produced by the construction of a railway line or a new road increasing the competitive advantage of places affected by it. The second type is rather more complex and may result from either a new external source of power or raw material being brought into use, or else from changes in the actual processing and so in the size of the various inputs. Of all these changes one of the best examples, although a very familiar one, is the iron and steel industry. By tracing its development, we can see the impact of technical change on location.

I CHANGES IN FUEL SOURCES
From its origins in the scattered ironworks of Europe, situated wherever supplies of charcoal and iron ore were available close to each other, the iron and steel industry was brought to its first technical crisis by the introduction of water power to drive bellows and hammers. The effect of this was to increase the scale of production and, with it, the demand for charcoal as fuel. In Britain this meant that by the sixteenth century the industry was concentrated in such wooded areas of southern England as Kent and the Forest of Dean, but that then, as demand for charcoal increased, it become impossible to meet the demand, especially since the southern forests were also having to supply timber to the shipbuilding industry of Tudor England. Consequently, there took place a movement of the iron industry away from its old haunts, in search of fresh fuel supplies. In its search the industry finally, and briefly, took root in the far west of Scotland, at about the same time that, back in England, the Darbys of Coalbrookdale were making the first experiments in smelting with coke.

The use of coal, both to make coke for the furnace and to raise steam for driving mine machinery, was a technical development of the eighteenth century in Great Britain, and it established what is, for most people today, the 'natural' association of coal and iron. But in a country as close to Britain as France, this association dates effectively only from the 1850s. France fought the wars of the revolution, and overran Europe,

Figure 37: The iron industry of England and Wales: furnace locations 1717 and 1849. The maps give an impression of the distribution of the industry in the late stages of the charcoal period (*on left*), when it still retained a connection with the forest areas of southern England and after a century or more of coal/coke smelting (*on right*). On the 1849 map, which was based on a Royal Commission's enquiries, many of the furnace *locations* possessed several furnaces. (Adapted by permission from B. L. C. Johnson, 'The Charcoal Iron Industry in the Early Eighteenth Century', *Geographical Journal* 117, London: Royal Geographical Society, p. 168, and A. Birch, *The Economic History of the British Iron and Steel Industry, 1784–1879*, London: Frank Cass, 1967, appendix III.)

with a native iron industry based on the charcoal furnace, though with help from the metal workers of the Meuse Valley in Belgium—an area to which belonged some of the earliest coke-using furnaces of continental Europe.

By the end of the nineteenth century, however, much of the iron industry was located on the coalfields, and all the largest concentrations were: in southern Yorkshire and South Wales in Britain; in the Ruhr in Germany, and western Pennsylvania in the U.S.A. Since that time, the industry has tended to free itself once again from this tie: the development of modern transport makes it no more difficult, and no more expensive, to transport coal than iron ore, so that we find coal and ore travelling to meet each other—for example, at a coastal location (Dunkerque, Trenton) where the ore arrives by sea and the coal by rail or canal.

2 CHANGES IN TECHNIQUE

The iron and steel industry is of interest because, although the products have been known and manufactured for millennia, the techniques of making them have continued to change right up to the present day. These changes centre upon two aspects of production: (a) the improvement of fuel use and (b) the making of steel, as opposed to pig iron.

(a) The first of these series of changes has had the effect of loosening the industry's long-standing tie to its fuel source: the individual weighting to be assigned to this input factor has been reduced. In the coal/coke phase, the process began with the introduction of Neilson's 'hot blast' in 1829. It was found that, by blowing hot air through the furnace, it was possible to cut coal consumption by as much as a half. The merging of iron smelting and steel making—formerly two distinct industries—into a single process in the integrated and continuous mills of the twentieth century led to further reductions in fuel input, since re-heating was no longer required.[12] Then in the last decade and a half further remarkable fuel economies have been achieved by the introduction into steel making of the oxygen-using LD process (named after the Austrian towns of Linz and Donawitz where it was developed). By blowing high-pressure oxygen onto the surface of the converter charge, fuel requirements have once again been cut by a third to a half. With all these developments continuing, the British Steel Corporation could report in 1970 that the heat input necessary to produce one ton of crude steel had fallen as follows:

[12] It is interesting to notice that, in some of the older steel-making areas, which date from the pre-integration period, the advantages of integration have been sought by linking the blast furnace to the steel mill by means of heat-proof railway trucks, on which the molten iron is transported to the steel mill exactly as if it were in a thermos flask. For example, a separation of some 10 km between the two parts of the industry on either side of Liège in Belgium is bridged by means of a constant procession of these railway trucks.

Therms

1955	339
1960	299
1964	276
1969	268

(b) Before the middle of the nineteenth century the making of steel was a slow, small-scale and therefore very costly business. It was produced in small quantities by hammering or by 'puddling'; yet there were any number of uses for which it was ideally suited in the new technology, if only the price could be brought down.

The first breakthrough came with the Bessemer converter of 1856. Bessemer's invention yielded cheap steel, in quantity—but only from non-phosphoric iron ores. In the U.S.A. in the 1850s, the newly-tapped Lake Superior ores were non-phosphoric hematites, and the industry based on them mushroomed with the demand for its new product. Great Britain was less fortunate. Its only important hematite ores were in Cumberland and although their presence was enough to draw a few units of the industry to north-western England, the majority of steel-makers had to use imported ores, such as those from Spain. When the Open Hearth furnace appeared in 1869, it made a better quality of steel, but still not from phosphoric ores.

Then in 1878–9 came the second breakthrough—the Gilchrist Thomas process. By lining the converter or hearth with a material of basic chemical reaction (in practice dolomitic limestone), the inventors succeeded in extracting the phosphoric slag without destroying the furnace lining. The new process attracted immediate attention, and nowhere more so than in eastern France. The Franco-Prussian war of 1870 had ended with the annexation to the new German empire of much of the iron ore area of Lorraine. Just how this area might have been revalued and the frontier redrawn if the Gilchrist Thomas process had been introduced ten years earlier is interesting to speculate: certainly, the process enabled the French on their side to expand steel production from the phosphoric ores notably in the years that followed.[13]

Since the 1870s steel-making techniques have continued to change. For one thing, the industry now makes extensive use of scrap to replace pig iron: some units are geared to 100 per cent scrap consumption. This makes it feasible to locate a steel mill in an area remote from either iron ore or blast furnace—in the vicinity, say, of a large city with a high mortality rate among its motor vehicles. For another, electricity has joined

[13] See R. Hartshorne, 'The Franco-German Boundary of 1871', *World Politics* 2 (1950), pp. 209–50.

charcoal,[14] coke and gas as fuel sources for the steel industry. Electrical furnaces account for about six per cent of British steel capacity and are particularly important in Scandinavia: they are expensive to operate, but have the advantages that they can function entirely on scrap and that they give a very close control over quality.

Over its long career, the iron and steel industry has been influenced in its location by a whole series of factors—fuel, ore supplies and markets, and today units of the industry can be found in places which represent all these influences. We have seen that, because of the size of the investment represented by a steel mill (p. 218), the industry feels the inertia effect of this investment as, perhaps, no other type of industry does. It is not altogether surprising, therefore, that over a period steel mills take on something of the distribution of giant whales stranded on the beach, each left there by a succeeding tide, and impossible to move once that technological tide has ebbed.

INDUSTRIAL REGIONS, OLD AND NEW

We saw at the beginning of this chapter that the distribution of manufacturing activity around the world is very uneven, and the distribution of large-scale, factory-based industry is still more strikingly so. Before bringing the chapter to an end, we must briefly consider the particular areas where it *is* concentrated—the industrial regions.

Industrial agglomerations may be of two kinds:

1   an agglomeration of plants all of which manufacture the same type of goods within an area, as in the case of the Yorkshire woollen industry or the cotton textile region of the Appalachian Piedmont

2   a grouping of industrial plants making many different types of goods, drawn together within a region by some attractive force which that region provides.

In the first case, the dominant regional industry is likely to benefit by the presence of a pool of labour skilled in the trades associated with it, by the opportunity for regionwide supply and marketing organization, and by the opportunity for specialization among the plants. In the second case, the various industries obtain the benefit of a very wide range of local supplies and of a balanced regional economy from which they all profit. In both cases manufacturers are attracted to an industrial region by the fact that such an agglomeration can sustain a well-developed transport network and a wide range of specialized technical and financial services; it is the

[14] Charcoal is still used in steel mills. In Brazil, in 1965, about one third of the blast furnace output was charcoal-based. See W. Baer, *The Development of the Brazilian Steel Industry*, Nashville, 1969.

existence of the agglomeration which makes this possible. Once formed, it tends to attract newcomers—at least up to the point where growing congestion acts as a disincentive and dispersal begins.

The earliest industrial regions of the western world can probably be identified as the region of the north Italian cities and the Low Countries, especially Flanders.[15] In both of them, the same factors can be seen at work:

1   the accumulation of capital resulting from trade, the eastern trade in the case of northern Italy and the trade of north-west Europe in the Low Countries;
2   the movement of a great variety of goods into and through these areas, since each served as an entrepôt region and handled a far wider range of commodities than was common in its period of growth;
3   urban growth and increasing population density, with a supply of labour therefore available;
4   a strategic situation in relation to the trade routes of the day.

Without trying to decide the exact sequence of these developments, we can see how *transport* and *capital accumulation* played the critical formative roles in these earliest industrial regions, one of which reached its zenith in the thirteenth century and the other in the fourteenth. Five centuries later, the same combination of factors was to create in the commercially active trading community of New England the first industrial region of the New World.

The several generations of industrial regions which have developed since the Industrial Revolution may be seen as the product of a variety of stimuli. One or two, like that of the southern Urals, have grown up on a basis of raw material supplies, in this case minerals and especially iron ore. But by far the largest group of these regions are fuel-orientated; quite simply, they correspond to the coalfields of Europe and eastern North America and, for that matter, of India and Japan too. Their names are the names of coalfields, from western Pennsylvania to the Ruhr, the Sambre-Meuse, the Donbas and Kuznetsk. The coal fuel formed the common element attracting a wide variety of power-using industries to the field,

[15] In the first half of the fifteenth century, the populations of Europe's leading cities are estimated to have been:

Venice	190,000	Milan	80,000
Paris	150,000	Ghent	60,000
Palermo	100,000	Brussels	50–60,000
Florence	90,000	Antwerp	50–60,000
Genoa	80,000	London	40,000

The importance of the two regions mentioned above is clear.

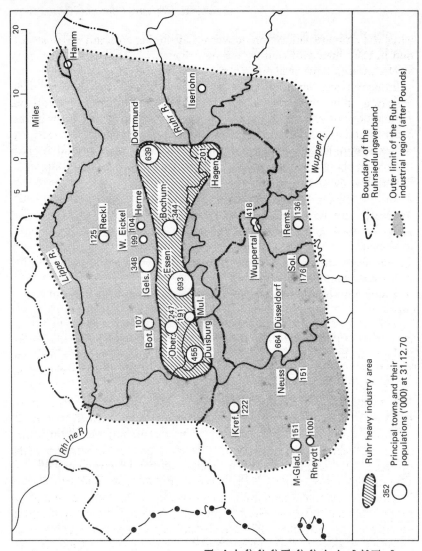

Figure 38: An industrial region: core and periphery. Taking the Ruhr as an example, the map identifies the core area, comprising the heavy industry belt, the centre line of the Ruhr coalfield and the line of largest cities, the area defined in 1921 as the Ruhr Planning Region (*Ruhrsiedlungsverband*) and the peripheral zone of light industries, textile towns and outlying industrial centres (as defined by N. J. G. Pounds, *The Ruhr*, London, 1952, figure 28).

Legend on map:

Miles | 5 | 0 | 5 | 10 | 20

Rhine R.
Lippe R.
Ruhr R.
Wupper R.

Hamm
Reckl. 125
W. Eickel
Herne 99 104
Recklinghausen
Gels. 348
Essen 693
Bochum 344
Dortmund 639
Iserlohn
Hagen 201
Bot. 107
Ober. 247
191 Mul.
Duisburg 455
Düsseldorf 664
Neuss 151
Kref. 222
M-Glad. 151
Rheydt 100
Wuppertal 418
Rems. 136
Sol. 176

Ruhr heavy industry area

352 ○ Principal towns and their populations ('000) at 31.12.70

--- Boundary of the Ruhrsiedlungsverband

···· Outer limit of the Ruhr industrial region (after Pounds) while the intimate connection between coal mining and railway construction in the nineteenth century ensured that these industries, when they arrived, would have available a highly-developed transport network.

Industrial concentration on a coalfield is, however, in a sense self-defeating. The larger the output of coal, the more seriously does the exploitation interfere with other, surface uses of the region; subsidence occurs and slag heaps occupy valuable space. Even on a field like the Ruhr, where a very high percentage of all slag is returned underground to pack the old workings, the centre of the region rapidly becomes congested. There then develops a secondary industrial region, on the fringes of the first, into which overspill takes place. The Ruhr, which has already been mentioned, offers a good example of this core-and-fringe situation. The core, the Ruhr coalfield of the post-1914 period, was worked at its peak over an area stretching approximately 85 km from west to east and 30–35 km from north to south—an area of 2,500–2,600 km^2. But the industrial region of which it is the core covers probably 8,000 km^2 and includes the valley of the Lower Rhine and the old iron-working and textile districts in the hill country south of the Ruhr; it extends far out into the North German plain and contains over 20 towns with a population of more than 100,000. Only about one third of the industrial establishments of the region are within the core; the other two thirds are located in the fringe. The financial centre of the region, Düsseldorf, is not in the Ruhr at all, but in the southern fringe.

With the gradual decline in the industrial use of coal, in fact, a new generation of industrial regions has grown up. Their growth is a result of favourable position for assembly of materials and marketing; they are in this sense transport-orientated. Such regions have been gradually growing, for example, around the capital cities and metropoli of the advanced nations—London, Paris, New York, Moscow, Sydney, Tokyo. Profiting on the one hand from their position at the hub of communications and, on the other, from the huge local market offered by the cities themselves, these metropolitan industrial belts occupy perhaps the most favoured positions of all today. That this is so can be judged, at least negatively, by the concern of governments to divert industry away from them, to prevent an over-concentration at the hub.[16]

[16] The measures taken by the French government may serve as an example: (1) France is divided into five zones, within which various subsidies and alleviations of taxes encourage the manufacturer to locate new plants. Zone 1, with the greatest financial incentives, covers the north-west and south-west of France, while in Zone 5, the inner ring of the Paris Basin, no payments or alleviations whatsoever are offered. (2) Within the Paris region, not only does the Ministre de l'Equipement have to authorize any and every new application for industrial construction of over 500 m², but there is a tax in certain areas of the region on all such construction of factories or offices, and a corresponding

Overcrowding at the hub has produced in the old industrial nations a last category of industrial regions, again generally transport-orientated, but seeking space and, in some cases, untapped labour reserves. In north-west Europe, one of the best examples of the new industrial style is to be found in the Campine (Kempenland) of Belgium, by Belgian standards an empty land of heath and forest, but whose population has one of the highest birth rates in Europe. Traversed by the Albert Canal and the main east–west motorway axis of the present European network, this region has everything to commend it to the modern industrialist. So do the rim-lands of the Alps and the United States' coast of the Gulf of Mexico, in both of which transport and labour factors are favourable while there is, in addition, a local power supply (hydro-electricity in one case and oil in the other) to support industry.

Meanwhile, new industrial development is occurring in Latin America and the former colonial areas of Africa and Asia. In due course, we may expect the emergence of industrial regions there, too. By 1961, the 'less indus-trialized' nations[17] accounted for 60·7 per cent of world population, and 27·3 per cent of world employment in industry which was reckoned, at that date, as around 150 millions. However, these millions of industrial employees produced only 8·0 per cent of the world's value added by manufacture.

The industrial development of the new nations has been, in most cases, determined but painful and, in some, wrong-headed. Typically, a start is made by obtaining capital and technical assistance on loan from an already industrialized nation—often the ex-colonial power—and erecting a high tariff wall behind which the new industries will be given a chance to get established. Industrial location is usually at port of entry, unless the development is related to a particular mineral or power resource, such as the Katanga–Zambia copper belt or the Owen Falls power scheme. Only by close agglomeration in the early stages can the industrializing country usually afford the necessary infrastructure—or, rather, it can afford the necessary services only over a fraction of its territory.

The choice of industry is likely to be critical, as we have already seen. The nations which are at this stage of development generally have abun-

---

[17] The term is taken, like the figures, from UNESCO, *The Growth of World Industry 1938–1961*, New York, 1965, pp. 230–31. 'Less industrialized' is there taken to mean countries where the value added by manufacture in 1958 was less than U.S. $125 per head of the population.

---

government payment to any firm which *vacates* premises in Paris and moves outside the city.

dant cheap labour and a dire shortage of domestic capital. Their advantages therefore lie, theoretically, in labour-intensive industries and simple technologies. On this basis, they can realistically hope in a short time to enter the export market and join the international manufacturers' 'club', to which we referred earlier, as junior members.

In practice, they have not for the most part followed this course, but instead have tried to make themselves independent of foreign manufactures (which cost foreign exchange) by protective tariffs, imported capital equipment and the production of quite sophisticated manufactures, up to and including motor cars. The result is a very high internal price level and renunciation of any hope of exporting their manufactures:

In practice, most governments have approached the question of international specialization by trying to replace all the imports which the country was physically capable of making, with little regard for cost.[18]

In these conditions, neither competition nor specialization is encouraged. At worst, a government monopoly in manufacturing may result. But it is not difficult to understand the reluctance of the new nations to throw their market for industrial goods open to international competition: that, after all, was the state they were mostly in during their colonial past. Even old-established manufacturing nations resort to tariff barriers to protect their own interests. But it would be a tragedy if a protectionist policy was pursued, in these lands where the standard of living is still desperately low, to the point where industrial goods, once imported cheaply and paid for with cocoa or cotton, should now be priced out of reach of the average consumer for the sake of a few hundred factory jobs and in the name of national self-sufficiency.

[18] A. Maddison, *Economic Progress and Policy in Developing Countries*, Allen and Unwin, London, 1970, p. 187. See his chapter six, 'Has Industrialization Been Too Costly?' Maddison points out that, for example, Brazil and Argentina in 1965 exported only two per cent of their respective outputs of manufactures, and that of the increase in India's industrial output between 1950 and 1965, only two per cent went into exports from there and 22 per cent into 'import substitution'.

9

Tertiary Activities: Services and Cities

The interest of economic geographers in tertiary activities is of comparatively recent date. They have, it is true, had a long-standing devotion to international trade, at least as represented by tables of imports and exports. But they showed no comparable interest in internal trade, either wholesale or retail and, prior to the second world war, they had probably produced more work on medieval fairs and trade centres than on contemporary distribution functions. Transport was thinly covered and administrative services, if they figured at all, were regarded not so much as a type of economic activity, as belonging more properly to the field of political geography.

All this has now changed, and it is not difficult to see why. The older economic geography, like the world in which it grew up, was preoccupied with the producer. Its problems were, by and large, production problems: how to feed the populations of a whole generation of new cities, or of old ones swollen beyond recognition; how to supply the industrial regions with the raw materials necessary for their manufactures; how to bring into production hitherto unused areas of the earth's surface. But in many parts of the world—at least, in those where most geographers operate—the problems of which we are conscious today are much more those of consumption than of production. In these technically-advanced lands the difficulty is not generally to get enough produced but to get enough consumed to support the producers. With this change has gone a shift in the balance of employment so that, as we saw in chapter two, the service occupations now employ as much as three fifths of the labour force. To exclude these occupations from a study of the geography of man at work would be both illogical and misleading.

There is another factor. The importance of the service functions has increased with the velocity and range of circulation of goods. Whereas formerly most goods, whether raw materials or manufactures, were consumed within the region of their production, we have today national markets, national advertising and, consequently, distribution over distances in the *internal* market which may run into thousands of kilometres.

Customers scattered in remote places expect to receive the commodities they order on the same terms as those who live in the city of origin. To organize delivery under these circumstances is a highly complex operation. To organize it at minimum cost to the producer and distributor requires the very careful siting of warehouses and distribution centres and the employment of large staffs. The longer the distances over which goods—everyday goods, not luxury articles—circulate, the larger the element contributed by distribution to total costs. It is no coincidence that in the U.S.A. with its huge and highly competitive internal market, in every single state of the empty west (and including Texas) employment in the wholesale and retail trades is larger than in manufacturing, while in five of those states there are more people employed in transport services than in manufacturing.[1]

If, as we saw in the last chapter, the activities which come under the heading of manufacturing cover a wide spectrum, that of the service industries is much broader still—so broad as to prompt the suggestion that they should be subdivided into *tertiary* and *quaternary* activities (see p. 37). They differ from one another enormously in the kind of skill they call for, the numbers of workers they employ and the income levels they support. Some of them, like hairdressing or freight handling, call for skills which are mainly manual, while others may demand mental agility or academic excellence.

We can recognize four main subsections of this group of activities. These are:

I DISTRIBUTION

This section includes all those involved in transport, in wholesale or in retail trade. Transport is essential at all stages of the production process, from the assembly of raw materials to the distribution of the finished product. Wholesaling involves the transformation of consumer goods from large lots to smaller packages or individual items, and may in practice involve a good deal of storage or warehousing. Retailing then covers the supply of goods and services to the individual customer, through shops and other consumer outlets. The number of workers involved in these distributive activities quite naturally has increased with

1   the range of circulation of goods
2   the variety and specialized character of goods and services.

----

[1] For the nation as a whole the ratio of employees in wholesale–retail trade to those in manufacturing is 2:3. The ratio of transport workers to manufacturing employees, nationwide, is 1:4·5.

In a community where the individual grows his own food and has the means to purchase only the barest additional necessities such as cloth and cooking utensils, the number of 'retail outlets' required is very small. As the individual's purchasing power increases, so does the variety of his purchases and the number of services on which he depends: not only can he afford a television set but he requires a repairman to maintain it, while the repairman in his turn needs to be taught his trade and to be able to obtain the spare parts for the set.

2 FINANCE

Within the financial category of activities the one which is probably of longest standing is that of the money-lender. Today, he still exists, of course, in his traditional capacity; in some societies he is still a dominant figure. But his rather crude function and cruder methods have been refined and expanded a hundredfold, to provide a whole infrastructure of financial services—banking, insurance, estate agencies and so on. Because of the interlocking nature of these activities, at any rate at the top of the hierarchy, they tend to coalesce into 'financial districts' in major centres, where the money supply is manipulated by what, to the outsider, are complex and often mysterious means.

3 ADMINISTRATION

Under this third heading can be classed all the activities of government, from the national scale to the local. In addition, in a country where education is wholly or mainly in the hands of the state, the teaching profession may be included within this subsection, although there are obvious difficulties about any hard and fast subdivision of this kind. The tendency of administrative staffs at all levels of government to increase is notorious: in the U.S.A., while the labour force as a whole doubled between 1940 and 1968, employment in 'government' tripled; it was, in fact, easily the leading growth sector of the economy over the period. It would not, however, be fair to think of this simply as the application of Parkinson's now-famous Law: it is also the case that, to make life pleasanter or safer, there is an ever-growing body of law to be administered and an increasingly complicated economy to keep running.

4 PERSONAL SERVICE

Under this last heading are usually grouped such activities as entertainment, the hotel trade and the medical profession—in other words, a thoroughly assorted batch of services. All of them have this in common, however, that the scale on which they develop varies very closely with the standard of living. They represent the true 'extras' of life, for even medical attention is a luxury to a large proportion of the human race, a luxury which has to be paid for by the patient unless it is available through government services or mission hospitals. Because they are extras, the value placed on these services may bear little relation to values in the remainder of the market: this subsection includes the world's most highly-paid 'workers'.

In a subsistence economy, the rate of generation of tertiary activities is very slow, once a few basic needs have been met such as those for spiritual and medical or pseudo-medical services. In Europe, the first concentrations of service activities arose in and around the courts and religious centres; that is, where consumption levels were higher than average. In order to improve their own or their capital city's image, the princes and grand-dukes would extend their patronage to court suppliers and court painters, gradually creating a group of tertiary activities in their *Residenzstadt*. Only much later did a rise in general standards of living make this a normal situation in every town and city, as we know it today. Overseas, the earliest such concentrations arose in the same way, around the native rulers and their courts, but the process was in most cases considerably speeded up by the arrival of a colonial power, which brought with it European standards of administration and the expectation of being served by the native population. Soon the colonizing power had provided itself with a large number of minor officials (the higher ranks of the service being closed to the native population) and a good supply of house servants. While independence may have made itself felt by changes at the top of the hierarchy, it has certainly led to no slackening in the rate of growth of the service industries; rather the reverse.

At the top of the scale of standards of living, the tertiary sector is constantly enlarging, for there seems no limit to the services which ingenuity can devise and market, once a community is living well over the subsistence level. Some of these new services are manifestly the product of accumulating wealth, such as the profession of investment adviser. Some are the result of higher standards being demanded in the field of hygiene and cleanliness, such as the post-war revolution in food packaging or the remarkable spread of dry-cleaning businesses for clothes. Others again increase efficiency in business by answering telephones or selecting secretaries. Clearly, this process of activity generation depends on convincing people that a need for service exists, of which they have previously been unconscious. A key role is therefore played by the sales staffs and advertising agencies, whose task it is to create demand where none existed and keep the tertiary sector continuing on its course of expansion.

THE LOCATION OF TERTIARY ACTIVITIES

The use of the term 'service industries' as a synonym for tertiary activities implies that they exist to serve people and that therefore they are located, generally speaking, where most people are. They belong to population concentrations or *central places*. Certainly, there are country school-teachers, and there are railway sectionmen in the middle of the Mojave Desert, but, characteristically, service industries grow up in centres and it is a fact that there are fewer and fewer country schoolteachers precisely because the education service is becoming progressively more centralized in the towns. This observable tendency for services to be concentrated in particular centres has given rise to a group of concepts known as *central place theory*.

There have always been types of human activity which depend on the presence of a group or community. In the earliest settlements, these were (1) defence, (2) exchange and (3) worship of the local deity, a com-bination of centralized functions which can be identified to this day in scores of European cities by the close grouping of castle, market place and cathedral. As time went on, the function of defence declined in impor-tance, but this was more than balanced by the expansion of other central functions such as administration, processing (which implies the assembly of materials at a central point) and the transport necessary to assembly and distribution.[2] As the number of workers necessary to serve these functions increased so, in turn, this rising population itself created a demand for further services. Two kinds of central function then grew up side by side—functions provided by the central place for its surroundings or *umland*, and functions meeting the needs of the service population itself. To the first kind of function the name *basic* economic activity has been given, while the second has become known as *non-basic*.[3] The first of these is 'basic' in the sense that it forms the main *raison d'être* of the central place; without it, there would be no need for centrality. Needless to say, the division between basic and non-basic is not necessarily clear-cut; a bakery may sell bread both to city customers and to those in the surrounding countryside, and the functions of central government apply to the popula-tion on both sides of the city boundary, even though the jurisdiction of the city itself may end there.

What decides *how many* services shall be grouped together in one central place and, in consequence, how many central places there shall be? Every

[2] As a spatial expression of these changing central functions one finds, time and again, in European cities, that the present railway station and goods yards are laid out on the site of the old fortifications, the arrival of the one coinciding with the removal of the other.

[3] See J. W. Alexander, 'The Basic-Non-Basic Concept of Urban Economic Functions', *Economic Geography* 30 (1954), pp. 246–61.

service presupposes a clientele and anyone establishing such a service will need to know two things about the clientele for which he is catering: (1) What is the minimum or *threshold* number of customers he needs to make his service pay. A community will only buy so many groceries or pairs of shoes and will therefore only support a limited number of grocers or shoeshops. (2) Over how large an area these customers are distributed. Every type of goods or service has a *range*, defined either as the distance people will travel to obtain it at a given price level, or the price increment they will pay to cover transport costs. The range of most everyday goods is small, although in detail it depends on shopping habits, and can be increased by deep freezes and travelling shop vans. But for these everyday goods most people want a source close at hand and, since they *are* everyday needs, the demand for them is high and consistent and the outlets that supply them are the most widely-distributed of all services.

But we know that, once we turn our attention away from everyday needs, there are many other types of goods or service which are needed only occasionally and which, in consequence, may require a much higher threshold to yield a livelihood to the operator. For these services—an occasional visit to a dentist or lawyer; a repair to electrical equipment—people are prepared to travel further or to pay more, or both, so that their range is increased also. Dentists are more sparsely distributed than filling stations, and shops selling furniture than those selling tobacco. It is possible, in fact, to estimate threshold and range and so to forecast what the frequency of dentists or tobacco shops will be, either in terms of population or in terms of distance from each other, given a particular population distribution.

If we imagine an area over which population is distributed perfectly evenly and movement is equally costly in all directions, we should expect the suppliers of each service to be distributed evenly also, at a distance from each other that would depend on threshold and range. These suppliers would divide up the territory between them and the pattern of their theoretical service areas would be one of adjoining hexagons. The hexagons would be smaller for some services than for others, and particular central places would be the centre of several hexagons of different sizes. In practice, the hexagon would be distorted from its theoretical shape by uneven terrain and unequal costs of overcoming the friction of movement in different directions: bus services rather than mere distance may decide in which town people go shopping. But the principle of subdivision of the territory will survive these distortions in detail.

Now it is reasonable to assume that, if there are a number of services which people use only occasionally, there are advantages in having those services grouped centrally. Not only does this enable people to make a single trip to the central place serve several purposes but, if the object of their trip happens to be a once-only purchase, like that of a suite of furniture or a television set, they like to be able to compare different makes of the same goods. In other words, from the consumer's point of view, if he is within an area where demand is sufficient to support three furniture shops, he would rather that those three shops were all together, so that he could readily compare prices and quality among them, than that they were distributed uniformly in the same way as groceries or post offices. Putting this in more general terms, we can say that, from the consumer's point of view, it is to his advantage if the more durable forms of goods and the more rarely-used services do *not* appear as soon as the demand threshold is reached, but are deferred until they can be provided and supported in multiple in a central place of larger size.

This leads us immediately to the idea of a hierarchy of central places, graded according to the variety of services which they offer. As the population of a central place, plus the population within the range of a particular service, reaches and exceeds the threshold figure, so the services make their appearance one by one, through the whole range until, at the upper end of the scale, we come to those which may occur only once within a country or region, in its metropolis. Generally, a central place in a higher rank possesses all the functions found in the lower ranks, together with some additional ones which they do not have.

The order in which these functions appear, and the threshold level of each, vary from culture to culture. Figure 39 offers for comparison two sets of figures, one for an American and the other for an English example. In the American case, the object was to calculate the threshold level for each type of service, by relating population to the number of existing (and, therefore, presumably viable) outlets.[4] The English list was compiled by simple observation over a 400–500 km² area, using parish populations. There are obviously wide discrepancies between the two lists, not only in the items that appear, but also in the size of settlement in which they first make their appearance. Some of these discrepancies we should expect, since there are services like bars and cafés which cater not only for the local population but also for passing traffic whose volume is not stated in these examples. Others may be combined under a single operator, as with the post office-cum-general store so often found in Britain. Other elements of the discrepancy may be looked for in contrasting shopping habits or standards of living in the two areas

[4] For the method used, see B. J. L. Berry and W. Garrison, 'The Functional Bases of the Central Place Hierarchy', *Economic Geography* 34 (1958), p. 149. The Berry–Garrison study was made in the state of Washington: studies which compare findings for the Midwest and the state of Georgia are, respectively, H. A. Stafford, *Economic Geography* 39 (1963), pp. 165–75 and J. B. Kenyon, *Annals of the Association of American Geographers* 57 (1967), pp. 736–50.

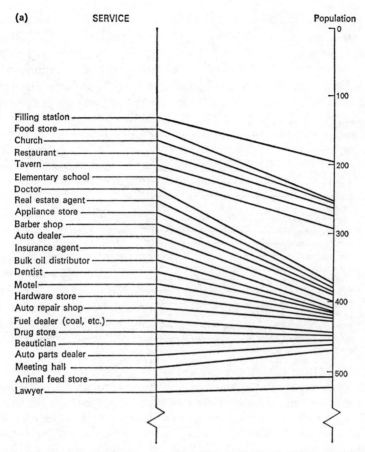

(a) SERVICE — Population

Filling station
Food store
Church
Restaurant
Tavern
Elementary school
Doctor
Real estate agent
Appliance store
Barber shop
Auto dealer
Insurance agent
Bulk oil distributor
Dentist
Motel
Hardware store
Auto repair shop
Fuel dealer (coal, etc.)
Drug store
Beautician
Auto parts dealer
Meeting hall
Animal feed store
Lawyer

Figure 39: Service thresholds: (a) American and (b) English examples of threshold populations supporting lower-order services. The American example shows thresholds calculated from the best-fit curve for 33 settlements in a county of the Pacific north-west: the English example is based on a simple field check of services within a part of south-east England, using parish populations for 30 parishes.

concerned. But within each culture area a certain regularity will emerge in the hierarchy, and this has been made the object of a very large number of studies by geographers and others in the past two decades.[5]

It must at once be added that this hierarchy, far from being immutable, is in a constant state of change. We have only to think back to the simple,

[5] See B. J. L. Berry and A. Pred, *Central Place Studies: A Bibliography of Theory and Applications*, University of Pennsylvania, Regional Science Research Institute, Philadelphia, 1965.

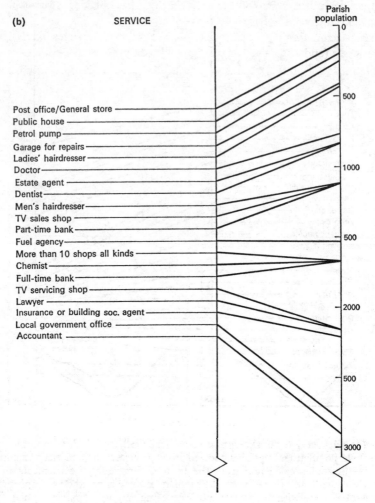

(b)   SERVICE

Parish population

Post office/General store
Public house
Petrol pump
Garage for repairs
Ladies' hairdresser
Doctor
Estate agent
Dentist
Men's hairdresser
TV sales shop
Part-time bank
Fuel agency
More than 10 shops all kinds
Chemist
Full-time bank
TV servicing shop
Lawyer
Insurance or building soc. agent
Local government office
Accountant

Figure 39b: *see p. 239*

three-tier hierarchy of hamlet–market town–regional centre in, say, eighteenth-century England to see the extent of this change. For one thing, the mobility of the consumer has greatly increased. The spacing of the market towns of western Europe was a product of horse and cart movement: ten km or so to market and ten km back on market day gave a spacing to these towns of twenty or, in more sparsely-settled areas, of up to forty km apart. But for a more mobile population today so dense a distribution of market towns is unnecessary: many of them—perhaps too many—have survived but they are not all actually needed. Today, they compete with each other for the available business, much of which has in any case transferred itself to the regional capital.

Other factors making for change in the hierarchy are changes in relative price levels (and so in the range of goods), the present tendency to buy

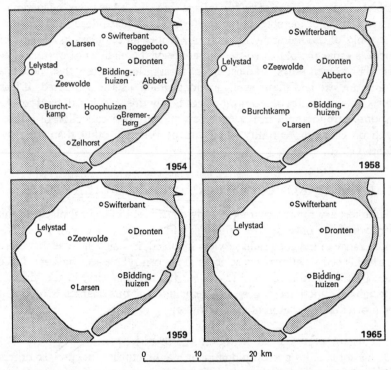

Figure 40: Changes in the need for service centres: an example from the Ijsselmeer polders. The four maps show phases in the planning of settlement on the future East Flevoland polder (see figure 29); the latest represents the realization of the plan. The number of planned centres was steadily reduced as social and economic changes in western Europe eliminated the need for the smaller service centres. (Reproduced by permission from M. H. M. Van Hulten, 'Plan and Reality in the Ijsselmeer-polders', *Tijdscrift voor economische en sociale geografie* 60, p. 73, Rotterdam, 1967, p. 73.)

outside the home goods and services which were formerly provided within it, and the much wider variety of needs which, say, a farmer has today than his predecessors had in the unmechanized days before the tractor and the milking machine. Then, too, some changes are produced consciously, by planners' decisions; the 'pole of growth' concept in effect represents an artificial stimulus to one particular central place, which is promoted in the hierarchy above its equals. The effects of such changes are perhaps most clearly seen at the lower end of the scale, where the loss of one or two service functions may make quite a critical difference to the status of a village or small town. In Britain, in recent years, the closure of the local cinema has been a common indicator of change; in the United States it has been the disappearance of the men's hairdresser or the local doctor; in France, it is often the village café which has been the victim of change. It is not merely that the smallest central places lose; it is also that the ranks of the hierarchy increase in number and gradations in front of them, so that the old three-tier hierarchy of the eighteenth century now has six or seven ranks. In most areas, observation suggests that there is a minimum size and number of functions which a settlement needs if it is to retain the dignity of a central place: below this size, it will tend to lose ground, atrophy and, in the end, become simply a collection of houses with no claim to centrality at all and no function other than the residential.

TERTIARY ACTIVITIES AND SPECIALIZATION

While tertiary functions are generally distributed in central places in the way which we have been considering and in accordance with the maximum range of the goods and services involved, it is also the case that there are local specializations. These occur (1) in central places which specialize in a particular function and (2) *within* the town or city, in the form of specialized functional zones. The remainder of this chapter is occupied by a brief consideration of each of these.

I CITIES WITH A DOMINANT SERVICE FUNCTION

Just as some cities possess a dominant manufacturing function, so others may have a service function which, in employment terms, is of outstanding importance. Each of the central functions we considered earlier is, or was, represented by specialist towns. The old defence function produced its garrison towns, most of them in Europe, but some in India and Africa too. The administrative towns are probably the most numerous at the present day. Heading any list would be the capital cities created specifically as the seat of government: Washington, Canberra or Brasilia. In Washington, almost exactly one third of the labour force is employed in the functional sector of government, as against a mere eight per cent in industry, of which more than half are in printing and publishing, an 'industry' for purposes of classification only.

But the government function is of at least equal importance to many lesser centres—state capitals and county towns and *chef-lieux*. They may be said to specialize by default of any other significant tertiary activity: they owe their prosperity, if not their existence, to the basic function of government and the non-basic business of servicing the bureaucrats and politicians. The presence of the administrative headquarters of a region has been recognized as a prize for the city which possesses it sufficiently valuable even to be worth fighting for—as the Italian city of Reggio Calabria literally fought in 1970, and lost the fight.

If we take the administrative function in its broadest context, then there are also towns which specialize even within this field. With the expansion of higher education, for example, the location of state universities and colleges has proved to be a powerful determinant of the levels of demand for services: to have 25,000 or 30,000 temporary residents is an addition to the strength of consumer demand which the merchants of almost any town will welcome in normal times.[6]

The distributive trades and transport functions have also tended to favour particular centres. This is most obviously true of ports, where goods are received, warehoused and shipped independent of the existence of either local manufactures or local demand for the products moving through the city. But it is also true of a growing number of inland cities which act as wholesale and warehouse centres, generally because they possess an unusually large *umland* for a city of their size. The best examples are the line of cities at the eastern edge of the plains in North America— Winnipeg, Minneapolis-St Paul, Omaha, Kansas City and Dallas-Fort Worth, with St Louis, the earliest city to play this role, in the position of a strategic reserve behind the line. The special function of these cities is the product of topography, population distribution and historic accident: that west of the cities, in about the position where the next regional centres should be found if the spacing were regular, are either semi-arid rangelands or unoccupied mountains; that the density of population—and the density of central places—is very much higher to the east than to the west of the line, and that America was settled from east to west and not the other way round. Instead of the regular honeycomb of service areas around central places which our theory would suggest and which are, in practice, found in the Midwest of North America, we find on the plains that the major centres have service areas distorted by being elongated in an east-west direction and that the central city itself, far from being *at* the centre, is close to the eastern edge of its service area (figure 41), towards which agricultural produce has traditionally flowed and from

[6] In the U.S.A., when new states were created, and particularly in the west where higher education was assured from the first by the system of land grant colleges, it was quite normal to apportion the main administrative functions to different towns and there was often lively competition among bidders for the state capitol and the university or colleges. In the administrative situation of the day, however, with poorly-developed government functions, the only consolation prize for a town which obtained neither the capitol nor the university was the state penitentiary.

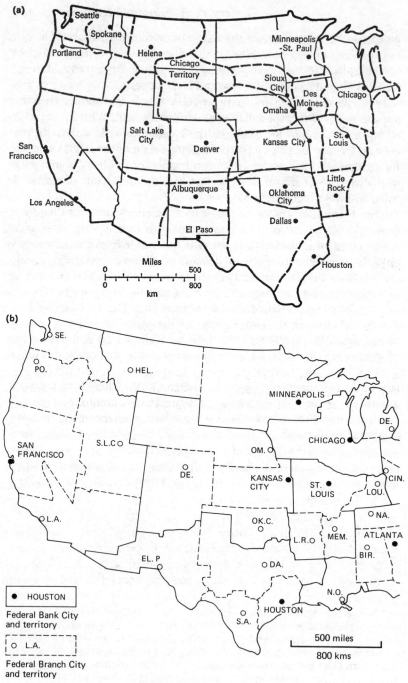

(a)

Seattle
Spokane
Portland
Helena
Chicago Territory
Minneapolis -St. Paul
Sioux City
Des Moines
Chicago
Omaha
San Francisco
Salt Lake City
Denver
Kansas City
St. Louis
Los Angeles
Albuquerque
Oklahoma City
Little Rock
Dallas
El Paso
Houston

Miles
0 ——————— 500
0 ——————— 800
km

(b)

SE.
PO.
HEL.
MINNEAPOLIS
DE.
SAN FRANCISCO
S.L.C
OM.
CHICAGO
DE.
KANSAS CITY
ST. LOUIS
CIN.
LOU.
L.A.
NA.
OK.C.
L.R.O
MEM.
ATLANTA
BIR.
EL. P
DA.
N.O.
HOUSTON
S.A.

● HOUSTON
Federal Bank City and territory

○ L.A.
Federal Branch City and territory

500 miles
800 kms

Figure 41: *see opposite*

which non-agricultural requirements have traditionally been supplied.

This same kind of distortion of the *umland*, a distortion which gives a central place special importance in the distributive trades, can be found elsewhere whenever the theoretical spacing of central places within the hierarchy is disturbed by some external factor—relief, sea or political barriers. As an example, we may consider the service centres on the edge of the Scottish Highlands. These carry on a distributive function greatly out of proportion to the size of their populations because they have, in effect, a double service area—their own, together with the territory which should belong to the *next* line of centres westwards or northwards, a line which, of course, does not exist. Not only do rugged terrain and scattered population discourage the growth of major centres in the west and north of Highland Scotland but, as on the Great Plains, all the economic movement into and out of the area is in one direction: there would simply be no function for this next line of major centres to fulfil.

While the cities which we have been considering specialize in the distributive service mainly because of their particular locational advantage, there is a sense in which, with the ever-growing volume of goods and services to be handled, every region *needs* a distributive focus and, if there is none, one has to be created. There was a very interesting redistribution of functions in West Germany, after the partition of the country cut the west off from its old focus in Berlin, and altered the shape of the national market area. In eastern Canada, there have for most purposes to be *two* distributive foci, Montreal and Toronto, because the French and non-French culture areas constitute, in an increasing number of respects, two separate markets: the dichotomy is, today, more marked than ever.[7] Perhaps the most interesting modern case, however, of the market creating the distributive service centre is that of Atlanta, Georgia, a city whose growth in this role over the past two decades has been out-

---

[7] On the role of the two cities, see D. P. Kerr, 'Metropolitan Dominance in Canada', in *Canada* edited by J. Warkentin, Methuen, 1967, pp. 531–55.

Figure 41: Metropolitan hinterlands of the western and central U.S.A. The two maps use different criteria to delimit these hinterlands; (a) shows the coverage of territory by major city newspapers and dates from the pre-radio, pre-television period when newspaper coverage was an economic indicator of much greater significance than it is now; (b) represents the system of regional sub-division actually used by the Federal Reserve (banking) System. The division of territory is based on major bank cities, whose areas are sub-divided between several branch cities. Both maps show how the hinterlands of the Midwestern cities extend westwards across the Great Plains, so that the metropoli are located, on the whole, at the eastern margins of their own hinterlands; that is, at the margin from which the original economic thrust into the area occurred.

standing. Never since the Civil War had the south-eastern region of the U.S.A. possessed a city whose functions made it clearly the regional focus, in large part because the south-east was a poverty region: income levels were low and so was demand for goods and services. But when, after the second world war, a new South began to replace the old, national manufacturers and advertisers found it worthwhile to establish south-eastern branches and, with what amounted to a 'situation vacant' sign out for a regional centre, Atlanta has successfully assumed this role.

2 FUNCTIONAL ZONES WITHIN THE CITY

In central place theory, the focus of each service area is treated as a point, and a point has by definition position but no magnitude. It is, however, obvious that, in practice, the service functions (some of which, like warehousing or marshalling railway freight, take up a great deal of space) will have to be grouped around the central point and that in a large centre, where the number of functions to be accommodated is considerable, there will be intense competition for space. In this competition, we shall expect that the main variable will be the price of space which each function can afford to pay and that this price will itself be related to the degree of centrality within the city afforded by a particular site. The functions which can support the highest price will obtain the advantage of the most central location.

Characteristically, space rentals rise very steeply at the centre of a city, to form a sharp peak at or around some point of maximum traffic circulation (figure 42). Although there may be a number of lesser peaks at major traffic foci in the suburbs, it is this central peak which represents the heart of the Central Business District (C.B.D.), the functional zone around which all the other zones are grouped. Because of the price of space, only the essentials of each central service are maintained here— offices, but not the warehouses whose stocks they control; publishers, but not their books; industrial headquarters, but not their factories. There are likely to be departmental stores and, on the other hand, highly specialized retail outlets: there are unlikely to be many food shops or garages—in fact, the centre of a large city is one of the worst places in the world to run out of petrol. It is not normally the case that government services are found in the C.B.D.—there is no special reason why they should be—but it is almost universally true that banks and other finance houses make up a high percentage of all businesses there. High ground rents in the C.B.D. are generally recouped by building or letting multi-storey blocks, so that the skyline of the city will in many cases reveal the whereabouts of the central core.

The size of the C.B.D. varies fairly directly with the population of the city (figure 43). From the country town with its single street of shops, or

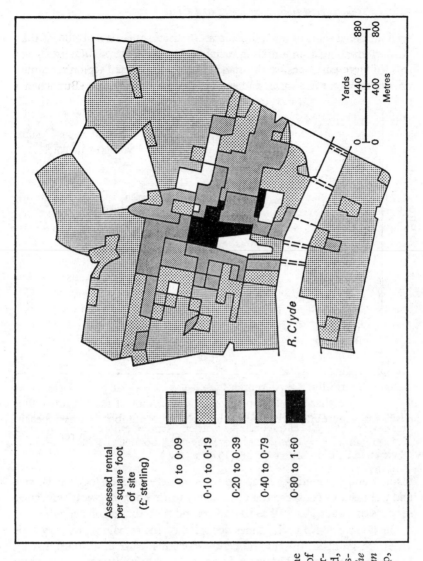

Figure 42: Land values in the city centre: the case of Glasgow. (Reproduced by permission from D. R. Diamond, 'The Central Business District of Glasgow', *Proc. of the I.G.U. Symposium in Urban Geography*, Lund: Gleerup, 1962, p. 532.)

Assessed rental per square foot of site (£ sterling)

0 to 0·09

0·10 to 0·19

0·20 to 0·39

0·40 to 0·79

0·80 to 1·60

R. Clyde

Yards

0   440   880

0   400   800

Metres

even its single-intersection business 'district', the size of the C.B.D. grows with population until it in turn may become large enough itself to be divided into sub-zones, with finance in one area, retail trade in another or entertainment in a third. In London, these subdivisions are particularly

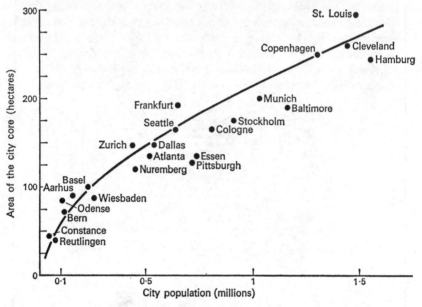

Figure 43: The relationship between the population of selected cities and the area covered by their central business district. (Reproduced by permission from K. Leibbrand, *Transportation and Town Planning*, London: Leonard Hill, Basel (Switzerland): Birkhaeuser Verlag, 1970, p. 122.)

distinct and fascinating. They are the product of increasing C.B.D. size and the need to conserve the advantage of proximity between associated services or outlets, as well as that of centrality to the region served.

Outside the C.B.D., the zones occupied by the remaining tertiary activities are grouped around the centre, together with those occupied by industry, amenities and housing. Urban geographers distinguish two main types of grouping, concentric rings and sectors. In the concentric ring model the functional zones are distributed around the C.B.D. in descending order of ability to pay the price of space, with the big space consumers in the outer rings. In the sector model, each form of activity runs out from the C.B.D. in a wedge, broadening towards the suburbs, with the different types of manufacturing, services or residential area graded by age, space occupance or planners' edict. Most cities conform partially to both models: the decisive factor is usually the transport pattern. One may often have, as with the old cities of Europe, an almost perfect series of concentric rings but slashed right across with a belt of transport-orientated activities. The line of the main routes of entry for transport into the city is usually marked by a belt of docks, sidings or terminals which not only attracts factories and warehouses but acts as an obstacle to transverse movement; it acts, in fact, as a very important sector in its own right. Along such an obstacle-sector, residential quality is likely to be poor and the transport barrier—any barrier within the city, for that matter—is a prime factor in producing urban blight. If a central place is to exercise all its various functions, then it must be possible for all the functional zones to communicate easily and swiftly with the C.B.D. and with each other.

Postscript: What shall we do with an Economic Geographer?

The geographers who began their careers in the years of expansion after the second world war set out with high hopes. Never before had there been so many of them, either as teachers or students. As far as tasks were concerned, those whose interest inclined towards economic geography confronted a relatively new and apparently limitless field of exploration—national and regional planning. In the wake of wartime upheavals of economy and landscape, planning was coming into prominence in most European countries, including Great Britain, and seemed to offer an ideal outlet for the energies of geographers. It is true that applied geography was still suffering from the damage done to its reputation through its misuse in Germany by a school of geopoliticians which had begun as a body of serious professionals and ended as a group of propagandists for German power politics. But there seemed no reason why geography in the future should be degraded in this way and, in the meantime, the geopoliticians had at least raised, even if they unworthily answered, questions about the philosophy of resource disposal which were clearly of fundamental importance.

If economic geography was to develop in the period ahead, it seemed likely that it would be in one or other of these directions—either through the application of geographical expertise to planning problems or as an organized body of thought on resource use, the emphasis being practical or philosophical according to the inclination of the individual geographer. In the event, however, development simply did not follow this course. Whether, in the 1950s, anyone could have foreseen the course that the development *did* take is an open question, and one that need not concern us here. But what happened was a very general, and bilaterial, disillusionment which grew up between geographers and planners; on the part of the planners because the geographers' knowledge was too unspecialized to fit them into the planning teams at the levels where they might be expected to begin working; on the part of the geographers because they found themselves involved in questions of local by-laws, sewers and rights of way which they were fitted neither by inclination nor by training to cope with. While one could reasonably conceive of a geographer as *heading* a planning team, it was more difficult to visualize him as fitting into a humbler niche, alongside engineers and architects, whose contribution to the planning process was much more specific. For those geographers who survived and remained, further training was required: many, however, left the planning field frustrated.

In the other direction in which development might have been anticipated —the evolution of a body of resource-use principles—little if any progress was made, by geographers at least. It is true that there has been a remarkable flowering of interest in the general subject of ecology; that is, in the conception of man as a part of nature, interacting with it rather than standing over against it purely as its exploiter. But in this geographers have been only marginally involved: indeed, one of the principal features of the development has been the entirely amateur status of many of those contributing to it. The subject of resource-use principles has, in fact, all too largely fallen into the hands of enthusiasts rather than scholars; hence in part the bewildering variety of views on resource potential to which reference was made in an earlier chapter. Had economic geographers concerned themselves in a more deliberate and objective manner with the subject, we might have been spared some of the propaganda and *ad hoc* policy-making with which it has in practice been surrounded.

There followed, for geographers in general, a period of deepening frustration, during which there grew up an anxiety that the field would yield no worthwhile tasks or objectives at all for the increasing number of workers crowding into it. If this anxiety has now been allayed— whether temporarily or permanently only time will tell—it was not on account of developments in either of the directions which might have been foreseen, but rather as a result of the growth of what undoubtedly sounded at first like a contradiction in terms—theoretical geography. Instead of the major progress coming at the point of practical application of the subject—among, so to speak, the by-laws and the sewers—it grew from a reversal of the previous sequence of thought; that is, from the creation of an abstract model of spatial distributions with which the reality might be compared. It would be unfair to suggest that by this means the geographer's lack of specialist training could be neutralized: certainly, it was not for this reason that the theoretical course was followed, but for its own sake. Nevertheless, the outcome of this development was precisely to replace the geographer's lack of specialization by a special interest in what has come to be called spatial or locational analysis, a specialization which he could now attempt to sell to planners and others, if and when he could convince them of its value. In the meantime, and quite apart from any answer to the always-dangerous question, 'But what *use* is it?', the development of this body of theory was leading geographers to adopt a number of techniques already in use in allied fields like economics and sociology, and to carry out with them new types of analysis of spatial patterns, in order to achieve a fuller understanding of existing landscapes.

The new techniques were, for the most part, mathematical in character but, as with many other techniques—such as the cartographic, which had been the geographer's mainstay for so long—the character of the technique matters less than the use to which it is put. In economic geography, the main uses have been to establish, and measure, the qualities of *location*, *association* and *concentration*: location of places or points relative to one another; association of two or more variables in the same place, and concentration of particular features or activities within a region or area.

What we have seen in recent years has therefore been a parallel development of (1) locational theory in economic geography and (2) new types of problem studies, the two lines of development naturally feeding each other. With the growth of locational theory there is associated a small group of names, all of which have become familiar to geographers in the past two decades after languishing in comparative obscurity for varying periods of time. It is a convenient generalization (which must be used with the caution that all generalizations demand) to say that locational theory has three godparents, all of them German: Joachim von Thünen for agricultural land use, Alfred Weber for industrial location and Walther Christaller for central place theory. Since von Thünen published his main work in 1826,[1] Weber in 1909 and Christaller in 1933, they have become familiar to, and appreciated by, geographers only slowly, and then largely through the intervention of a newer generation of theorists like Hoover, Lösch and Isard.[2] Whether, or to what extent, this work is geographical rather than purely economic it would be invidious at this point to stop and discuss: certainly, it has commended itself to a large number of workers trained as economic geographers, who are now operating in this field. Their success can only be judged by the measure of improvement they are able to bring about in the validity of generalizations which have, in the past, been made by geographers using a much more limited range of techniques and on the basis of induction from empirical studies.

Meanwhile, the range of these empirical studies has broadened. In general terms, the nature and number of the variables included in such studies has been enlarged, and enlarged to include such intangibles as the

---

[1] A complete edition of Von Thünen's work, however, appeared only in 1875. See Andreas Grotewold, 'Von Thünen in Retrospect', *Economic Geography* 35 (1959), pp. 346–55.

[2] References to work by all these writers will be found in the list of Suggested Readings.

diffusion and circulation of ideas, as well as of plants or animals or cultural artifacts. Studies of circulation and central place systems aid the businessman looking for the best location from which to serve a territory. They feed into a newly-recognized subfield of economic geography, the geography of marketing; they have, in other words, a direct bearing on money making and money saving. Other studies relate to the level of economic 'health' of particular areas, while studies of regionalization are of direct interest to planners and administrators at every level. As a further dimension in all these types of study, it may then be of value to distinguish between the real environment and the real circumstances of production on the one hand and, on the other, the environment as people perceive it and react to it. For the *perception* may generate behaviour which is stubbornly immune to the classic assumptions of the economists, like least-cost and maximum-profit choices.

It is to be hoped that this concentration of interest on locational analysis will not, however, lead to a narrowing of the field of economic geography as a whole. To concentrate on location as if it were the *only* geographical attribute, or as if in itself it contained the quintessence of geography, would be a denial of mainstream thought over a century or more, and of the long-held view that the content of area, as well as area itself, is what geographers study. In particular, it is to be hoped that economic geography will develop, if belatedly, an interest in the assumptions on which resource use should be based. There is already a sufficient tendency for purely statistical assumptions like mean and best-fit to take on a life of their own in policy making, without geographers lending weight to the trend. To a field of policy in which emotion and enthusiasm have in the past been allowed to contribute far too largely, economic geography has surely much to contribute both of vigour and of expertise.

Notes on Further Reading

Chapter One
The late 1960s and early 1970s have seen a tidal wave of literature about resources and conservation, to add to the series of textbooks—mostly American—which were produced by the earlier wave of the mid-1950s. A reasonable starting point for further reading would be the works of one of the Calders—either Nigel Calder's *The Environment Game* (Secker and Warburg, London, 1967) and *Technopolis* (MacGibbon and Kee, London, 1969), or Ritchie Calder's *The Inheritors* (Heinemann, London, 1961) and his earlier works. From these one could pass on to the naturalist-ecologists like F. Fraser Darling and, if only as a tribute to an important figure of the immediate past, Aldo Leopold: see *A Sand County Almanac* (Oxford, New York, 1949) in which he set out the principles of the ecological school. See also J. Black, *The Dominion of Man* (Edinburgh University Press, 1970).

Little of this literature is specifically by geographers, but they contributed a number of papers in the collection of *Readings in Resource Management and Conservation* edited by I. Burton and R. W. Kates (University of Chicago Press, 1965). On the relationship of population to resources, a good short source is W. Zelinsky, *A Prologue to Population Geography* (Prentice-Hall, Englewood Cliffs, N.J., 1966) chapters 9–13: see also A. J. Coale and E. M. Hoover, *Population Growth and Economic Development in Low Income Countries* (Princeton University Press, 1958).

Chapter Two
The subject of input–output ratios is well covered on the agricultural side, but less well on the industrial. On agricultural inputs see M. Chisholm, *Rural Settlement and Land Use* (Hutchinson, London, second edition, 1968): W. Alonso, *Location and Land Use* (M.I.T. Press, 1968); A. N. Duckham and G. B. Masefield, *Farming Systems of the World* (Chatto and Windus, London, 1970), and W. C. Found, *A Theoretical Approach to Rural Land-Use Patterns* (Arnold, London, 1971). On the industrial side, see M. Chisholm, *Geography and Economics* (Bell, London, 1966).

The subject of labour quality and supply can be pursued by referring to texts such as L. C. Hunter and D. J. Robertson, *Economics of Wages and Labour* (Macmillan, London, 1969).

Chapter Three
A basic text is R. S. Thoman and E. C. Conkling, *Geography of International Trade* (Prentice-Hall, 1967). One of the best sources of comment

on contemporary trends in trade is the periodical *Foreign Affairs* (quarterly), while the recent history was dealt with by P. L. Yates, *Forty Years of Foreign Trade* (Allen and Unwin, London, 1959). See also J. W. Alexander, 'International Trade: Selected Types of World Regions', *Econ. Geog.* **36** (1960), 95–115.

The problems encountered in the course of setting up free-trade areas can be studied in the voluminous materials issued by the European Economic Community, while similar problems in two other continents are covered by P. Robson, *Economic Integration in Africa* (Allen and Unwin, London, 1968) and M. Yudelman, *Agricultural Development and Economic Integration in Latin America* (Allen and Unwin, London, 1970).

On the question of aid to underdeveloped countries, see either H. G. Johnson, *Economic Policies Towards Less Developed Countries* (Allen and Unwin, London, 1967) or R. F. Mikesell, *The Economics of Foreign Aid* (Weidenfeld and Nicolson, London, 1968).

Chapter Four

A general transport geography is J. E. Becht, *A Geography of Transportation and Business Logistics* (Brown, Dubuque, Iowa, 1970). Among the means of transport and their impact, railways are well covered: see, for example, A. C. O'Dell and P. S. Richards, *Railways and Geography* (Hutchinson, London, second edition, 1971); H. Perkin, *The Age of the Railway* (Routledge, London, 1970); J. R. Kellett, *The Impact of Railways on Victorian Cities* (Routledge, London, 1969). Water transport is usually covered only regionally, but ports have received some recent attention, e.g. in J. Bird, *The Major Seaports of the United Kingdom* (Hutchinson, London, 1963) and *Seaports and Development in Tropical Africa* edited by B. S. Hoyle and D. Hilling (Macmillan, London, 1970). For roads, there are chapters 1–4 of C. A. O'Flaherty, *Highways* (Arnold London, 1967) and for airways K. R. Sealy, *The Geography of Air Transport* (Hutchinson, London, third edition, 1966).

Freight rates are well covered by R. J. Sampson and M. T. Farris, *Domestic Transportation: Practice, Theory and Policy* (Houghton Mifflin, Boston, 1966) and particular aspects of cost-distance by J. W. Alexander and others, 'Freight Rates: Selected Aspects of Uniform and Nodal Regions', *Econ. Geog.* **34** (1958), 1–18 and J. F. Johnson, 'The Influence of Cost Distance Factors on the Overseas Export of Corn from the United States Midwest', *Econ. Geog.* **45** (1969), 170–79.

On transport policy, there are a number of international studies carried out by the Brookings Institute in its Transport Research programme, e.g. *Transport and National Goals* edited by E. T. Haefele (Washington, D.C., 1969). An excellent short study is R. I. Wolfe, 'Transportation and Politics: The Example of Canada', *Ann. Ass. Am. Geog.* **52** (1962), 176–90.

The 'climax' network of Yorkshire is examined in J. H. Appleton, 'The Railway Network of Southern Yorkshire', *Trans. I.B.G.* **22** (1957), 159–69: see also his *The Geography of Communications in Great Britain* (O.U.P., London, 1962). For another network study, see D. W. Meinig, 'A Comparative Historical Geography of Two Railnets: Columbia Basin and South Australia', *Ann. Ass. Am. Geog.* **52** (1962), 394–413.

Chapter Five

G. Manners, *A Geography of Energy* (Hutchinson, London, 1964) has already been referred to in the text. This apart, one of the best sources is formed by the publications of the European Coal and Steel Community, Luxembourg, especially as these deal with energy policy. As a summary of such policies, see R. L. Gordon, *The Evolution of Energy Policy in Western Europe* (Praeger, N.Y., 1970): for the U.S.A., consult *National Petroleum Policy: A Critical Review* edited by A. E. Utton (University of Mexico Press, Albuquerque, 1970).

On the petroleum industry, see P. R. Odell, *An Economic Geography of Oil* (Bell, London, 1963) or C. Tugendhat, *Oil, The Biggest Business* (Eyre and Spottiswoode, London, 1968). W. E. Pratt and D. Good, *World Geography of Petroleum* (Princeton University Press, 1950) though comprehensive, is now out of date.

On specific aspects of the British situation, see J. R. James and others, 'Land Use and The Changing Power Industry in England and Wales', *Geog. J.* **127** (1961), 268–309; T. M. Thomas, 'The North Sea Gas Bonanza', *Tijds. voor econ. en soc. geog.* **59** (1968), 57–70, and R. T. Foster, 'Pipeline Development in the United Kingdom', *Geography* **54** (1969), 204–11.

Chapters Six and Seven

The ground covered by these chapters is largely that dealt with by D. Grigg in his *The Harsh Lands* (Macmillan, London, 1970); see also his 'The Agricultural Regions of the World: Review and Reflections', *Econ. Geog.* **45** (1969), 95–132. Other useful base texts are L. J. Symons, *Agricultural Geography* (Bell, London, 1968), and A. N. Duckham and G. B. Masefield, *Farming Systems of the World* (Chatto and Windus, London, 1970). On specific farming systems, see C. Clark and M. Haswell, *The Economics of Subsistence Agriculture* (Macmillan, London, second edition, 1966); L. M. Cantor, *A World Geography of Irrigation* (Oliver and Boyd, Edinburgh, 1967) or, alternatively, R. M. Highsmith, 'Irrigated Lands of the World', *Geog. Rev.* **55** (1965), 382–9; P. P. Courtenay, *Plantation Agriculture* (Bell, London, 1965) and J. Chang, 'Agricultural Potential of the Humid Tropics', *Geog. Rev.* **58** (1968), 333–61. A useful guide to the progress of agricultural technology is formed by the annual *Yearbook* of the United States Department of Agriculture.

On land reform many studies, chiefly on Latin America, have been published by the Land Tenure Center, University of Wisconsin, Madison (list on request) and a summary to date for Latin America was given by R. J. Alexander, 'Nature and Progress of Agrarian Reform in Latin America', *J. Econ. Hist.* **23** (1963), 559–73. D. Warriner, *Land Reform in Principle and Practice* (Oxford, 1969) deals with Indian and Latin American examples: see also her *Land Reform and Development in the Middle East* (R.I.I.A., London, 1957) and R. P. Dore, *Land Reform in Japan* (R.I.I.A., London, 1959). For an up-to-date picture of the progress of reform S. H. Franklin, *The European Peasantry: The Final Phase* (Methuen, London, 1969) is also useful.

Chapter Eight

Basic references are R. C. Estall and R. O. Buchanan, *Industrial Activity and Economic Geography* (Hutchinson, London, 1961) and E. W. Miller, *A Geography of Industrial Location* (Brown, Dubuque, Iowa, 1970); while for a view of the factors affecting individual industries and processes, it is hard to improve on E. B. Alderfer and H. E. Michl, *Economics of American Industry* (McGraw Hill, New York, third edition, 1957). There are numerous histories of industrialization in the United States; for Europe, see T. Kemp, *Industrialisation in Nineteenth Century Europe* (Longman, London, 1969). Several studies have been made of the British steel industry, e.g. H. R. Schubert, *History of the British Iron and Steel Industry from c. 450 B.C. to A.D. 1775* (Routledge, London, 1957) and A. Birch, *The Economic History of the British Iron and Steel Industry, 1784–1879* (Cass, London, 1967), but none covers the entire period of its growth; see, however, N. J. G. Pounds, *The Geography of Iron and Steel* (Hutchinson, London, fifth edition, 1971) and Pounds and W. N. Parker, *Coal and Steel in Western Europe* (Faber, London, 1957).

On industrialization of the underdeveloped areas, see A. B. Mountjoy, *Industrialisation and Underdeveloped Countries* (Hutchinson, London, second edition, 1966) or A. Maddison, *Economic Progress and Policy in Developing Countries* (Allen and Unwin, London, 1970).

Chapter Nine

There are not at present any geographies of tertiary/quarternary activities as such, but most economic geographies devote at least a section to them, and marketing at least has been the subject of three recent texts: D. Mulvihill, *Geography, Marketing and Urban Growth*, (Van Nostrand, Princeton, 1970); J. E. Vance, *The Merchant's World: The Geography of Wholesaling* (Prentice-Hall, 1970), and P. Scott, *Geography and Retailing* (Hutchinson, London, 1970). These can be supplemented by studies of marketing and services in specific centres, e.g. for London see A. E. Smailes and G. Hartley, 'Shopping Centres in the Greater London Area', *Trans. I.B.G.* **29** (1961), 201–13 or W. I. Carruthers, 'Service Centres in Greater London', *Town Plan. Rev.* **33** (1962), 5–31; for Chicago see, for example, B. J. L. Berry and others, *Commercial Structure and Commercial Blight* (University of Chicago Press, 1963) and, for the United States generally, S. B. Cohen and G. K. Lewis, 'Form and Function in the Geography of Retailing', *Econ. Geog.* **43** (1967), 1–42. As a contrast, the quite different setting of marketing in Africa can be studied in *Markets in Africa* edited by P. Bohannan and G. Dalton (Northwestern University Press, Evanston, Ohio, 1962) or A. K. Mabogunje, *Urbanization in Nigeria* (University of London Press, 1968).

There is a very large literature on the city as a service centre: a good starting point would be one of the smaller urban geographies like J. H. Johnson, *Urban Geography* (Pergamon, Oxford, 1967), from which one could move on, say, to B. J. L. Berry and F. E. Horton, *Geographic Perspectives on Urban Systems* (Prentice-Hall, 1970). This might then be supplemented by *The City in Newly Developing Countries* edited by G. Breese (Prentice-Hall, 1969).

Postscript
    The problem of where to start on the literature of the new geography
is a real one. Perhaps the best point to begin is with the final chapters
(31-3) of J. W. Alexander, *Economic Geography* (Prentice-Hall, 1963),
and to move from there to H. H. McCarty and J. B. Lindberg, *A Preface
to Economic Geography* (Prentice-Hall, 1966). The basic works of the
forerunners are *Von Thünen's Isolated State* edited by P. Hall (Pergamon,
Oxford, 1966); A. Weber, *Theory of the Location of Industries* (University
of Chicago Press, sixth impression, 1968) and W. Christaller, *Central
Places in Southern Germany* (Prentice-Hall, 1966). These lead one on to
E. M. Hoover, *The Location of Economic Activity* (McGraw-Hill, New
York, 1948) and A. Lösch, *The Economics of Location* (Yale University
Press, New Haven, 1954), after which P. Haggett, *Locational Analysis
in Human Geography* (Arnold, London, 1965) and his later works provide
guidance on subsequent development. The application of the classical
models to real situations is then tested in studies like R. Sinclair,
'Von Thünen and Urban Sprawl', *Ann. Ass. Am. Geog.* **57** (1967),
72–87 and R. J. Horvath, 'Von Thünen's Isolated State and the Area
round Addis Ababa, Ethiopia', *Ann. Ass. Am. Geog.* **59** (1969), 308–23.
Christaller's south German work has been followed up in a long series
of other area studies, starting with J. E. Brush, 'The Hierarchy of
Central Places in Southwestern Wisconsin', *Geog. Rev.* **43** (1953), 380–
402, and covering parts of all the continents.

Index of Place Names

(This index lists the main places used as examples of the principles discussed in the book. General entries for Great Britain and the U.S.A. are omitted, however, since references to them are so numerous as to occur on almost every page.)

Index of Subjects